Praise for *Pretty Baby*

"Compelling, thought-provoking, and wonderfully written, Chris Belcher's *Pretty Baby* is a revelatory examination of queerness and sex work. I couldn't put it down; I read it in one sitting without even intending to. Every page is gorgeous, every page a reckoning."
—Alex Marzano-Lesnevich, author of
The Fact of a Body

"*Pretty Baby* is an unflinching, layered exploration of sexuality, queerness, and power that isn't afraid of gray areas or contradictions, honest in its blurred lines as it moves between realms: between a rural blue-collar upbringing and academia, between academia and sex work, between sex work and sex."
—Lilly Dancyger, author of *Negative Space*

"Captivating . . . Belcher's pen is at once graceful and scathing as it prods the complexities of desire—the ever-present dangers of straight maleness, the sometimes complicated haven of female queerness."
—*Electric Literature*

"*Pretty Baby* is a book packed with all the analysis of class, power, sexuality, and embodiment we might want from a gender studies professor, but spun together by a pro domme into a story that holds you tight and lovingly cuts you open."
—*BOMB* magazine

"Belcher is able to infuse a book regarding sexuality, gender, and class with a humor that is rare and, thus, something to treasure. . . . The glory of the book, beyond Belcher's sharp mind and tight lines, is the ways in which Belcher finds egress from social and financial constriction through her sexuality and sex work. The ways in which the two worlds that, on paper, seem disparate—academia and the sex dungeon—are defined by notions of power is something Belcher explores with acumen."
—*Lit Hub*

"Fascinating and wonderful . . . Belcher uses her experiences as a young queer person in rural America and as a lesbian dominatrix in one of the biggest, most economically disparate cities in the country to explore the ways in which shame infiltrates and influences every corner of our society. . . . She shows how omnipresent the power of shame is and raises questions about how we can take that power back."

—*Autostraddle*

"[Chris Belcher] balances the raw and shocking . . . with incisive takes on the economics of sex work . . . and the freedom she found in it. The result is an illuminating personal look at the power and politics of sex."

—*Publishers Weekly*

"Riveting . . . Belcher's inquisitiveness and vulnerability persist, or rather insist, even as her protagonist matures. Her tale is thus a cascade of openings. . . . In *Pretty Baby*, theory is indissociable from practice, and the abstract cleaves to the concrete. This beautiful first book is as real as they come."

—*Public Books*

"Intriguing connections . . . bound together expertly by a sharp-eyed exploration of gender dynamics, labor politics, and capitalism that weaves itself through everything."

—*Xtra*

"*Pretty Baby* is a collage of moments pieced together, seamlessly building the narrative of Belcher's life. . . . These images are woven together so that one memory shares space with the next until the entirety of Belcher's journey becomes clear. There is little filter offered to readers in this memoir; this is a brutally honest collection of images focusing on a life spent redefining what it means to be feminine."

—*Southern Review of Books*

Pretty Baby

a memoir

Chris Belcher

Avid Reader Press

New York London Toronto Sydney New Delhi

AVID READER PRESS
An Imprint of Simon & Schuster, Inc.
1230 Avenue of the Americas
New York, NY 10020

First Avid Reader Press trade paperback edition June 2023

AVID READER PRESS and colophon are trademarks
of Simon & Schuster, Inc.

For information about special discounts for bulk purchases,
please contact Simon & Schuster Special Sales at 1-866-506-1949
or business@simonandschuster.com.

The Simon & Schuster Speakers Bureau can bring authors
to your live event. For more information or to book an event,
contact the Simon & Schuster Speakers Bureau at 1-866-248-3049
or visit our website at www.simonspeakers.com.

Interior design by Lewelin Polanco

Manufactured in the United States of America

10 · 9 8 7 6 5 4 3 2 1

Library of Congress Cataloging-in-Publication Data has been applied for.

ISBN 978-1-9821-7582-5
ISBN 978-1-9821-7583-2 (pbk)
ISBN 978-1-9821-7584-9 (ebook)

For my mother

Author's Note

I crafted this book from memories. These memories have beat themselves around inside me, have broken and splintered, one against another. And after it all, I've translated them into story. I have tried to be faithful to the truth of those memories in the translation.

There are people in this book who have shared experiences with me, who have their own memories, their own truths. I've changed names and identifying details to provide those people and their memories some distance from mine.

Very early in my life it was too late.
—Marguerite Duras

You only remember the bad stuff.
—My sister

Prologue

• •

I float on my back in a client's saltwater swimming pool, high enough up into the hills that the traffic on Sunset is faint. A house looms above me, three stories tall. It looks as if it could tip over at any moment and crash into the pool before tumbling down onto the Strip. Although houses in the hills are never truly private—neighboring balconies compete for the same view of the city—the courtyard is fenced, and an overgrowth of bougainvillea makes me feel like I am alone. I *am* alone. At that moment, the client has disappeared inside the house, has left me floating, gone to retrieve a bottle of champagne.

The pool water is hot. I said as much when I first waded in and the client told me he kept it that way, heated to ninety degrees so he can enjoy early-morning laps and hosting beautiful women in February, the coldest month of the Los Angeles winter. It is the first time I've been in a pool purified by salt, and I'm surprised by how still it holds me afloat. I suspend, effortlessly, and close my eyes, knowing that a woman should never close her eyes alone at night in a strange man's pool. I am afraid of him, not because of anything he has said or done, but because I know I am supposed to be. Which makes closing my eyes, letting my ears sink beneath the surface to muffle the radio, feel like a dangerous game. It's gratifying, knowing I can take such a gamble and win. Like people who use heroin—only once. We all have to find out what we're made of.

My girlfriend, Catherine, is sipping whiskey in New Orleans. Technically, she's in New Orleans to see clients—submissive men in town for grocery-store expos or poultry-industry conferences or management-guru lectures. Better yet, medical-sales conferences. Dental professionals' associations. New Orleans is a hot spot for conventions, and so it's also a hot spot for touring sex workers. A pro dominatrix can throw up a Backpage ad and easily pay for her hotel, buttery chargrilled oysters, beignets, and other indulgences, and still fly home with a roll of cash in her boot.

Catherine scans the New Orleans convention center website for events that seem like they'll draw crowds of repressed male submissives with money to burn. After helping them burn through that money, she will stay down there a few extra days to party with her best friend, a woman who used to be a domme in Los Angeles but left to be a bigger fish in a smaller pond. She is known, at least to herself, as the Queen of the Quarter. In LA, if you called yourself queen of anything, you'd be called delusional by everyone else.

Catherine had texted me late the night before to ask if I cared that she fisted her best friend's roommate, since it was just for kicks, and I did care but I couldn't explain why, so I said it was no big deal. This morning, I imagined her waking up and ordering breakfast, fried green tomatoes with rich remoulade and crumbly biscuits to ease her out of yesterday's decisions, and I got jealous for more than one reason.

Catherine taught me how to do this work, and it feels

good to do it without her for the first time. To take my own risks: risks I probably would have judged her for taking. Somehow, the risks we are willing to take ourselves terrify us when taken by those we love.

I stand up in the shallow end and watch as the client reappears on a top-floor balcony, then starts to descend a staircase that zigzags down the back of his house, way down deep, three stories into the canyon where the saltwater pool suspends me. He walks over to the water's edge, and I see his neon-white chest hair peeking out of the bathrobe he's wrapped around his body. The robe has replaced the suit jacket and jeans he'd paired with New Balance sneakers earlier in the evening, an outfit that announced to the entire restaurant that he'd paid me to be there. He bends down and places the champagne bottle and two flutes on the terra-cotta tile, near the edge of the water. I think of Catherine's primary rule—no glass by the pool—and smile to myself. With Catherine out of town and my job a secret, no one knows where I am or what I am doing.

The client doesn't ask for my permission; he just drops the robe and dives in naked, dispelling the welcome anxiety I had been steeping in, that feeling of inching closer to the front of the line, a roller coaster tearing away with screaming passengers right in front of you. I can no longer imagine him strangling me to death. Now that he's naked, I concede: I am not going to die tonight.

"I love a saltwater pool," I say when the client comes up for air, filling the silence with a compliment.

He treads water, demonstrating buoyancy, then grabs for the edge.

"Salt water's denser," he explains, like a fourth-grade science teacher. "Easier to float."

I take a flute and pour myself some champagne, then push away from the pool deck, glass in hand. I revel once again in the possibility that something terribly bloody might happen.

When I was a kid, our backyard pool's chlorine was bitter enough to singe your sinuses. My father was a summertime chemist, testing pH balances, skimming dead things from the surface, setting little whirlpools to life behind his net. At twelve, I was desperate to free myself from the previous year's bikini top, its pre-growth-spurt elastic cutting into the skin stretched taut over my expanding ribs. I paddled my feet underwater, hands on my sides, pulling the fabric away from my body and letting the water rush in over my nipples.

At twenty-seven, I spin around in the salt water, close my eyes, and picture my dad and the client together, holding hands at the pool's edge, and then vanishing, at once, into thin air.

"Wanna take off your top?"

The client speaks and I open my eyes, shake my head, and take a sip of my champagne. I wouldn't dare bare my tits to him. Not for some sense of propriety, or fidelity to Catherine, or the rules of dominance and submission; I won't show my tits because they are small.

Our family pool was aboveground. My parents explained that we couldn't have an underground pool because we lived too close to the railroad tracks and the boxcars full of coal, clambering down those rails, would crack the liner. I'm certain that was a lie told to explain why they had enough money to give their girls something pretty great, but not enough for something *really* great: a deep end and a diving board.

Those railroad tracks were right at the back of our small lot, and I learned from a young age to stay away when I heard the whistle sound as it crossed Midway Drive, the street half a mile down the tracks. I would never say I grew up on the wrong side of the tracks—the other side was a few acres of swampy marshland that was rumored to be a dump site for runoff from the coal-washing process, conducted at the power plant a few miles down the highway. It peeped and chirped its swamp song loudest in the summer, proof of life when Dad's pool chemicals drowned out the stink.

When I turned eighteen and left for college, my mom asked me to come back one weekend to have my blood tested for C8, a chemical used in the production of Teflon. A chemical company with a plant just upriver from where we lived was paying for blood testing and medical monitoring of residents who may have had chronic exposure to the carcinogen. Unbeknownst to us, we swam in it every summer off the banks of the Ohio River. Seventy thousand people in the river valley turned over their blood for testing.

No matter. I'd gotten myself to California, where I use the cast-iron skillet my grandmother gave me before I left— no more Teflon poison—and I float in saltwater pools. I buy water bottled at the source. I know that if I drink too much champagne while remembering the railroad tracks, I might start to ramble about the chemicals used to wash coal, and the polyps on my uterus, and my persistent tonsil infections. I set the glass down on the pool's edge and swim toward the client, determined not to embarrass myself.

• •

I was in the middle of my twenties, at the beginning of a PhD program in the humanities, and at the end of my financial rope when I met and fell in love with Catherine, a woman who worked as a professional dominatrix in a BDSM dungeon that had been running for decades out of an unassuming house on a stretch of Venice Boulevard that had never been in a movie. I knew next to nothing about professional domination, but I needed money to stay in LA and Catherine promised to teach me everything there was to know about torturing men to get it. The key to success, I would learn, had little to do with skills in rope and a lot to do with how well you can mask your fear when you find yourself alone with a stranger.

I found that I was good at masking myself.

I learned the basics of bondage to hold men still and the art of tease to keep them hard. My worth for the span of an hour was measured in blood vessel and meat. Sometimes, I penetrated them, their hairy legs spread high and wide. Those things I did for money felt like sex. Other things did not. I had a regular who liked me to stand barefoot on the side of his head for twenty-minute intervals. I asked Catherine if this could damage him, break his neck or crack his skull, and she just shrugged: "I don't think so."

But there was no way to know for sure.

I regularly fed dog food and ketchup-covered Little Debbie cakes to a man who pouted and begged for more, rooting around on a filthy tarp like a starved piglet. I once dressed a guy up in leather puppy gear without realizing he wanted to role-play *bad dog*, and spent the better part of an hour running from a two-hundred-pound man drooling and humping and growling and nipping at my legs. He wouldn't listen to my safe word. He claimed he hadn't been properly trained and didn't know that command.

Most of the time, the guys who came to see me would simply suck on my toes and jerk off while I called them mildly offensive names.

Other women prodded me for my shame when I told them I was a sex worker. They scanned me for my tenderest bits, listened for the cadence of my voice to change when I went running for my defenses. My manicurist, the woman who microblades my eyebrows—her tiny scalpel nicking cuts into my forehead, filling them up with ink—the professionals who women become intimate with in the upkeep of their femininity, all asked me, in one way or another, if I was ashamed of myself.

My aesthetician, for example, said that when she hooked up with guys she didn't know, one-offs from Tinder, or guys who picked her up at happy hour, she'd be fine when it was happening. But afterward, she said, when she was back at home alone, she hated herself.

"Getting paid for it must be worse," she prodded, hoping I would reassure her that *Yes, I feel like a whore, and feeling like a whore feels bad, so you can thank your lucky stars that despite all the other indignities you are likely to suffer at the hands of men, you haven't suffered this.*

I never hated myself for being a sex worker, but these questions still ignited my shame. It must have been there, buried in a place I couldn't access because I needed the money, and needing the money is always more present than anything we might have to bury inside.

There was a place where, absent the questions, shame still bubbled to the surface. It was the place I tried my best to hide.

In a grad school seminar, in a bright room with bright people, my classmates discussed queer theorist Eve Kosofsky Sedgwick's claim that *we distinguish shame from guilt because guilt attaches to what one does, whereas shame points to what one is.*

We talked about the ways that shame is contagious. It spreads across the blushed faces of those who witness a shameful act. I imagined my classmates witnessing what I had done the night before—the force-feedings or the cock teasing—and my cheeks flushed. They didn't know who I was—that I was broke, that I would do things that they presumably wouldn't do to stop being broke—and the threat of discovery was always with me, vibrating against the surface of my skin.

In the essay, Sedgwick describes a thought experiment she assigned when lecturing on shame to other grad students like us. She asked them to imagine a man walking into their lecture hall, stark raving mad, pissing on the floor. Although they would rather be anywhere else in the world than in that lecture hall, watching the breakdown of another human, witnesses to such an act are unable to look away. Shame floods them. They avert their eyes, hang their heads. Then they raise them, take another look. Shame moves us simultaneously in two directions: revulsion and empathy. *I am nothing like that. Look at me, there I am.*

Look at me, there I am.

1

When I was ten, my parents caught me messing with my father's *Penthouse* collection. A small utility room opened next to the bathroom in my childhood home. I wasn't allowed inside. A hot-water tank sat in the corner, and when one of us took a shower, a faint knock came from the inside, like a ghostly third sister. The opposite wall was stacked floor to ceiling with my dad's hunting gear and a gun case, locked. A neat row of polished rifles and shotguns. I sneaked inside sometimes, pried my fingers into my father's things, smelled his dirt, gun oil, and sweat. He had old coins and photographs of people I didn't know. Once, with my little sister distracting our babysitter, I dragged a chair from the dining room into that utility closet, determined to investigate the things my dad kept on top of the gun cabinet.

I had seen pornos before, in my friend's basement, packed into boxes ready to move out because her dad had cheated on her mom. As far as I could tell, the magazines on top of the gun cabinet were evidence that my dad was doing the same. Those women looked me right in my kid face and spread themselves open with manicured fingers.

I took the whole stack.

I hid the women who spread themselves open under my bed for days until I got a chance to escape, then ran with them down the railroad tracks that marked our property line. I threw them one by one off the overpass, into the creek below, where we fished for crawdads and minnows. Letting my legs dangle over the concrete ledge, spray-painted with swastikas and declarations of teenage love, I dammed up that tiny trickle of a creek with what I saw as my father's infidelity. Despite my moralizing, I too felt the white-hot throb of desire that Dad must have felt for the centerfolds.

Weeks later, when he noticed they were gone, I was the only possible suspect, my sister still too young for perversion. First, a spanking for the immediacy of his anger, and a subsequent grounding for a chance to think about what a pervert I had been. I passed the time alone in my bedroom, masturbating to what I had seen in the magazines. My father's betrayal became my own body's. I never got to tell my parents that my intention was to save their marriage, a lost cause even then. If I had set out to be the good daughter, the hum between my legs betrayed me. I kept my mouth shut and accepted what I had coming.

An obsession with losing my virginity came soon after.

It wasn't about pleasure, or scratching an itch. I could do that myself, with or without the magazines. If I tipped myself to just the right angle under the bathtub faucet and squeezed my toes like a fist, my pulse would stop thrashing between my ears and travel down. If I swiped my mother's back massager and put it between my thighs—hidden like a fugitive in the tight space between bed and wall, boom box turned up to drown out the electric hum—I could undo my insides entirely. It wasn't hard to steal the massager. My mom was a shift worker, in and out of the house with a lunch box and hard hat like a man. She actually used the massager to beat down her worn-out back.

Without surveillance, I had gotten away with it for years. I got caught only once, on a summer vacation when Dad stayed home and we brought my grandma with us to South Carolina: a fresh pair of adult eyes. On an overcast day, no good for the beach, we went to see a movie.

My vigilant grandmother asked the teenage theater attendant if the film was suitable for children as he took our tickets to *A League of Their Own*. He ripped them halfway and handed them back without comment.

"It has Madonna in it," she whispered, loud enough for me to hear. I didn't know what Madonna meant, but the teenager gave in, said we would be fine, and I was excited to find out.

After the movie ended, when we left the air-conditioned theater for the stifling minivan that had baked in the sun during our matinee, I climbed onto the floor behind the driver's seat and draped my yellow blanket over myself to find a different kind of relief from a different kind of heat. Suspicious of a kid under a blanket in the humidity of a Carolina afternoon, my grandma snatched it up to find me underneath, hands down the front of my shorts.

"Quit that!" she shouted. "It's nasty!"

I pulled it back out of her hands and threw it into the front seat, denying I'd been doing anything nasty underneath it. I wasn't even masturbating to Madonna. I was masturbating to the alcoholic coach, played by Tom Hanks, who stumbled into the women's locker room and took a long, drunk piss in front of all the lady baseball players.

None of that was why I wanted to lose it. When I thought of pleasure, I thought of lukewarm faucet water and the back massager. I thought of a chipped-white daybed squeaking under my weight while I squirmed and squeezed a pillow between my thighs, staring up at my Spice Girls poster. In the years of "MMMBop" and "Wannabe," Scary Spice would eventually dethrone the middle Hanson brother as my number one girl crush. A boy was unnecessary. I didn't want to lose it for a boy. I wanted to lose it because I wanted to be the first.

I was the first of my friends to start my period, and I relished being the most adult twelve-year-old in the room. It meant that I knew the answers to all the most important questions like, *Will I have to tell my dad?* and *What if it comes in class?* I dispensed advice like the tampon machine that should have existed in our elementary school bathroom. *No, it doesn't feel like peeing. Always keep a pad in your desk, just in case. Yes, it hurts.* I reveled in the power given over to me by those doing the asking, and I wanted to hold on to it. For a twelve-year-old girl, power is hard to come by, and you take it where you can get it.

At recess, in the year I started bleeding, an older boy who had been held back for a second year of sixth grade lined a bunch of girls up against the concrete wall that separated the cafeteria from the playground. He was slightly browner than the greasy-haired white kids who had already learned casual racism from their parents. His friends called him *spic* like it was a nickname and not a racial slur. There in the line, he walked from girl to girl, making each of us tug our shorts down a little so he could check for hair.

"If you have hair," he said, "you're not a virgin," peering into each girl's underwear while his friend Eric kept watch for teachers who might interrupt the inspection.

I had a little.

"I am though!" I insisted. "I swear!" I may have wanted to lose my virginity, but I wasn't going to have it taken away by a sixth grader's speculation.

He gave me the go-ahead to zip up my Levi's, but he didn't believe me. He called Eric over from his post, doing crowd control by that point on the half-moon of boys watching and the long line of girls waiting. He grabbed the waist of my jeans himself and pulled them away from a stretch of my skin that had never before been touched.

"Look," he said to Eric, and Eric looked.

A few days later, Eric scribbled a note that asked if I wanted to be his girlfriend and gave it to a boy who gave it to a girl who gave it to me. I said yes. Having a boyfriend would get me that much closer to losing *it*, for real, on my own terms.

Being Eric's girlfriend meant sitting next to him on the school bus and calling his house in the evenings. I hadn't liked Eric before, and I didn't like him any more after weeks of listening to him play *Donkey Kong* with his brother through the phone. He laid it down each time it was his turn to take the controller. I sat on the line, listening to the mashing of his thumbs.

The issue of body hair that brought us together would also tear us apart. A month into our budding romance, Eric started sitting at my table at lunch. The unforgiving fluorescent lights of the school cafeteria illuminated the fine, dark hair covering my forearms, and Eric said he didn't want a girlfriend who had more arm hair than he did. He said it in front of the whole table, and all the boys laughed. All the girls tugged down on their shirtsleeves. Twelve-year-old masculinity is just as fragile as it will be when those boys grow into men. I got home from school and shaved my entire body, a soft layer of protection gone. Freshly shorn, I hunkered down with my best friend, Becca, to plot the ends of our innocence.

Becca and I were in the same sixth-grade class, and on the last day of the school year, our teacher let us watch movies all day long. She laid her blond hair and gray roots down on her desk, exhausted after a year of babysitting restless kids whose parents sent them to school with lunch boxes full of white bread peanut butter sandwiches and Mountain Dew.

Becca was a tiny girl with stringy black hair and glasses thick enough to magnify her eyes if you looked at them from certain angles. Our classmates sat distracted by the brick of a television mounted in the corner of our classroom. A bulletin board's trim drooped down over Crayola kid hands, traced and decorated: Thanksgiving turkeys. Our teacher had given up all the way back in November.

Becca pulled my notebook off my desk.

"Let's write the pact," she whispered.

We had already decided to have sex that summer before junior high began. If our parents had discovered their twelve-year-old daughters were planning to fuck, they would've likely taken us straight to the psych department of a pediatric hospital, or interrogated us to find out who was the instigator.

I'd been fascinated with sex for as long as I could remember. Before I had my period to brag about, I told my friends that I watched my parents do it every night through a hole in their bedroom wall. There was no hole in their bedroom wall, my parents were rarely home at the same time, and I'd never seen anyone have sex, at least not in person, only on late-night Cinemax and HBO. But telling the story made me feel powerful. It made me feel powerful, that is, until a girl in my class told her mother and her mother called mine and my mother screamed, "That isn't true! What in the hell is wrong with you?"

She started watching me more closely in the bathtub and with the back massager.

Other girls my age talked about horses and dance routines. Other girls went to church. There were around fifteen hundred people in town, five hundred homes, but there were nearly twenty churches dotting both sides of the Ohio River across a ten-mile radius around my house. There were even more churches farther out in the country, where hands were laid and tongues were spoken. My parents dragged us to a hellfire-and-brimstone Baptist church every so often and always on holidays, where I got the sense that church existed for judging the behaviors of others—noticing those among us who were living in sin, asking them to let Jesus take the wheel—and my parents felt they were the ones being judged, never the ones doing the judging. Mom fell asleep in the pew each time we went and humiliated my dad, jolting herself awake with a loud snore when her head nodded, mouth open, chin to chest. Mom wanted Dad to remove his hat inside like all the other men, but he was self-conscious about his bald spot, and so he refused. Neither seemed to me cut out for organized religion.

At church, I watched grown men kneel at the altar and weep, begging for the keys to God's kingdom. Humiliated on their behalf, I prayed only that the spirit didn't grab hold of me and carry me to the front of the church, where I would be prayed over by a sweating man called Brother Graham. His breath smelled like the mothballs my grandma told me were poison but were still scattered in small packets across the floor of her bedroom closet.

I attended summer Bible school at my friends' churches, where stout church ladies gave us watered-down orange

Kool-Aid and off-brand Oreos. It was more arts and crafts than hellfire and brimstone. When the pastor asked who among us wanted to join God's army, I stood up with everyone else to take my place among the ranks, even if they were in service of a God whose orders I couldn't hear. I knew that if you got saved at the beginning of the week you could get baptized in the pastor's pool at the end of the week, and nothing sounded more fun than jumping into a pool with all of my clothes on.

To maintain appearances, I would entertain Jesus and horses and dance routines and all the other childish topics my friends favored, but I couldn't wait until we were alone so that I could talk about sex with Becca. Besides our parents, the only people we were sure had done it was the cast of *The Real World*, and there was nothing I wanted more than to grow up and be on *The Real World*.

MTV wasn't allowed at my house, but Becca's mom was younger than everyone else's, and she recorded *The Real World* on VHS tapes so that she could keep up when she had to work evenings. A note from my mom would give me permission to take the bus from school to Becca's house, where we had access to boxes full of adult programming on tape. When the bus dumped us at the bottom of Becca's long driveway, we would run up the hill to her old two-story house, crumbling off the wooded mouth of a holler, and down the stairs into a windowless basement family room. I could have cared less about Pedro Zamora's commitment ceremony with his partner, the first same-sex commitment to air on television, twenty years before gay marriage would be legalized in the United States. We fast-forwarded past all talk of his dying.

Our obsession with the show had only grown two seasons past San Francisco, when we watched Miami's frat boy

Mike bring a girl home to soak in the house Jacuzzi. Room-mate Melissa joined the two, and the trio eventually ended up in the shower together, sending the rest of the cast into a frenzy of speculation about a wild threesome. Dan, Flora, and Sarah broke a window trying to watch the girl-on-girl-on-boy action. Becca and I sat close to the screen, eating Fun Dip and licking our sugary fingers. It was the first time I heard about girls making out with other girls.

Nineties teen culture was obsessed with virginity. Tai deals the harshest insult on *Clueless* when she calls Cher *a virgin who can't drive*. On *Beverly Hills, 90210*, virginity was Donna's defining characteristic.

"You can make all the *90210* Barbies have sex," I explained to my sister. Brenda and Kelly, Dylan and Brenda, even Brenda and Brandon. "Everyone except for Donna."

Donna didn't do it; that's what made her Donna.

The Real World's producers cast a virgin on almost every season, and if I couldn't relate to anything else on the show, I could relate to them. New York: Julie, a sweet Southern girl who was shocked by all things sex in the city. San Francisco: Rachel, a good Catholic girl who flirted with bad-hygiene bad-boy Puck. Boston: Elka, whose father forced her to sign a contract promising that she wouldn't drink, do drugs, or have sex on TV. The show's virgins were proxies for its mostly teenage audience, lying awake and wondering who might be having sex in the next bed over.

Genesis Moss was not a virgin. She looked like a lesbian Drew Barrymore: bleach-blond hair, crimson lips, black leather, the archetype of nineties hard femme. On the Boston season in 1997, Genesis spent most of her time in queer bars, befriending local drag queens, not wasting her breath on the people MTV had cast to confront her homosexuality.

Until the scenes set in the youth center where the Boston cast worked, there were never kids on the show. But in that youth center, a girl—younger than Becca and I by a few years—said to Genesis, "I don't like gay people." With bobble-head excitement, the girl's voice singsonged when she said it: "I just have a feeling that I hate them."

Them: gay people.

I wonder who that kid grew up to be and if she, like me, watches that scene over and over again on YouTube.

"When I grow up and go to college," I said when Becca stopped the tape, "I'm going to be a lesbian like Genesis."

Something about the way she hurt, the way her hurt rallied her housemates around her, made me want to be her. I wanted repercussions.

"If you want to be a lezzie," Becca said, "you should go for it."

She was a good friend.

After the episode, Becca got up to retrieve the magnifying hand mirror out of her parents' bathroom so we could pluck our eyebrows into thin lines like Genesis and Drew Barrymore in *Mad Love*, a movie we rented on more than one Friday night sleepover. In it, Drew is so sexy that the boy next door can't help but watch her through her bedroom window every night. He uses a telescope, and I couldn't wait until a boy wanted to watch me through a telescope. I hoped my neighbor in college would have one.

I knew one lesbian outside of *The Real World*. Our elementary school bus driver wore faded Wranglers and work boots and moved like her legs had been built around a motorcycle. She held on to her belt buckle and talked rough, only when she had to, only when us kids were so bad we forced her hand. Her manliness was a reliable topic of conversation, but we never got the chance to observe her behavior off the bus. That is, until our summer sleepaway camp hired public school bus drivers to take us all the way across the state. That trip involved pit stops.

It was two hours of interstate between us and home before the bus sputtered to a stop and kids pushed and shoved their way down the stairs and into McDonald's. Six of us squeezed ourselves into one booth, dunking chicken nuggets into sweet-and-sour sauce as the driver passed us by, walking hips first into the women's restroom. We had already learned the art of surveillance. Our parents watched us; older brothers watched us; teachers watched us.

And I had already been accused. Earlier that year I got the cartilage of my right ear pierced at a kiosk in the mall. An older girl on that same bus we were riding to camp saw it, still red and oozing, and called me *gay*.

"The gay ear," she called it. *My ear*: gay. I flushed with anger when she asked, "Are you gay or something? You pierced the gay ear." I had only gotten the piercing to impress older kids. MTV taught me that older kids were impressed by piercings and by gay people. MTV couldn't have been more wrong.

To protect ourselves, we girls enacted the art of surveillance upon others.

"Follow her in! Let's see how she pees!" someone squealed. Everyone else stuffed their mouths full of fries, not wanting to be the one caught looking. Rumor had it, the bus driver was worse than a lez. People said she was a man in disguise, and a bad disguise at that. If she peed standing up, we'd know for sure.

Desperate as ever to be the brave one, I peeled my thighs off the plastic booth and headed for the bathroom. A friend who was usually much nicer than me trailed behind, misbehaving in anticipation of sleepaway-camp independence. The driver was already in a stall by the time we slipped inside, so we crammed ourselves into the one beside her and locked the door. I kneeled down, looked under the stall, and saw those dirty old work boots, toes pointing directly at the toilet.

"She's a man!" I shouted at whisper volume. "She's a total man!"

We burst out of the stall, out of the bathroom, and flopped back down into our booth, where we dunked our remaining nuggets in sweet-and-sour sauce with grubby, unwashed hands, and recounted what we'd just seen to all of our friends. I was first in line to load back onto the bus, took a seat at the rear, and watched each girl pass by the driver, holding back laughter that I prayed would go unnoticed. I knew that the driver was probably just placing a layer of toilet paper down onto the piss-stained toilet seat, but that wouldn't have made for a good story.

If you didn't want to be like the bus driver, if you didn't want an older girl to tell everyone that you pierced your gay ear, there were many tactics you could try to make their suspicions fade. But there was only one thing that would make them disappear, once and for all.

"Okay." I looked Becca in the eyes on that last day of our sixth-grade year. "Let's write the pact."

At the school year's close, fresh sheets of paper were hard to come by, but I flipped toward the back of my notebook— past MASH games, vocabulary lists, and pages of miscalculated math equations—until I found a clean page. I took Becca's pen and started sketching a blueprint of the clubhouse: the place where we intended, that very summer, to have sex.

The clubhouse was an abandoned announcer's booth at a decrepit rodeo arena, crumbling behind the Little League baseball fields on the outskirts of town. A few times each summer, the road to the arena would be lined with horse trailers, and I would walk down with my mom to watch the cowgirl barrel racers and little-boy calf ropers. The cowgirls looked like pretty men: strong and dirty, and always from out of town. I liked the way they tucked their button-down shirts into their blue jeans and got dusty all the way up to their elbows. By the last day of sixth grade, the cowgirls hadn't come to town for a couple of summers, and the announcer's booth was just another neglected structure in a neighborhood becoming more run-down with each passing year.

The arena was at the end of Midway Drive, a street I liked because the name reminded me of a carnival, throwing dull darts at a wall of balloons or sinking a Ping-Pong ball into a revolving island of goldfish bowls. But there was no carnival excitement to Midway Drive, just a flat, pothole-littered street lined with single-story, single-family homes.

Railroad tracks cut across Midway, carrying coal trains to and from the power plants just outside of town. They carried us as well, a pathway of wood and steel that cut through thick brush from one shitty subdivision to the next. We balanced on rails like delinquent gymnasts, smoking cigarettes out of sight from passersby. At one end of Midway was my house and the highway, State Route 2. We called it *the main street*. Not *Main Street*, which might suggest a small theater, or a diner, or a bookshop—we didn't have any of that. We had *the* main street and Midway Drive, the baseball fields and the Methodist church. We had the run-down rodeo arena where I missed seeing the cowgirls at Midway's end. Beyond that, the river, another place we weren't allowed to go but often went.

Becca and I walked from my house down to the old rodeo arena and climbed up onto the splintered wooden fence that the cowgirls used as their perch between events, drinking Budweiser and kicking their boots over the sawdust and summer earth. Once, we found a case of hot Busch Light inside the clubhouse, hidden under a mess of old newspapers, just inside the door. Some teenagers must have stashed it there for safekeeping.

Becca and I decided it was a gift from the devil, since that's what we imagined adults might say if they knew we had discovered a case of beer. We tore open the cardboard box and shared one, taking turns gulping and turning away from the other to swallow it down, turning back to pretend that we liked it. After a whole can of cringe swallows, we stumbled back to my house for my mom's gardening tools. We planned to dig twenty-three twelve-ounce-can-size holes in the soft tilled arena dirt, each hole an individual hiding place for a can of beer. We planned on digging them up and presenting them to our future boyfriends, as soon as we found the boyfriends and could bring them to the clubhouse. We dug the holes and planted the beers, but forgot to ever dig them up again.

The blueprint of the clubhouse—the one we drew on the last day of sixth grade—spelled out our intentions. One of us would take a mythical summer boyfriend to the top-level announcer's booth, her preteen body stripped down on the tobacco spit–stained wood floor. The other would use the ground floor: the less desirable option, the bottom bunk. Like novice skydivers who can only jump if they strap their bodies to another, we had to lose it together.

To ensure that we wouldn't be able to see each other, Becca and I had already gone to the clubhouse to lie on our backs in the exact places we intended to do it. I added tiny drawings of boys and girls in stick-figure coitus to the blueprint of the clubhouse, next to the pact. An older sister by nature, I claimed the top bunk.

I swear that I will have sex this summer, I wrote in purple gel ink.

I passed the notebook to Becca, and she signed her name. She passed it back, and I carefully signed my own.

We hadn't yet secured the boys, but we did have crushes from the previous summer. Both boys were from out of town and would be back in a few weeks to spend their summers with their grandparents. My crush, CJ, only lived in the next county over, but he had a thicker accent than mine and a wide, slow smile. For *wash* he said *waarsh*, like my mother. His mother must not have policed his grammar like mine did. She didn't want me to grow up and sound like her. I got soap in the mouth for saying *ain't*, and there he was claiming he *don't got no* . . . whatever. That would have never flown in my house, where country grammar, like cussing, was forbidden for children but fine for adults.

CJ was a year older than me and wore tight jeans and cowboy boots. He even had a cowboy hat. The first time I saw him, he was sitting on his grandmother's porch, wearing that hat, taking a knife to a branch, whittling it into a sharp point. I shouted from the road, asked if he wanted to go for a walk, and he jumped up to join me. We headed for the railroad tracks, and as soon as we came up on some boys I knew from school—boys wearing sagging cargo shorts and Nike sneakers, not cowboy boots and hats—one of them asked, "Who's the faggot?" The hat sat on a shelf in CJ's grandmother's guest room for the remainder of the summer.

You couldn't tell the difference between the two boys in our blueprint, but we labeled the horizontal figures underneath them *Becca* and *Christina*.

Dotting the final *i* in my name, my pen flew across the room as our teacher yanked the notebook out from under my poised right hand. All the blood drained from my face and limbs and pooled somewhere I couldn't quite locate.

I would be grounded for the entire summer.

My parents would forbid me from seeing boys.

My dad would, once again, pull the *Tiger Beat* posters down off my bedroom walls.

My mom would call Becca's mom, and our prospective boyfriends' grandparents.

I would be forced to wear a chastity belt. I had seen one on HBO's *Real Sex*, a show my friends and I watched at sleepovers after we heard our parents snoring softly in their bedrooms upstairs or down the hall.

The teacher walked back to her desk with the drawing, stared at it, then stuffed it inside where we would never, ever be able to get it back.

"My dad is actually going to kill me," I whispered to Becca.

"Don't worry," she replied, her eyes back on the TV screen, trying to pretend that whatever the teacher got, it was no big deal. "Don't have a cow."

Don't have a cow: an ethos, a way of life I was never able to live.

"You don't understand," I repeated. "You don't understand my dad."

My dad inherited his moods from his father. I never met my paternal grandfather, but my mom described him as a kind and quiet man, but also a man with bad nerves. They were so bad, she said, you could watch the muscles of his arms dancing, just below the surface of his skin. My grandmother locked up the knives after a first attempt, but you couldn't confiscate a man's guns.

Dad lived with his parents in his childhood home, next door to a sausage factory, when he met my mom. She was living down the road in a two-bedroom trailer with my half brother. Dad would sleep at the trailer park, but every morning he retreated to his parents' house, trying to keep his mother proud and his father alive. You could hear the pigs screaming and smell them shitting and dying at the sausage factory, but it was still better than a trailer park.

My parents had been dating for five years when my dad found his dad dead. Before the body was cold in the ground, Mom demanded they get married.

"Do it now," she said, "or your mother will never let you leave."

I arrived two years later, when my dad's grief subsided and my mom got a job good enough to support a baby. Years into manhood, Dad was still being a boy. All through deer season, from late September to the first of each year, he needed to be free. He worked construction, but that only ever ran for a few months at a time. My birth was planned down to the month: January, after deer season ended, when my father would be available for late-night feedings and early-morning diaper changes. Mom told me the yelling started long before I arrived.

When I did arrive, my dad loved me, in his way. He had a badgering sense of humor and liked making me laugh. His thick black beard and mustache would tickle me when he kissed my face, and he loved sending me running and screaming. He would sneak up on me and put his beard on my shoulder, chase me with his chin jutted out like a weapon. On good days, this would send me into fits of laughter. On bad ones, he would tickle me until I cried, or rip a few hairs from his face and lay them on me when I wasn't looking. The loose hairs sickened me, made me gag and cry and push him away. This too made him laugh, until it went too far and each of us left the other feeling unloved. He'd go outside to sulk; I would curl myself around my mother's legs like a kitten.

Dad wanted me to be tough, and so taught me to fire a gun. On an autumn Saturday when I was eleven or twelve, he took me by the hand and led me back into the woods behind my grandmother's house, toward a little creek called Broad Run that drained off the hill into the Ohio River. With his ruddy complexion and perpetual farmer's tan, he was athletic as ever in the forest. He stomped over underbrush with a quiet authority, while I kicked up leaves and sang songs about the woods until he told me it was time to quiet down.

We stopped in a patch of sunlight, filtering in through the tree cover, and Dad pulled the rifle that had been slung across his shoulder off his back and propped it up against a tree. He unzipped the leather case to let the gun breathe. He crouched down, looked me in the eyes, and told me that knowing how to shoot was key to survival. A woman couldn't always count on a man. He had invested a good deal of prayer into his hopes for a son, but when God didn't make good on the return, he found it his duty to equip his daughter with the same means of survival he would have passed on to a boy. I would learn to hunt.

Dad picked up the rifle. I'd seen him handle guns all my life but hadn't been allowed to touch them myself. He stepped behind me, pressed the rifle's butt up against my bony shoulder, took my right hand in his, and fastened my index finger around the trigger. He took my left hand under his left, showing me how to hold it steady under the barrel. He held me like that, wrapped into him, and told me that he used to hunt squirrels with his own dad when he was a little boy. This was his grandfather's gun, he said, his father's daddy, and when he explained that to me, his lips touching the crown of my head, I knew I was supposed to understand the gravity of inheritance. Instead, we fired, and the rifle's kickback frightened me. I cried all the way out of those woods.

Dad was obsessed with the family tree. He often sat me

down in the living room, turned off the TV, and laid a chart out in front of me like a map. He traced lines across the browning paper, teaching me who was who and what they did with their time on this earth. People who feel themselves disinherited often become fascinated by the idea of inheritance. He drove the whole family to Civil War battle sites where a great-great-great-uncle lost his life. These were noble men, he would tell me, no matter what side they were on.

"They died fighting for their country," he said, contrary to the truth.

I listened to his spiels about battle lines and numbers of dead, but as soon as I got a chance, I darted off to make believe I was somewhere else, in the shadow of Confederate monuments. As I got older, my disinterest in heritage made it clear to him that fathers and daughters were just not the same as fathers and sons.

I never found out what my father would have done to me if he learned of my sex pact with Becca. My sixth-grade teacher never reported our blueprint. Maybe she knew what we didn't: that we wouldn't actually do it with those boys in the old rodeo clubhouse. Instead, we played kickball with them, and they taught us karate. We played in the creek and chewed on honeysuckle. That summer, we weren't ready. Imagining we were was the fun part.

Becca would get there before me, but it would still take another year for her to meet the older boy who would rid her of virginity.

Roller-skating had been our religion since that summer we didn't lose it. Becca and I would show up at the skating rink a few towns over in matching crop tops and tiny cotton shorts so short that the piece of cotton between our legs was no wider than my index and middle fingers. Once, the rink manager told us to go home and change. Since my grandma had dropped us off and gone about her day, Becca and I sat in the parking lot for hours smoking cast-off cigarette butts and waiting for her to come back and collect us. That's where we were sitting when we finally got to talk to Brian.

Brian was one of the oldest and best skaters at the rink. He rode his blades like a god, his wheels seeming to hover an inch off the ground as he slid back and forth, tricking and twirling while everyone else braced themselves for impact. He had already fucked two other junior high girls and told us about it. We had been trying our best to look like the kind of girls you could tell about fucking.

Becca lied to her parents, said that sixteen-year-old Brian was our age. She also said he was just a friend.

"I'm in love," she gushed in secret. Becca had asked Brian for photographs of himself and pasted them inside her notebook, where she used to paste photographs of our favorite actors. I knew she meant it when she said she loved Brian because she ripped out Jonathan Taylor Thomas, Devon Sawa, and Andrew Keegan. There was only Brian. I knew that I had never been in love because I never would have ripped out Jonathan Taylor Thomas.

Just like she and I had scouted the clubhouse, Brian had already chosen the place to do it: a field down the road from her house, just out of sight of neighboring homes and the highway. She walked me by the spot half a dozen times, psyching herself up before the opportunity presented itself.

"I'll tell you everything," she assured me. There was nothing yet to tell, but I already missed being the one doing the telling.

When it was over, Becca picked and saved the leaves of grass and clover that had been smashed under her body. They were smeared with her blood. She could prove that it happened—she had evidence. We put the clover into a ziplock bag and saved it to use for love spells. If Becca let me burn it, I thought, my own virginity might get lost too.

But once Becca lost hers, she lost all her friends with it. "Slut," the girls in our grade said to her face. "Fugly slut," they said behind her back. I never defended her—afraid I'd be taken down myself—and by the time we got to high school, everyone had forgotten that I had been her best friend. She started hanging out with boys. Not the kind of boys we wanted to hang out with: the popular ones who drank whiskey and smoked pot, but still played sports. The boys who became Becca's friends huffed gas and set fires out in the woods.

I was still in pursuit of loss, but what happened to Becca taught me to go about it differently: she didn't wait for me, but she taught me to wait. I knew that there was some kind of power girls got from fucking. It was the power those porno women had when they spread themselves open for my father. It was the power to make me ache between my legs and the power to make boys barter for a look. It was the power to bring down a marriage.

But that kind of power, it can turn on you.

2

. •

I wasn't even the second of my friends to lose it.

Katie had a perpetual tan—maintained in her stepmother's tanning bed—and a small smattering of freckles across her nose. Not a mess of them like mine. My mom teased me for them, even though she had a mess of freckles herself. She said we looked like we got hit with piles of shit, thrown through a locked screen door. Unlike Becca—before or after she lost it—Katie was popular, and becoming her friend felt like an achievement.

Katie lived down the street from brothers who had just moved to our town from New York—the state, unfortunately, not the city. They were dark-haired Puerto Rican boys with a strange-sounding last name who were trying too hard to preserve each and every hair that sprouted from their cheeks and chins. They played soccer instead of football, spoke Spanish with their mother, and attended a Catholic high school forty minutes from our town, making them even more deliciously mysterious. We said they were Italian because we had a notion that Italian boys were sexy and had no concept of where or what Puerto Rico might be, much less what its boys were like.

Freshman year of high school, Katie called me her best friend and the younger brother, Max, her boyfriend. The older of the brothers, who was shy and a little less cute, would become mine. I thought I'd placed a safe bet, seeing as he was older, but Max was the fast one. He was ready. I kissed the dry-lipped older brother and bided my time. But when I went to his house after school, he just played Nintendo 64 and reached over with a clammy hand to give mine a squeeze in between games while the screen flashed *Game Over.*

On a bus ride home from school, a few months into our respective teenage romances, Katie pulled me into a seat, a couple of rows from the back, where the bad kids sat so they could do bad things like rub snuff. Not that the lesbian bus driver, who we still thought was a man, gave a shit about rednecks rubbing snuff. She rubbed snuff herself and spat the juice out the window, the spray sometimes coming back through and hitting the good kids who sat in the first four rows behind her. Unlike Becca—a permanent fixture of the last row—Katie could move between front and back. But this was a back-of-the-bus kind of day, and Katie pulled me in close to tell me without hesitation, "I'm gonna have sex with Max."

"Today?" I asked, incredulous. "Do you have a condom?"

Katie and I, and a few other neighborhood kids, had been trying to procure condoms for months. When Becca and I were still friends, we stole a bunch from the only pharmacy in town. We wanted to show our friends how to use them, to show the boys we knew how: our own personal sex education, since no one else had stepped in to provide it. It didn't matter much that we had gotten it wrong—we claimed that girls held the condoms out while the boys took aim, thrusting into the rubbers and the girls at the same time. It was clear that no one was having sex, since that sounded logical.

Thankfully, when Becca hooked up with Brian, he already knew what he was doing.

After our robbery, the pharmacy put the condoms behind the counter. A sign hung under the empty pegs where they should have been: *Must be 18 or older to purchase family planning items. Ask at the pharmacy counter.* The pharmacist was also a local pastor who knew everyone's parents. Through what we thought would be a harmless theft, Becca and I probably doubled the town's teen birth rate.

"Max got some," Katie assured me. "He even tried one on."

My friendship with Katie had picked up right where my friendship with Becca had left off. Together, we learned how to be girls. After years of bleeding into embarrassing, crinkly pads, Katie showed me how to use a tampon. She had just started using them herself and didn't understand how to remove the applicator, so we waddled around the neighborhood, full up with cardboard, in pain. We already knew girlhood to be painful, so it seemed normal enough to us. It took another friend more carefully reading the instructions for us to realize that it wasn't. We looked through Katie's step-mom's bathroom cabinet and found bottles of Summer's Eve douche, letting us know that we were dirty. We started swiping bottles every once in a while, douching before we walked to the baseball fields to eat snow cones and distract the boys deep out in left field.

On the day that Katie decided to do it with Max, she gave me a hug: a little too long, a little too scared. Like the tampons and the douching, she must have known it would hurt. I went home and sat catatonic in front of the television. *TRL* was on, ". . . Baby One More Time" inching closer and closer to number one. I watched Britney, like Katie, act like a woman when she was only just a girl.

At football games in my cheerleading uniform, and afterward on the dim-lit gymnasium-turned-dance-floor, I moved my body like Britney's. If I hadn't had sex yet, it wasn't for lack of trying. Earlier that year, before I'd even scored my older boyfriend, I'd set out once more, in earnest, to lose my virginity. I'd known for weeks that my parents would be out of town for my sister's gymnastics competition. It was the first time they'd agreed to leave me at home alone overnight, and from the moment they acquiesced, I'd been planning to betray their trust. I'd already picked the boy and imagined exactly what I was going to do with him.

My parents had agreed to let me stay home on account of a friend's birthday party, to be held where many such occasions had been held: in an undecorated community center, fluorescent lights switched off halfway for ambiance. It would be the perfect place to secure the guy. The birthday girl had swiped a bottle of peach schnapps from her parents, and we passed it around in a Sprite bottle, accounting for at least half the courage it took to set my plan to motion. The liquor made me feel big and dumb, but in a nice way, like a clumsy puppy. I bragged to anyone within earshot that I was going to take a boy home to have sex, hoping that the boy I'd picked would hear me and inquire.

He was the birthday girl's cousin: Michael, a varsity basketball player from a few towns over, with a smooth, blond bowl cut and a girlish mouth. I had just made the varsity cheerleading squad, an honor for a freshman, and first spotted him when our school played his. He and I had barely spoken at Dairy Queen, where we all hung out after the game, but social capital made us a fine match. Plus, after seeing what had happened to Becca, I knew that doing it with a boy from another school would be a smart choice. When it became clear that an encounter was unlikely to occur naturally,

I told one of my friends to tell one of his friends that I wanted to hook up with him, and in no time he gestured me over to where he sat in a folding chair, at the center of a group of boys all the girls wanted.

I crouched down next to Michael and he told me he'd heard that I wanted to *hang out*, and asked if I had some other girls I could bring. Two equally popular boys looked around the room like he wasn't asking for them. It took me no time to convince two girls to join. Neither was a cheerleader. They had social climbing to do.

On our way out, Katie grabbed me by the elbow and asked if I wanted to wait for someone I loved.

Sex came before love—it came before everything else—I was sure of it. Even Brian fell in love with Becca for a little while, after they'd done it. I pulled away from Katie, and the six of us, popular boys and aspirational girls, made our way back to my empty house.

The boys didn't take off their shoes before tromping across my mom's new carpet and sprawling their gangly boy limbs across her couch. The whole house changed with boys in it. It smelled like sweat, and the Axe body spray they used to mask it. When my family returned, I hoped they wouldn't be able to follow their boy scent.

Before I lost my nerve, I took Michael by the hand and led him straight upstairs to my bedroom. I yelled a warning from the top of the stairs: "Nobody smoke in the house!"

I shut my bedroom door behind us, and we lay down on the twin bed, side by side, under a smattering of glow-in-the-dark stars. In my fantasies, boys' lips were soft, and they tasted like strawberry lip gloss. In reality, I knew boys' mouths to be too wet or too dry, rancid like morning breath from afternoons spent dozing in the back of classrooms, or cottony from bong hits. Michael's lips were soft, and when his tongue brushed against mine, I could taste the chewing gum he must have swallowed, evidence that he cared about what I thought of him. I unzipped his jeans and slid my hand through the slit of his boxer shorts. His dick was soft and warm, lost in a mess of pubic hair.

I'd seen plenty of porn. Me and Katie and some other neighborhood girls borrowed VHS tapes from older boys on our bus route, juniors and seniors who never would have spoken to us if it weren't for our interest in their porno collections. I didn't want to watch the porn as much as I wanted them to know we were watching the porn. An hour of nasty girls next door or MILF extravaganzas, and our after-school snacks—baby carrots and Cheese Curls—looked like bowls of dicks. The next day in the cafeteria, we would poke each other with corn dogs or bananas and make barf noises that would offend anyone not cool enough to be in on the joke.

In these pornos, the guy's dick was always hard before the kissing even started, but I still knew, somehow, that it was my job to get him into it. I'd never had a boy's dick in my mouth, had only given one hand job that must have chafed because it lasted two hours of the bus ride back from summer camp. But I tugged Michael's pants down like I knew what I was doing and took him into my mouth. I tried to bob up and down like the porno women, but there was nothing to bob on, just my nose smashing into his bristly pubes.

When I realized that the blow job wasn't going to work, I pulled myself off the boy, off the bed, and took off all my clothes: a new tactic. The move that turned me on the most, the one I had to look away from in my friends' living rooms lest I get turned on right there, in front of everyone, happened when the porno men said to the porno women, "Baby, baby, sit on my face." I pretended that Michael had said it and answered in kind. He licked me, timidly, and I gave it a minute or two before I craned my head to look down at his crotch, where I saw that, still, nothing had happened. Nothing was happening in mine either, but that was less obvious.

I climbed off of him, laid down at his side, and pulled the blanket over myself. I turned to see him in the blue light of winter, leaking in through my bedroom window, and he looked like he might cry. Then, as quickly as I'd removed them, he sat up and pulled on his jeans, zipped them, and his face changed. He no longer looked hurt; he looked like he might hurt me.

Michael didn't kiss me one last time, he just left without a word, and I scrambled to get dressed before he descended the stairs. I followed, hoping to pretend that nothing was wrong. When we turned the corner into the family room, where I was pleased to see the others had relocated—out of the living room we weren't supposed to live in—the other boys jumped up to give high fives. Michael just shook his head, like he was walking off the court after a missed shot at a free throw. He went outside to have a cigarette alone. His friends called me a cock tease.

Katie shed her virginity like skin she'd grown out of, an unnecessary layer put on during the morning chill and thrown off in the afternoon sun. When Becca lost it, I hadn't been ready, and so I observed her transgression with a fascination absent envy. Her boyfriend was too unpopular, too poor, too old for her. Once it was Katie's turn, I really wanted it to be me.

I ended up giving my virginity as a sixteenth-birthday gift to a boy who loved me. I had been wrong about the love part, after all: it had come first. We had been dating since Tim's fifteenth birthday, and on the morning he turned sixteen, he opened his front door to find a drag-race-ready Mustang sitting on his front lawn, under a giant red bow. I loved him almost as much as his mom did, giving him something that she couldn't afford.

That night, he drove us in his shiny new car up to the cemetery behind the Baptist church where I'd sat silently, on so many Sundays, next to my dad and sister while my mom did her best with the hymnal. Tim held my hand tight while he drove, and I was afraid that a deer might leap to its death at the front end of his new car, but I loved the way his fingers felt between mine: knuckle to knuckle, bone to bone, they ached. I brushed the fine golden hairs of his arm absentmindedly with my free hand.

The church was far enough outside of town that no cops would drive by on patrol, but close enough that the gravestones were illuminated by the orange glow of the power plant across the road, its chimney stack belching pollutants into the night air, our own private atmosphere.

It was cold outside, but Tim laid a blanket down on the near-frozen ground next to the car, and another for us to crawl underneath. He played sweet songs on his car stereo from a CD he burned just for the occasion. When he took off my jeans and pushed his dry fingers inside me, his nails were jagged, and they scratched me a little on the inside. I had been meaning to ask him to file them for months, in the buildup to the real thing, but I never got up the nerve. I wasn't going to make a big deal about it that night. It was his first time too, and his birthday, and I didn't want to ruin it.

It hurt when he pushed himself inside me, but not as much as I thought it would, not as much as I wanted. For all my efforts, I needed it to leave a mark. Tim told me he loved me. It wasn't the first time he said it, but it was the first time I was certain that he meant it.

After that, boys sought me out. I discovered that sex—if not virginity—meant much more to them than it did to me. I learned that once you'd given it up, boys could smell your potential. They'd lean into you in the cafeteria line. If you were caught in the hall alone with them after the bell rang, they'd corner you.

Older men too. The health teacher who also taught sex ed—nothing more than a lecture on the sights and smells of STDs—would let the girls who had already fucked play video games on his desktop computer while the rest of the class read about the diabetes that had already claimed some of their grandparents' legs from the knee down. Somehow, he knew who to pick. He would hover over us, brush his hips up against our backs. At lunch, we would hang around in his room. He would let us sneak outside for cigarette breaks behind the baseball dugouts. He would sometimes ask us to sit on his lap. He would eventually go to prison for worse.

I wanted so badly to feel like I was grown—for sex to change me. And it did. But once it was over, I stopped caring much about it. I loved Tim, but when I was with him, I imagined he was a girl on my cheerleading squad. I lay beneath him and stared up at the glow-in-the-dark stars that were peeling, one by one, off my bedroom ceiling. I imagined wanting something more, not yet knowing what it would feel like, or what it could be. I thought of the lukewarm faucet, and I still had that back massager, electrical tape wound around its cord so it didn't shock me, or worse, quit working. I sometimes had orgasms. I never got pregnant.

Tim and I broke up, like high school sweethearts do, and that made it harder to maintain my popularity without sleeping around. I avoided finding myself alone with boys I never worried about before. I learned to hold them at bay without seeming like a bitch. I was a girl-who-fucked without a boy-to-protect-her. One night, I gave in and let a friend fuck me on someone's couch after a party, just so he'd leave me alone long enough that I could fall asleep.

Before I'd done it, I thought that fucking would make me powerful because the *Penthouse* centerfolds were powerful. Genesis from *The Real World* was powerful. Britney Spears was powerful. Katie was powerful. What I would come to understand was that even these girls, they really weren't. Not like I thought they were, anyway.

Once you fucked, the fucking was no longer about you and your power. It became about boys and theirs.

3

• •

The summer already hurt. I peeled sunburns a little too eagerly, tugged at translucent sheets of skin, pulled to the point of tension, then snapped them from the good flesh that I managed to keep safe under a ratty T-shirt. Reminiscent of past summers' loose teeth, worked over with a diligent tongue to the point of their hanging on by only a bit of root, then poised there like a nearly sated itch, knowing one more wiggle could drop the thing, I worked at the shedding until the point of inevitability, at which I was never willing to fully let go. My sunburned shoulders ached at the margins, blood welling there like jagged state lines on a map.

I tried to break bones all summer; I wanted to show up for the first day of seventh grade with a cast. On the playground swing set, I swung as high as possible and let go beyond the apex, at that point where the swing had ascended as far as it could and then even farther, before gravity persisted and the chain caught. I did it with a friend who also wanted a cast. She broke her arm; mine stayed intact. I suffered two concussions—one on a trampoline, one on a bike—the kinds of injuries that leave the kinds of scars over which no one fusses. I believed myself invisible, and I wanted scars that showed.

Late that summer, a new voice pierced our ears each evening, sharp and wavering, pitching somewhere between cowboy yodel and castrato, a sound that echoed across the neighborhood like a tornado warning.

"JESSEEEEEE!"

The way her mother yelled gave me a headache, but the way Jess moved through my world would heal all of it twice over.

Newcomers were few and far between—people were more likely to leave our town than to stay. Leaving was also rare. So, I was surprised when Jess moved in from somewhere else. Not Pittsburgh or Cincinnati: somewhere rougher than a city. Somewhere in the South that taught her to survive the country. With her fuzzy head of strawberry blond hair and pink flushed cheeks, she would have fit right into a peach orchard, but I only saw her against grays and greens. The West Virginia autumns never lingered long enough to notice her in season.

Jess moved into a house just a few doors down from mine, so I noticed her sitting on her new front porch, looking lonely, not too long after she arrived. When a new kid came to town, I wanted to be their first friend—their best friend—and to accomplish the task, I capitalized on loneliness. No one would have lined up to be best friends with Jess. Her accent was thick and her family was poor and she acted like a boy. But her strangeness didn't repel me: it drew me in.

The day after I spotted her, I rode my new ten-speed mountain bike up and down the street past Jess's shitty gray house and shitty yard, its grass high and littered with plastic kid toys that would eventually get chewed up and spat out of a lawn mower like confetti. I saw her tinkering around in the shadows, out in the garage with her dad's tools scattered across the oil-slicked concrete. When I passed by for the third time, she caught on and inched out toward the end of her driveway, basketball in hand. Mesh shorts hanging down past her knees and a baggy T-shirt made Jess look like a boy, but unlike boys our age, who mostly still pretended that girls didn't exist, Jess practiced spinning the ball on her fingertip to impress me. She did it with one foot in her driveway, one in the street, like an animal testing the danger at the edge of her territory.

My driveway had a hoop, and hers did not. I stopped my bike to point that out, and Jess followed me home, dribbling all the way. I thought my parents might ask why this girl looked and acted like a boy, and worked an answer over in my mind: she's not from here, I would say. That's just how girls are where she's from. As if I knew what girls from anywhere else were like.

When they did meet Jess, my parents didn't show concern about the fact that she acted like a boy. I was the only one who even seemed to notice.

"My dad put it in," I explained, once I had Jess standing under the hoop. "I don't like basketball really. You can use it, as long as my dad isn't parked here."

She sank three shots before saying thank you.

Dad installed the hoop above the driveway, his truck topper barely clearing the net. I'd asked for a basketball jersey for Christmas that year, so he thought I wanted to play. But I'd only asked because *Seventeen* magazine did a spread on hip-hop fashion (for white girls) in which all the white girls wore oversized basketball jerseys with their short shorts. I didn't get the jersey, I just got the hoop.

I wasn't coordinated enough for basketball, but I was one

of the best tumblers in my gymnastics classes. Never the best, but close. The best girls were the stupid-brave ones; the ones who flung their reckless bodies into the air like they didn't have necks to break. The small and skinny and stupid. My legs grew thick with muscle that I hesitated to use. My calves would catch like a shotgun blast when I set off to run the length of the floor. I'd throw my arms over my head, feet over my arms, into a roundoff that I finished by jumping higher than anyone else in class. But I always hesitated before throwing myself backward into a tuck or handspring, barely making it over. What held me back was mental, not physical. My sister was the stupid-brave one, and she would become the gymnast.

"Why don't you girls use that basketball hoop I bought you?" Dad would ask every once in a while. He wasn't talking about *us girls*. He was talking about me. I never appreciated anything he did for me, and this question, more than anything, served to prove that point. I wouldn't answer, knowing silence to be the smartest choice, and Dad would scoff, would walk out of the room without argument. He also understood silence to be his best option.

That was before Jess.

Hands on his hips like a proud coach, Dad would step outside to watch Jess and me play one-on-one. He knew special when he saw it. I would reach toward her, freckled limbs moving all around me, Dad standing right there, admiring Jess from the carport. She'd lunge at me like a puppy, letting me take hold of the toy from its mouth, but just long enough to pull it back again. I'd try to impress her, to put up a fight, to get my sweat all over her, but it was useless in the end. She needed a boy to play with just about as badly as my father did.

Jess hadn't yet shorn her sandy waves into the boy's

cut she would sport as a teenage butch, a small black comb pulled from her back pocket to run through it when she got nervous or bored. She was not yet a danger to him, nor to his daughter.

After Jess realized that I was an unworthy opponent, she invited neighborhood boys over to provide a challenge. Listening to Jess heckle the boys through the open window while I picked over green beans and pork chops at the kitchen table, I complained that they'd taken over *my* basketball court.

"You never played out there anyway," Dad shrugged.

I, too, only wanted the toy once it had been pulled away.

Eventually, I accepted the court as hers and sat under the elm beside the house, pretending to read books and swatting at mosquitoes while Jess beat the boys. They never did what you expected boys to do when they'd been beaten by a girl. They didn't hurl insults at her. They didn't whine. They didn't even call each other pussy. Either they didn't consider her a girl at all—given her looks, her height, her mannerisms, her talent—or they simply respected her. I would wager it was the former.

I grew to love watching Jess beat the boys. I watched as her sports bra soaked with sweat, a wet creep from her armpits down to where her cutoff T-shirt started and I had to stop. Her fine, golden armpit hair was starting to sprout and show in the sun. She was a year older than me but didn't seem to notice her own puberty. I'd already started shaving my armpits in anticipation, so if the hair was coming in, I never saw it. Jess was rough, and I sanded myself smooth. I had long brown hair, straight teeth, and boxy gymnast thighs that I hated. I was getting closer to pretty, but the boys didn't yet watch me the way that I watched Jess.

When we got a bit older, my friendship with Jess moved

from my driveway to the pool hall in town. A gas station with a low-ceilinged, fluorescent-lit back room operated like a bar without booze, an adult arcade: a pool table and a few video poker machines. If you were over twenty-one, you could buy beer in the front and carry it to the back. Teenagers were allowed inside, and the adults who hung around there were the types who didn't mind furnishing alcohol to minors. They didn't even kick us out for smoking cigarettes. Everything about the place was illegal.

In the heyday of the pool hall, Jess bet a drunk she could beat him and did, winning his professional pool cue in its very own black leather case. I watched and chewed up my cuticles, knowing she had nothing to pony up if she lost and sensing he wouldn't take *nothing* for an answer. Then, I watched her win with the exactness of a mathematician and a magician's finesse, like I always had.

When girlhood gave way to high school, when my mom got a raise and we moved to a bigger house on the hill at the end of our street—so close that when we unloaded the last of the boxes and went back for the dog, we let her into the new house and she ran right back to the old one—we left the basketball hoop behind and my dad installed a pool table in our brand-new garage. He grew up with a pool table in the basement, and my mom figured billiards was a good skill for girls to have, in case we should end up in a bind in a bar, needing to place a bet. Until then, it was a good idea to keep my ass out of the pool hall.

"I was a shark back in my day," Mom bragged. She never stepped foot in the garage.

Once my dad got the game room set up, Jess swung that drunk's pool cue in its leather case over her shoulder and carried the thing everywhere.

"I'm comin' over," she'd mutter in my direction as she

stepped off the school bus behind me. Never a question—a declaration of intent. Jess sauntered up the hill to my house five minutes behind me and walked into our garage like it was hers, like she ran the joint.

"Why is that lez over here?" a cheerleader friend asked one day after school, her body hung halfway out my bedroom window, smoking a cigarette. She flicked the butt into the yard and ducked back inside. I didn't have to check the backyard to know exactly what lez she had seen outside my house.

Jess never came out as gay. She didn't have to. When we got to high school, old friends developed new senses and the words *dyke* and *lez* replaced *weirdo* and *loser*. And so, at school, me and Jess weren't friends—we weren't even neighbors, as far as I was concerned. We shared an art elective, but we didn't sit at the same table. When I passed by for a new pastel stick or to sharpen a pencil, I'd glance at her drawings and they were always the best in class, but I never complimented her.

"I don't, like, invite her over," I told my cheerleader friend. "She just comes when she feels like it." I clicked the remote through the channels and landed on MTV. "She's friends with my sister."

"Your mom shouldn't let her around your sister," she replied.

I knew Jess was harmless to my sister, but I wasn't so sure about myself.

Alone on my front porch after my friend left, I pulled my knees in close to my chest, swaddled myself in my cheerleading hoodie, and watched Jess walk down the side of the highway, sucking down a Marlboro Red in full view of the town cops who drove by but never bothered ticketing her for underage smoking. I watched her flick the cherry tip of her cigarette. Sparks ricocheted off the pavement as she turned down the street where her house sat quiet, awaiting her return. Other nights, I'd watched her walking hand in hand with her girlfriend, Sasha. It was a miracle no one ever swerved to hit them, walking like they did deep into the evening, looking like two skinny fags in love. I watched them, squeezing my thighs together in a private gesture equal parts disgust and desire.

Sasha was rail thin. She covered her buzzed head with a beanie that drooped down over sunken eyes, even in the summer. If she were shameless enough to shave her head, that beanie suggested otherwise. Jess never said anything about getting a girlfriend. One day, she just had one. It must have been simple for her and Sasha to find each other: you could tell both of them were queer from a mile away.

I was sure that Jess met Sasha the same way every kid met Sasha: looking to score booze. She would buy cases of beer for plenty of underage kids. She did it especially for girls, and that was how I knew her too.

"Fuck, y'all, I can't get it, not worth it," Sasha would say when we asked, shaking her head in refusal.

You always had to ask her twice, but we knew the drill.

"Please, Sasha," I would beg, smacking my gum between my teeth, a gesture I thought would look sexy but felt stupid as soon as I started. "If we get busted, we'll say some old dudes bought it for us outside Minute Mart."

Sasha would start to soften.

In a couple of years, my guy friends will make me go into our dealers' trailers to buy bags of weed, sure that a girl will get a fatter bag. I will smack my gum the same way, standing in a dealer's dirty living room, trying not to sit down on the couch where he'd put his hands on my boxy thighs before weighing out an eighth of an ounce. The boys probably learned it from Sasha.

Sasha would take a drag off her cigarette and shift her weight from one ratty Vans sneaker to the other, her sharp hips jutting from left to right. After this ritual, she'd snatch the money we'd pooled together from my hand and count it aloud: "Ten, fifteen . . ." She'd tug up on her sagging jeans.

"Fuck, fine, but I'm gettin' myself a forty, so you ain't gettin' no change."

An hour later, Sasha would park her car behind the library and cross the railroad tracks to a rendezvous point on the riverbank, where she could drop the case of beer without anyone catching the handoff. But Sasha didn't ever leave the scene of the crime. She'd crack her forty right there and stay put.

The boys would light a campfire on the riverbank, and I'd step to the periphery with any other girls down there. The boys learned that throwing soda cans and Bic lighters into the flames ignited a thrum of possible injury, another layer of good high. If you didn't watch them, they'd ask to borrow your lighter and modify it so that the flame would shoot up five inches. My friend Jon was the best at it: he could do the whole modification one-handed, inside his pocket. He went crazy for the smell of singed eyelashes, and he'd just as soon do it to a girl as a boy, even though the girls had more emotional investment in keeping their eyelashes intact. As the summer sky turned from blue to black to blacker, we'd stumble drunk and hungry up off the bank and across the tracks, our shoes sticky with red Ohio River mud, incriminating every last one of us.

"Keep your ass off that riverbank!" my mother would say if she caught me coming home with river mud on my shoes. She was always telling me to keep my ass out of places—the riverbank, the trailer park, the strip mines outside of town—because she knew what it felt like to get stuck. Like me, my mom had been trouble for her parents since she was small.

Born left-handed and assumed by the laws of Appalachian folklore to be marked by the devil, she was forced to eat and write with her right hand, a cruelty that stunted her language until puberty. Despite having four siblings, she was the child her mother sent to the neighbors' houses to ask for a cup of *sha-sha-sha-sugar*. Like throwing a kid who can't swim into the deep end, she was forced to be the one who asked.

Mom got pregnant with my half-brother in October, two months past her fifteenth birthday, the weight of the stutter still thick on her tongue. She didn't tell anyone until March, when her ninety-five pounds became a hundred and ten. Her parents forced her to marry the boy who got her pregnant in April, and she conveniently had the baby when summer break began, right after her sophomore year of high school. It was 1972, not even a year before the Supreme Court made a decision on *Roe v. Wade*. She told me this story once my half-brother had grown into a man, when I was fifteen myself and needed a warning. She dropped the date without saying she would have terminated the pregnancy, but it was clear to me that she would have.

At fifteen, my mom, a child bride, moved to the other side of the county to live with her child groom. After the baby, no one knew how she would get to school in the mornings, much less graduate. But the vice principal of her high school lived on that side of the county, and Mom was able to catch a ride with him to and from school, at least until she'd had enough of his pleas to fool around before the morning bell rang. There was no question anymore that she was the kind of girl who did such things. It would have been easy to bow out of school, to quietly join the ranks of local dropouts. But she was determined to graduate, stutter or no stutter. Baby or no baby. Ride or no ride.

She transferred schools and walked across the gymnasium

stage at sixteen, with just enough credits to graduate a year ahead of schedule, baby and husband and parents all together on the bleachers. When she caught her dad's eye, she held up her diploma and yelled, "Told ya!" He was the one who most underestimated her. That day in her cap and gown, she must have felt free, but she was stuck as anything.

Entrapment would make her into a mother who was impossible to fool. She took no cheap thrills in punishing her children, but she did what she could to warn us away from the same trailer park she had once landed her own ass in.

More than mine, Jess's mother was overly protective. On evenings when her screeches for Jess to come in past curfew didn't turn her daughter up, she'd walk door to door, searching. If we heard a knock an hour after sundown, it would likely be Jess's mom.

"Jessie here? She s'posed to be home before nine!" Her brow would knit itself into a furrow so deep it looked painful.

"Not here." A door closed.

"Try over at that nasty thing Sasha's house," someone might suggest under their breath.

At our house, my dad would say, "Check out in the garage."

"You see 'er, tell 'er to get home!" Her mother nodded good-nights to those parents who had a better handle on their babies.

The next morning on the bus, everyone would laugh at Jess and her mother.

"Did you get your ass spanked last night?" some boy or another would ask.

"I'll spank you, faggot," Jess would reply, refusing humiliation. The boys would stand down.

Some nights, I watched from my porch as Jess and Sasha turned off the highway, down a path carved through thick brush beaten down by boys riding ATVs and men hunting squirrels. By then, it was overgrown, and the two of them stepped softly, picking their way through thistle and thorns and poison oak. I watched Jess's ball cap point left, toward town, then right, toward the power plant, before they disappeared into the thicket. She made sure no one saw them go in there. But I saw.

The next time I was alone with Jess, sitting on that same front porch, I asked her if she and Sasha went back in the woods there to smoke pot.

"Next time," I asked, "can I come?"

Jess laughed and told me that she and Sasha fucked in those woods by my house. It was the first time Jess admitted, at least to me, that she had sex with Sasha. They walked hand in hand, sure, but so did plenty of teenage lovers who weren't stealing away to fuck in the woods. They couldn't find any privacy at home, she said. Someone was always lurking, watching her around all the corners in that town. I had been one of them: one of the many waiting to catch Jess in the act. I was disarmed by her admission, and wondered if she could smell the curiosity wafting out from between my legs.

"It's deer season," I said, trying to recover. "Y'all better be careful."

Every year we heard tales of kids getting shot, their rustling footsteps mistaken for those of a doe.

The possibility of a desperate, teenage fuck in the woods, of being mistaken for a deer by a hunter trying to feed his kids, horrified by the life he'd taken—and being watched by the neighbor girl, who secretly wishes to be part of what you're about to do in the dirt—all these possibilities hung there, in the space between Jess and me, alone together on my front porch.

4

• •

I loved the internet because it was a place where I could lie as much as I wanted, whenever I wanted, to whomever I wanted. These lies were made possible by my mom's hard labor. When I was in junior high, she saved $100 from each overtime shift she worked to buy us the desktop computer that would turn our dining room into our *computer room*. In that computer room, I would lie and lie and lie.

I met the first real victim of my lies on AIM. He asked the question that all men on the internet asked me—*A/S/L?*—and I answered with my favorite lie: *18/F/Massachusetts*. He told me he was *Daniel, 21/M/Scotland*. I named myself *Josephine* and based my character on Joey from *Dawson's Creek*. Over months of emails, I made love confessions lifted directly from the show's dialogue, praised by TV critics for its intelligence and wit. He said he was a college student with a broken heart that he needed to mend. He said he might be able to study abroad in Boston, to see America and meet me, and I had no reason to believe he was lying, so I had to break it off.

Every day, the same question from a different guy, and every day, I would give a new answer, variations on my standard responses. Sometimes, I told the boys that I was a lesbian, and they asked me to cyber with them anyway. I never said no.

By the time a girl named Sam asked the question, I had gotten bored of lying. I told her the truth: *16/F/WV.*

She responded, *16/F/PA.*

Where in Pennsylvania? I typed, faster than I'd ever typed before. I'd been to Gettysburg with my parents, walked Civil War battlefields on midnight ghost tours. I knew that it was possible to drive in one straight shot from West Virginia to Pennsylvania.

Sam was even closer than Gettysburg. She was only a three-hour drive from my hometown; I calculated the distance on MapQuest as soon as her message with the town's name appeared on my screen. My pulse raced. I had never spoken to anyone online that, with a little determination, I might meet face-to-face. I had a driver's license and no more qualms about lying to my parents than I had about lying to people from the internet. Nothing was holding me back from Sam.

Our online friendship escalated from exchanging deep song lyrics to confessing our insecurities, our equally destructive coping mechanisms, and our mutual frustration with our fathers—hers absent, mine not absent enough. I looked for her screen name every time I logged on. She lived most of her life on the internet, but when she wasn't online, I read the lyrics she posted in her away messages. I searched for her favorite bands on Napster and burned whole CDs of songs that told me she was offline.

Sam asked me for a photograph of myself, but there weren't any good ones on the family computer. In the folders of uploads from my mom's digital camera, I was slumped over holiday gift refuse in the dorky pajamas she'd bought me to match my sister on Christmas morning. I only wanted Sam to see me wearing makeup. I closed the folders and dug through a shoebox of photos I'd taken on disposable cameras, picked out a sophomore-year cheerleading shot, and carried it over to Katie's house because she had a scanner and we did not. I got home with the photo on a disc, uploaded it to the computer, and emailed it to Sam.

I look fat, I typed—lied—in the email, inviting her to correct me. As far as I was concerned, *U look skinny* was the nicest compliment one person could pay another.

Sam replied with a shot of her gazing up at the camera with sad puppy-dog eyes. I knew immediately that it was the kind of photo you would use to get a girl off the internet to like you, and it worked. I liked her boyish short hair, spiked up at the top with cement-strength hair gel, her near-black pools-for-eyes, and slightly crooked teeth poking out from between her lips. Her photo only revealed her arms and her face, but I imagined her belly warm against mine. I could tell from the picture that Sam was queer, but weeks of chatting passed before she typed, *I've got something to tell you . . .*

I told Sam that I knew she was gay but not that I had imagined it, had pictured her doing gay things and pictured her doing them with me.

Did you guess when you saw my picture?

Yeah, I typed, trying to leave it at that.

Are you? she asked.

My heart thrashed against my ribs. If Sam was gay, it meant something about me too, about why I'd sent her the photograph and burned all those CDs. It said something about why I kept talking to her, weeks after I saw her picture, looking as queer as Jess but worse. Jess was queer, but she was *our* queer. Sam was a stranger.

I logged off. I wasn't sure if saying *me too* or *I'm not* would have been more inaccurate, but typing the word *gay* on my shared family computer was not a risk I was willing to take, one way or the other.

In the days after Sam came out to me, I jumped on the trampoline with my sister, let her curl up into a ball while I pummeled her around, yelling, "Popcorn!" until I was exhausted from bouncing and she was exhausted from squealing but still begged me to keep going. I played softball with Dad. He threw me pop-ups and grounders, and when I caught them, I hurled them back fast, like he was really the first baseman and we were really teammates mounting a defense. He put his arm around me and asked if I wanted to go across the river to get milkshakes from our favorite spot. I sucked down my chocolate banana shake and pretended that nothing had changed because I knew that everything had.

When I finally did log back on to AIM, Sam told me she had been worried I'd never speak to her again. She said she'd cut her ankle with a razor blade, thinking that she ruined our friendship. I thought that was terribly romantic, but instead of saying so, I sent her back some Garbage lyrics.

I didn't want Sam to think I was gay, but I didn't want her to think I was not gay either.

My heterosexuality was not theoretical; I had acted on it. I'd had a boyfriend, and I'd had sex with him. We'd had sex in a hot tub. We'd had sex outside in a field. We'd had sex on a pullout hotel bed while my mom and sister slept in the adjacent room. We'd gotten caught having sex by his mom, and she'd told my mom to put me on birth control. After our breakup, I'd had sex with other boys. None of them were remarkable, but all of them were proof that I wasn't queer.

I just want a lesbian friend, I told myself. A lesbian friend besides Jess, who'd never even uttered the word *lesbian*, at least not to me, and who'd never left the state of West Virginia, at least not since she moved into that house down the street. I wanted a lesbian friend from the eighteenth largest city in Pennsylvania, close enough to Pittsburgh that you could call it a suburb and people might believe you. What counts as city life is relative to the country life of the country girl. Having a lesbian friend who lived in the eighteenth-largest city in Pennsylvania made me feel a little less country. It felt like having an online boyfriend, another person I could easily fool.

Sam didn't really know anything about me. She didn't know that my heterosexuality wasn't at all theoretical. She didn't know that my parents grew up in my hometown and would never leave it. She didn't know my cheerleading coach, who told me that my tumbling was coming along but my smile needed work. She didn't know that I hated school but got good grades because it was so easy I had no reason to fuck it up. She didn't know anything that I wasn't willing to tell her. With Sam, I could be whomever I wanted to be. I could be the kind of person who had gay friends. I could even be gay.

In 2002, the internet didn't yet feel like a place where teenage girls met charismatic strangers and ended up on TV shows about missing persons. When I asked my mother if I could go stay for a few weeks in June with a friend from the previous year's summer camp, she agreed to drive me three and a half hours north and left me in a McDonald's parking lot with few questions about the girl who looked like a boy, waiting there to pick me up. Not until my mom walked out of McDonald's with the large black coffee and two apple pies that would fuel her long drive home; not until she handed me a hundred-dollar bill, and said, "That's gotta last you two weeks"; not until then did I realize what I was actually doing. I wasn't there to make a lesbian friend. I was there because I was a lesbian.

Sam's homemade Sleater-Kinney tank top was tucked into her baggy jeans, held together with a silver studded belt. She grinned at me like a girl with a crush, her crooked teeth nibbling into her bottom lip on accident. Her bleached-blond hair was still a little spiked on top from what must have been yesterday's faux-hawk, but fuzzy and soft around the temples, where I would touch her soon after my mother left. Looking Sam over, from top to bottom, I knew that my mom must have suspected I was queer. That she would be thinking about it all the way home.

"Be good," she said like a warning, and I blushed.

And then she was gone.

Sam drove us to her house and introduced me to her pet rats and tarantulas, but all I could see was the framed photograph of her ex-girlfriend sitting on a bookshelf between the creepy aquariums. Sam had told me about this girl over chat. I knew that she had cheated on Sam with more than one boy and tried to kill herself when her mother found out that she was bisexual. Holding her picture, I forgot all of that. I saw only that she was prettier than me: big boobs stretched her cool black LOSER T-shirt taut across her chest, and her lips shimmered dark under purple lipstick. She would have looked good standing next to Sam, their wallet chains clinking against each other. I was envious, but I had decided all the way back in junior high that I was never going to wear Goth clothes or try to kill myself.

I dropped my duffel bag onto a clear patch of carpet in Sam's messy room and brought out photographs of my own: proof of the life I'd been telling her about for months on AIM. Flipping through the stack, she paused at a photo of me kissing a neighborhood boy who I hoped made her feel how I felt about her big-titted ex. It wasn't a moment I would have chosen to preserve on my own: not a truth, but a dare. Someone had swiped my disposable camera and saved the kiss for posterity. I had packed it in case I needed to remind myself that I wasn't gay. Looking at it between Sam's fingertips, I remembered that the boy in the photo had drooled through his braces when we kissed, and when he pulled away, I had to slurp up his spit, else it would have spilled out of his mouth and down the front of my shirt. I wasn't worried about my shirt, but I was worried about his ego, so I swallowed.

"Is that your ex-boyfriend?" Sam asked, her voice smaller than it had been before she'd seen it.

"No, just a friend," I said, and shrugged, like it was none of her business.

I was trying as hard as I could to draw a boundary between the life of the photographs and the life I was testing out on Sam's bedroom floor. The drunk cheerleaders holding up bottles of Hot Damn! cinnamon schnapps, the cute stoner boys rolling joints, me and my friends showing off our belly button rings—those were photographs of my life, and this was something else. But Sam didn't make it to the end of the stack before she leaned in and put her lips on mine. Her heavy hand rested itself, certain, on my thigh. I had walked into her bedroom less than two hours before and already her mouth was on my neck. Meanwhile, my mother's car wasn't even safely off the interstate.

Sam and I spent two weeks sweaty, fucking for hours a day in her mom's two-bedroom, one-bathroom trailer without air-conditioning. We barely left except to walk to McDonald's or Subway, where I would order double and eat until I felt sick. The sex made me ravenous, but I hated leaving Sam's bedroom, tiptoeing out, past her mom, into the kitchen. She looked up at me from her recliner like she could smell her daughter on me, and surely, she could. Sam brought me bowls of cereal in bed, and cheeseburgers she fried herself. When the calories revived me, I pulled her back in and pushed her hands down under the covers. I had never been so hungry in my life. Sam didn't yet know how to move her fingers inside a woman. When she got it wrong and prodded at me clumsily, I accepted the pain of it. I couldn't see her as anything less than perfect, and so I blamed my own body for anything that hurt.

Sam's rats, tarantulas, ball python, and giant cockroach, all of them creaked and shifted in their glass cages through the night while we slept among them in that cramped room. Sam told me she loved these creatures because everyone else found them unlovable, like her. I touched her face and kissed her all over and told her that she was the most lovable creature I had ever seen. I'm sure there were girls like Sam where I lived—girls who were strange, who were hurt and who hurt themselves and found beauty in it. That tragic kind of beauty that can intoxicate teenage girls. If those girls did exist in my town, they weren't cheerleaders, so I never knew them. I had to leave to find one.

On the final night of my visit, Sam and I clung to each other and cried ourselves to sleep. In the morning, a bang on the bedroom door woke us up. My mom had arrived early, and I barely got to say goodbye. Both of our mothers stood in the living room, making small talk while I finished packing. We didn't even close the door for one last kiss. The next day, Sam wrote to say that one of the smaller tarantulas had gone missing from its cage and she found it after I left, smashed to death under some blankets.

Without me, Sam had *Final Fantasy* and her bass guitar and her brooding loneliness. I didn't know what I had anymore, without her. The life of my photographs was waiting for me when I returned, but I had a hard time recognizing myself in it. I had work to do, perfecting my back hand-springs for cheerleading camp, getting in shape for summer softball—but all I wanted to do was to wrap myself up in bed, close my eyes, and remember what it felt like: the feeling of Sam.

Softball could have been a distraction from the heartache, but I found myself wary of Jess—afraid my queerness would be detected by association—and paranoid that my dad might notice. She was the team's pitcher, and he was the coach. Every summer since I was small, he turned whining girls into ballplayers. Girls worried about sweating, about getting dirty; girls fussed with their ponytails. Ballplayers didn't mind dirt, they invited it. Girls sat in the dugout and talked about boys. Ballplayers kept their heads in the game. Dad had all kinds of trouble with girls. It was hard enough to ignore the things his own daughter must have done in her boyfriend's bedroom. He didn't need to hear that kind of talk from benchwarmers.

Jess never spoke about boys, and she was the closest thing he had to a real ballplayer.

"If it weren't for her trash mouth . . ."

"If it weren't for her trash attitude . . ."

"If it weren't for her absolute inability to respect authority . . ."

Jess could really be something, Dad insisted.

"She could make all-state," I agreed.

"No, *you* could make all-state," he said. "Jessie could win a scholarship."

Anyone could tell that Jess was gay, but my dad didn't yet care much about gay people. He had no reason to care. He wouldn't care until he found out about me. His anger with Jess was not motivated by something so simple as homophobia. There was something else he needed to stamp out of her.

"Jessie! Are you with us?" he'd taunt her when she

showed up to practice high as a kite, her eyes glazed, staring at nothing in particular somewhere way out over second base. He ran a step behind her when she trotted off the field, clapping his hands like an animal trainer on an agility course, trying to get his dog to pick up the pace.

"I wish he'd just take her out and spare us all the lecture," the second-string pitcher complained.

In the July heat, dust kicked up from cleats to lungs, and when you wiped your sweaty face on your T-shirt, it would come off brown as mud. Everyone knew that, in that kind of heat, you could fake fainting to get out of practice early. You could do it once a year and the coaches were none the wiser. Aside from the first practice of the year, anyway, when fainting was all but expected. At that first practice we ran laps until someone puked. Until someone puked, we ran.

Jess showed up to one of those miserable July practices white around the mouth and collapsed, not fifteen minutes in, at the pitcher's mound. This collapse wasn't the fake kind. Ballplayers never faked it, only girls in the outfield. Jess was a ballplayer, and hers a ballplayer's collapse. She was out cold, crumpled into a pile of oversize boys' workout clothing. I bounded toward her from third base, saw the beads of sweat pouring from her freckled face onto the pitcher's mound before the coaches ran toward her with water and pushed me a few feet back, out of their way.

When she came to, Jess puked right there on the field. She wiped her forearm across her lips and grabbed a bottle of water from my dad. She swished some around in her mouth, then spit it dramatically, doling out a punishment to the earth. The assistant coach, another girl's dad, stepped back to give Jess room, his hand outstretched to her broad shoulders. My dad spat in the dirt just like Jess had done and walked away.

"Druggie!" he yelled, kicking dirt across the puke-splashed ground. He slumped in the dugout, sat in silence for the rest of practice.

When he was a senior in high school, Dad got a baseball scholarship himself, to a small state school, where he studied history and pitched. He dropped out when his shoulder failed him. Jess betrayed Dad just like his shoulder.

Then, one day, at practice, she punched him.

Jess pitched a ball that he called below the strike zone. It was low, but not that low. A generous umpire may have given it to her. But Dad was the umpire at practice, and he wasn't generous. He knelt there on creaking knees to guide her into the zone, but she didn't make it. I watched from third base.

Jess didn't like the call, and she let him know it, threw her arms up and called, "Bullshit!"

Dad jumped up from behind home plate, his eyes wide like they got behind our fence, our yard, our vinyl siding, our insulation, our drywall, our paint, like they got inside our home, where he jumped up off his recliner and came at me.

Everyone can see this, I thought. *Everyone is watching.*

My dad shared the secret of his anger with Jess and the whole team. It had always been concealed, known only to our family of four. No matter how often she hung around in our garage, Jess was not family.

She stumbled back from him, braced herself, and threw her fist into his face. His salt-and-pepper mustache, yellowed at the lips with sweet tea stains, bloodied.

When we grow up and away from the town that raised us, I'll ask Jess, "Do you remember hitting my dad?"

She'll say she doesn't. She doesn't think she hit him. Maybe she did? Sounds like her.

But she'll remember that I wanted to.

5

. •

My mother kept our family photo albums stashed inside the end tables that hugged either side of our living room couch. That summer, after I came home from two weeks at Sam's, I pulled them out, looking for versions of myself that I recognized, turning up versions that I did not.

Lying on the carpet of my bedroom floor, paging back through time, I flipped to the photograph of the pretty baby contest.

In 1985, my parents entered me in my first and only beauty competition: our county fair's pretty baby contest. My mother took the stage in a wood-paneled room, held me up like a prize-winning blueberry pie, and I took home the blue-ribbon. This big win became part of my family's lore, my parents often reminding me that, at eight months, I was the most beautiful girl in the county. Hell, in all of West Virginia, as far as they were concerned.

I had seen the photo many times before, but this time I noticed my mother's hair. Her wild copper curls were cropped short on top, while the back hung down long, below her shoulders. I pulled it out from under its cellophane, held it up close to examine it. I didn't recognize my fat baby face fighting for air under lace and tulle, but I did recognize my mother's haircut.

"Mom! Oh my God!" I screamed down the stairs the way I did to mark any minor emergency: my sister swiping clothes from my bedroom, my Discman batteries dying. I heard Mom drop a laundry basket and make her way upstairs to find me leafing through the photo album, another nonemergency in a long line of nonemergencies.

"What?" she asked, annoyed that she'd run up to find that nothing terrible had happened behind my bedroom door.

"Mom, when I was a baby, you had a *lesbian haircut*!"

I laughed at her misfortune, certain that whatever had happened to me in secret that summer, it would never result in an ugly lesbian haircut.

Mom snatched the photo out of my hand, sucked her teeth, and smiled. She tapped it a few times in her palm and then handed it back to me.

"I got that haircut to piss off your father."

• •

Every August, roaring big rigs rolled down the state highway to our county from some other county. They carried big-top tents, funhouse mirrors, and the masses of steel and wire that carnival workers somehow turned overnight into the Tilt-A-Whirl, the Rock-O-Plane, the Ring of Fire. They hosed down the rides, cleaned off the puke and cow shit from their last stop. They replenished the stock of goldfish swimming circles in their plastic bags, awaiting the first kid who will sink a Ping-Pong ball into a bowl on the midway, winning himself a new pet for a week, until it dies. My parents planned on going in 1985, as they had every year before and would every year to come. But in 1985, they weren't just going to see

Marie Osmond sing "Paper Roses" on a hot summer night. Their baby was pretty; everyone said so. They wanted to take that blue ribbon home.

They had struggled with me, a colicky baby, loud and unhappy. My aunts and uncles, even my own grandmothers, wanted nothing to do with me until my stomach settled and I unclenched my little fists, unfurled the baby pain that made me scream late into the nights for my first year on earth. At least I was pretty.

Mom gave me no context for how or why he said it, only that days before the fair began, she and my dad got into an argument and he called her a bitch for the first and the last time. To hear her tell it, she didn't make a fuss. The argument ended when she walked straight out of the house and drove to the local beauty parlor, where she interrupted the gray-haired old ladies who had paid good money for that hour of gossip. She slammed the door behind her, bells jingling to announce her arrival, as if there would have been any way to miss her.

"Make me look like a bitch," she demanded.

What she wanted was a mullet, like Joan Jett's, or Cher's.

"A real bitch haircut," she called it, "rock and roll."

Mom didn't use the word *mullet* when she told me the story, but *mullet* is what she meant.

"You call me a bitch, I'll show you a bitch," she growled in my direction, as if I were the one who had said it, not my father.

"It wasn't a bitch haircut, Mom," I called out to her as she left my room. "It was a *lesbian* haircut."

I slid the photograph back into the album, walked downstairs, and slid the album back into the cabinet. I walked back up to my room and slid myself deeper into the closet. A few weeks later, I would return to school for junior year. I may have had lesbian sex, but I had a decidedly *straight* haircut.

At the end of a still-hot September day, buses lined up as they always did in the school parking lot, belching their diesel fumes into our lungs. I glanced up at one that was headed to another part of the county and spotted two lesbian haircuts, dyed Manic Panic red and purple, smashed together, sharing a single pair of headphones, too close for my comfort. Ever since summer, I had been carrying around a secret that sloshed around in the pit of my stomach and ended up in the cotton crotch of my underwear. When I saw the two girls together like that, earlobe to earlobe, thigh surely pressing into thigh, everything I had done with Sam bubbled up into my throat. The want for what they had swarmed inside me and exploded in a scream.

"Fucking dykes!"

I yelled it loud enough that everyone around me stopped to see who I was and who I was about to fight.

Manic Panic Purple turned, saw me, and opened the bus window. She yelled nothing in return, just stuck her head out the window, placed the V-spread of her first two fingers over her mouth, and wagged her tongue fast and hard, looking me right in the eyes until the bus pulled away. Her pentagram necklace, the least menacing thing about her, dangled out the window.

When I got home, I took the stairs two at a time, closed my bedroom door, and lay down in the spot on the carpet where I flipped through our family photos. I found Manic Panic's picture in another set of albums: my high school yearbooks. I turned to her page in every year. I noticed the blond roots peeking out from under her tenth-grade black-dye job, the eyebrow ring she added junior year. She armored herself against popular girls like me, but I knew we had the same tender parts underneath.

Someday, I will try to kiss her at a gay bar in a town an

hour away, and she will reject me right there on the dance floor.

The days got shorter and colder, and I spent hours of each one burying the queer version of myself in letters to Sam. I finished my work in geometry or French and flipped to the back of my notebook, where I wrote declarations of love, intentions for marriage, more than a decade before gay marriage would be legalized. We loved each other in those letters like we didn't know anyone would hate us. We wrote like Matthew Shepard hadn't been tied to a fence and left for dead when we were in eighth grade, like all the movies they'd made about him weren't showing up on our TV screens that summer we fell in love. Off-screen, an effeminate boy at school got his fingers slammed inside his locker, and I saw him sitting outside the office, bloody hand on ice, waiting for someone to collect him and say, "Stand up for yourself like a man!" I figured it was only a matter of time before he ended up on TV.

After school, I started driving over the river to Ohio, forty minutes to the nearest Blockbuster, where I rented *Boys Don't Cry* and *The Laramie Project*, *High Art*, and *Gia*, and retreated with them to my bedroom. I locked my door, and my walls lit up with the cool blues of queer tragedy. Not so much steeling myself against the coming pain as stealing it for myself, I became obsessed with the ways the world would come to know and hate me.

Sam already knew about hatred. Detectable in her shyness, and her haircut, which had gotten shorter and shorter since middle school, Sam's queerness had already made her a target. In her letters, she asked me to take her away from her high school where no one spoke to her, from her mom's house where the checks kept bouncing and the phone kept getting turned off. When the bills were paid, Sam complained, her mom kept the phone line hot, taking the computer into the living room, where she could spend her days online, finding guys who wanted to cyber. She invited internet boyfriends from all over to come stay, and when Sam couldn't sleep under the noise of their fighting and fucking, she wrote me letters to drown out the noise. We hatched plans to get her out of there, to live together—me in college, her in the Air Force—in an apartment she promised she could pay for once she finished boot camp. Our letters were the kind that can only be written by lovers who had been hurt, but not in a particular way, not by each other.

One day when I was at school, my mother read a fat stack of them. I found her at four o'clock in the afternoon, perched on my bed, hunched over the letters, scanning the words for some recognizable version of her daughter, the pretty baby she'd held in her arms at the county fair. She had unfolded them one by one, and when she tried to hide what she had done, she couldn't fold them back. Nimble teen girl fingers had creased the paper, carefully, a booby trap for snooping parents. Sam had folded them into the shape of birds. Mom folded in on herself. The early stages of arthritis swelled her guilty joints. What she read couldn't be unread, and it changed everything.

I stood in the threshold to my room, sick to my stomach. Mom got up off my bed and handed the letters over to me like someone who'd borrowed a book and dog-eared the pages, written all over the margins, and was nervous to return it.

"Are you going to cut your hair?" was the only question she asked.

"No!" I screamed. "Get out!"

I pushed her out of my room and slammed the door behind her hard enough that it jarred my molars. Angelina Jolie watched me cry from a dozen different angles, her face printed over and over from internet fan sites and taped to my bedroom walls. That dirty secret I kept to myself became one I shared, unwillingly, with my mother. What were once damp, hidden things had been pulled out of my dark places and smeared like mucus onto a microscope slide.

Mom paced outside my bedroom, insisting, "We won't tell your father."

I heard her walk down the stairs, open and close cabinets, and ascend again.

We won't tell your father became "Please don't tell your father."

I stood in front of my mirror, pulled at my long brown locks, frizzed at the roots, baby hairs making it wilder than I'd have liked. I always had to glue the flyaways back with a thick layer of plasticky hair spray and when I took it down, it would crunch and flake under my fingertips. Pulling it up and tying it with a bow had been the finishing touch of my high school cheerleading uniform. It was the hair that boys tugged on in middle school when they were trying to figure out how to flirt. It was the hair that my first boyfriend held on to, pushing my head down as far as he could get it on his dick, his slime coating the back of my throat like a sinus infection.

After my mother asked the haircut question, I wanted to see it lying on the floor behind me, like she had seen her own: my mother with her bitch haircut.

For weeks, I ignored her pleas to talk, to show me that she could understand me. No matter how many times she told me she still loved me, it felt, suddenly, like she loved me *despite*, which is surely a thing that mothers are capable of doing but that children are better off not knowing. A thick scab started to form over the hurt, and I was careful not to pick at it.

Gender made Jess queer before sex. She just couldn't find it in herself to be a girl. It was the same with Ben and David, the two boys at school whose queerness was suspected, then confirmed. Ben was the only boy in the marching band's color guard. He frosted the tips of his hair blond, fussed over dirt on his khakis, and could sit for an hour of class just picking fuzz off his sweaters, disgusted by the disorder of garments. He practiced twirling a flag on his front lawn. He didn't even have the decency to hide himself around the back.

David was tougher than Ben, and no one said shit to his face because they knew he would respond in kind. Dressed in florals and pastels, he sewed his own clothes and looked like an extra from a made-for-TV movie about Woodstock or Studio 54. A line of girl friends followed him like baby ducks down the hallways of our school. Neither boy's sexuality required a reveal, but I knew that mine would.

After my mother found out, she spoke to another mother, asked her to encourage her daughter to be kind to me. Her daughter had never been kind to me. That daughter spoke to another daughter. Someone asked me, and I didn't deny it. Someone else asked, and I remembered how much I liked being the sort of person that other people asked about.

The things I did were being spoken about, and once it started, I couldn't stop it, any more than my mother could unread the letters. These things I had done with Sam—and would soon do with Grace—they became more than things I had done. They became who I was.

6

• •

Jon pushed his face into mine. I closed my eyes and imagined that we were back in the sixth grade playing *touching tongues* at recess, hidden inside the playground slide with lunchtime milk still fresh on our breath. I opened my eyes and could see his facial hair growing in wild, causing inflamed white pustules to raise under his skin in the places where it wasn't yet strong enough to push through.

I had passed him—innocently, I thought—walking with his friends along a path beaten down by ATV traffic, cut between two subdivisions, one half-built and abandoned when the power plants up the highway started shutting down and laying off everyone's fathers. All the stoners and teenaged drunks hung around there, safe from the everyday violence of parental unemployment.

Jon had less violence in him than some of the other boys I knew. If a conflict was brewing, he was the type of guy to light a joint and pass it around to distract everyone. At that moment, you couldn't tell it. Jon's friends backed up, formed a circle around us. They knew the conventions of a fight. They also knew that guys shouldn't hit girls, but they didn't know if

I counted as a girl anymore. Either way, no one was going to stop Jon from defending himself against what I'd done.

"You wanna fuck like a man," he yelled, right in my face, "you better learn to fight like a man!"

I braced for impact.

But Jon turned away from me, stormed off into the woods, through briar patches that must have cut up his arms and legs—some pain at least, for one of us.

Eventually, after a few weeks of silence, Jon and I made up without apologies. Maybe he knew what I didn't: that his anger would be the least of my problems. What had once been rumor had become a cold, hard fact. I was not only a dyke but a dangerous one, converting innocent girls with big curls and doe eyes, girls who should have belonged to boys like Jon.

In the months that followed my coming out, a few of my friends made it clear that I was no longer welcome to sleep over, their bedrooms roped off like yellow-taped crime scenes, the crime imminent if not yet committed. I stopped getting invited to parties where I might try to fuck one of them.

To remedy the fallout, I had sex with a boy from school and made sure everyone heard about it. I told myself I did it because I wasn't ready to give up being straight, but the truth was that I knew I could get away with it: that Sam would never find out, that she would go on loving me and saying so in her letters.

When friends asked if I was bisexual, I said, "I don't know," because I didn't.

"What about your girlfriend?" a fellow cheerleader asked. "Does she know that you're hooking up with guys?"

Of course Sam didn't, and my silence on the matter was all the answer anyone needed. I hated myself for hurting her, but not enough to stop.

"Matt really likes you," the friend scolded, "so maybe you should stop messing around with him if you're gay or whatever."

I stopped getting invites to parties where I might fuck a boy from school.

Grace took their place.

She sat next to me in art class, where she wore short shorts and crop tops and complained about the air-conditioning. Our art teacher told Grace to put on some clothes the next time she left the house. Her Daisy Dukes were the problem, she said, not the thermostat. Grace in more clothes would have been a relief to me as well. On more than one occasion, I'd glanced down to watch pale pink goose bumps raise golden spikes of hair across her thighs and imagined laying my head there to feel them on my cheek. I hated myself for imagining it: she was a pretty straight girl who had just started dating Jon, who'd been one of my closest friends since grade school. Besides, I had heard that lesbians were predatory, and I didn't want to be a predator.

"I have hypothermia," Grace whined, putting her head down on the table. "I can't be creative when my limbs are going numb."

"Suit yourself, Grace," our teacher quipped, "the world will go on spinning without your aesthetic contributions."

Our art teacher was in her thirties and unmarried and used words like *aesthetic*. That was as close to gay as any adult I had ever met, and I loved her for it. I did my best to impress her with still life drawings of silverware. Grace printed Grateful Dead bears off the internet and colored them in to look like tie-dye.

After school, I started visiting Grace at the house where she babysat a yard full of dirty blond babies. She would watch the kids while their mom ran errands and drove from house to house, selling her OxyContin and Vicodin prescriptions. No one called them opioids, or mentioned an epidemic. Sticky sweetness covered every surface in that house, like the floor was coated in a thousand dropped lollipops and your shoes would smack like chewing gum when you tried to pick up your feet. I felt down the legs of my pants for places where I might have backed up into a table covered in dried Kool-Aid, or one of the kids had wiped a snotty hand on my jeans. Grace fit in there, hoisting babies up onto her hips with the skill of a seasoned mom, putting their whole dirty hands into her mouth to make them squeal.

Grace never asked me anything about being gay. She knew, of course, everyone knew—but she still wanted me around. If I said I was going to leave a hangout early to call Sam, Grace never asked who she was or how she was doing. *Don't be an aaaass-hole*, she would say, in her thick-as-molasses accent, and continue talking about whatever she'd been talking about before I said I might not be down to hang out all evening. Like a country dad content to drink beer in his recliner and avoid his feelings, Grace asked no questions, provided no commentary, just gave me room to ignore it altogether on the promise that I'd stay.

We hung out almost every weekend, drinking beers with boys who would someday become teenaged fathers, dropouts, shift workers, a few of them dead by thirty. A batch of heroin cut with fentanyl will eventually take out half the town's trailer park, one lifeless body left when the Narcan supply runs out. The lifeless body will belong to Justin, the only Black kid in my graduating class, and I'll wonder if the emergency response workers got to him last because his lifeless body felt like less of an emergency. When we were kids, everyone called him "Boy-Boy." That was the name printed across the back of his basketball jersey in middle school. Only in college would I realize that his nickname was what all the adults in town referred to him as—boy—never by his name.

Me and Grace and the boys pooled lunch money and scraped together the change from all our parents' car ashtrays until we had that magic $40 for an eighth of weed. We cruised country roads, making stops at one busted backwoods trailer after another, searching for a dealer willing to sell a bag to a car full of teenagers. When the evenings got colder and the boys got wilder on Wild Turkey and pills, Grace and I clung to the last hours of after-school daylight alone. Out back behind my house, we passed a joint between us. I watched her lick her finger and leave a snail trail of saliva dabbed around the burning cherry to slow its pace. We could enjoy it, for once, no boys around to bogart the whole thing. Without warning, Grace puffed and passed and blurted out that she liked me as more than a friend.

I was stoned, slow, and before I had a chance to react, she leaned in and kissed me with chapped lips and a stiff tongue. My mouth was dry from the weed. *I miss Sam*, I thought, but didn't say.

As soon as the kiss was over, Grace pleaded with me not to tell anyone. Her spit didn't have time to dry on my lips before she wiped her mouth and smeared her shame all over me.

I called Sam and told her what had happened. I blamed it on the weed, not my own cowardice or desire. I never thought I would kiss Grace, but once Grace kissed me, I started imagining a life with her kissing me always. A life with a real girlfriend who lived in my town, who would sleep over and go to prom and take me to the movies. I imagined picking Grace up for school every morning and kissing her in front of my sister, who wouldn't mind. She would just roll her eyes and say, "Get a room," like she used to say to my boyfriend, Tim. Sam sobbed into the phone, and I cried too, listening to it, as if it wasn't me who had been wrong, as if it were my right.

Before long, Grace and I found ourselves on the floor of a stranger's house, half a dozen other drunk kids sprawled out around us, crashed after a party none of us were allowed to attend. We kissed again, in the dark this time, as quiet as possible, without questions. I slid my hand into the front of her shorts and tried to make her come the way Sam had taught me. I was too scared to ask her if it worked. When I was with Sam, I felt like I was building a secret; with Grace, I felt like I was telling it. She had a curiosity, and it was my duty to satisfy. Grace didn't touch me in the ways that I touched her, but at school on Monday, she broke up with Jon, and somehow, he knew exactly what had happened.

After that, I called Grace my girlfriend, but she never held my hand at school. She didn't call herself queer or ask her parents for tickets to Ani DiFranco or buy rainbow stickers from Spencer's at the mall. She didn't tell people we were in love. She wasn't like me.

But small secrets burn through small towns like a match dropped in a dry October cornfield. Grace's mom worked at a salon where people talked, and it wasn't long before she caught wind of the rumor that her daughter was hanging out with a gay girl, and the gay girl may have gotten hooks into her daughter.

Without warning, Grace started avoiding me at school. I watched her from across the gym, laughing with her old friends, the ones who had looked down on her when she started dating Jon and pitied her when she started hanging out with me. After school, I called her and she didn't answer.

After that, I waited and she didn't call back. I didn't even care that Grace couldn't be my girlfriend anymore; I just wanted to hear what her mom had done to her. I wanted to tell her what I was afraid my dad would do to me.

Days into her silence, I pushed a note through the slots in her locker.

> *Get a bathroom pass in 3rd period. 1:30 out the side door. I need to talk to you.*

We had snuck through the school's side door before, pushed ourselves through the hole in the fence that separated school property from the Walmart parking lot, where we could hide between parked cars and share a cigarette. It was the last place we'd kissed. Grace wrote me back by lunchtime, and I found her note in my locker just before third period.

> *I'll meet you in the first-floor bathroom. I can't get caught.*

She wasn't taking any more risks with me.

I'd already been out of class long enough to raise suspicions when Grace swung open the bathroom door.

"Whatcha wanna talk about?" she asked, as if she hadn't been five minutes late, as if she didn't know.

Grace's eyes darted around the bathroom and she checked under the stalls to make sure the coast was clear. She turned her back to the door, planted her feet, and folded her arms around herself, a pose of plausible deniability.

I tried to break her posture—to pull her into me—but she resisted.

"Don't touch me," Grace whispered. I saw tears well up in her eyes, but knew she was not willing to spill them.

"You can't just stop speaking to me," I said, knowing good and well that she could. Losing Grace wasn't going to break my heart. We had never said "I love you." She was barely even my girlfriend. We had only become close a few months before the romance started, and I was growing accustomed to seasonal friendships. But her abandonment was a harbinger of what was to come and I knew it.

I tried again to pull Grace into me. She went soft then, and our bodies collided, just as my third-period teacher burst into the pink-and-white-tiled restroom. She'd suspected smoking but found something worse. She grabbed Grace's shoulder and spun her around, held her there by the arm, her fingernails gouging deep enough into flesh that she would have lost her job under normal circumstances. These weren't normal circumstances. No one would care about the little half-moons of proof like track marks on the kid in question. The teacher had seen on Grace what she'd heard about me. When she let go, Grace ran out of the bathroom and back to class without a second thought about what would happen to me.

My punishment for inappropriate behavior in the girls' bathroom: for the next month, I would need to ask the teacher on duty to watch over my restroom visits. If I couldn't conduct myself like a "normal" girl, a teacher would have to escort the "normal" girls out before I would be allowed in. If I behaved myself with supervision for a month, they'd consider letting me back in on my own.

Grace was pulled out of class and told to stay away from me, or else her parents would be notified. Turns out, that wouldn't be necessary.

I hadn't spent much time with Grace's mom. She worked

a lot, and Grace never invited anyone over to her house, never said why. So, when our phone rang after school and I jumped to answer it, I didn't recognize the voice. I knew only that the woman seething, "Faggot, you little faggot," was an adult because she used the gender-inappropriate gay slur—*faggot*—and anyone my age would have known *dyke* to be a better fit. When I heard Grace crying in the background, I realized who the voice belonged to, what I had done to deserve it.

Like a lover desperate to hear her sweetheart over oceans of distance, the crackle and pop of a poor connection, I strained through her mother's insults and listened to Grace insist: "We didn't do anything, Mom! It isn't even true!"

Fear that I would soon be lying like Grace dried my tongue, and I hung up the phone without saying a word. I still hadn't told my dad about Sam, about Grace. He would be home from work in an hour or so, and all I could think was *he knows*.

But he didn't. Not then. And by the time he found out, Grace and I would be long finished with whatever it was we had started.

It had been over a month since Grace stopped sitting with me in art. It had been over a month since she'd stopped hanging out with me at lunch. It had been even longer since she'd invited me anywhere after school. It was well into our parentally imposed separation when I found a note in my locker: *I'll be babysitting tonight. Come over.* I stuffed the note into my backpack before anyone could see it, but reached inside and read it again, secretly, a dozen times that afternoon.

The winter sun was almost down by the time school let out, so it wasn't late when I pulled into the driveway, parked where a busted old Jeep Cherokee usually sat, and stepped over the Barbie cars and BMX bikes in the yard. Before I even got a chance to knock, Grace opened the door. Without a word, she pulled me through the living room and kitchen, avoiding the kids, who I could hear down the hall, playing in one of their bedrooms. She pushed me into the kitchen pantry and kissed me, apologizing over and over for the awful things her mother had said.

We slumped onto the floor and I put my arms around her. She pressed her shoulder into my chest and I let her cry like I was the strong one, like my embrace could make it better when I knew that it couldn't.

I told her that I wanted to talk to her, but I didn't want to make things worse.

"They couldn't get any worse," she said, and I could tell that she meant it. This meeting was more than a risk for her. It was a last resort.

Then, the front door slammed.

"Where is she?"

The voice from the phone rose through the house like a flash flood.

"I know she's here, Grace!"

Grace jumped to her feet, tumbled out of the pantry and into the living room, where she swore to her mother that I wasn't there.

"You're scaring the babies," Grace admonished, and I heard one of them cry out for her from down the hallway.

"Whose car is in the driveway?"

"Mom! It's not her car! I don't know!"

Grace swore that she was alone. Swore that she was babysitting. She swore, and I listened and trembled and waited for it to be over.

Doors opened and slammed.

Grace cooed to the babies that everything was okay.

The slamming got closer still. I could feel the floor shake under heavy footsteps, my ass still planted on the pantry floor. The door swung open, and ugly yellow kitchen light washed over me, cowering in the corner with the boxes of Hamburger Helper and canned vegetables.

I tucked my head into my knees, covered it with my arms, waiting for a blow.

Grace's mother grabbed me by the elbow, pulled me up to my feet, and spit at my face. I jerked away from her and ran from the house toward my car. She chased me, first through the yard, then down the driveway, then down ten miles of highway in her bright blue pickup. I drove the speed limit, crying all the way home, watching her curse me through my rearview mirror. She kept her headlights on my bumper until I turned into my driveway, where I saw my dad outside, unloading his truck.

I resigned myself to my fate: this was how he would finally find out about me.

But she kept driving.

Inside, I headed straight into the shower to wash the spit from my hair. Like all the other moms I knew, Grace's mom loved gardening and Garth Brooks and summer evenings down by the river, wine coolers with friends and bass boat fishing. She had three children, who she also seemed to love. And she had just then chased another woman's child down a dark highway, hoping her seventeen-year-old life might extinguish, front end twisted around a guardrail or tree.

The next night, she called my house again.

My mom picked up this time, and received a warning: Keep your gay kid the fuck away from my daughter or else.

"That's all she said," Mom told me, changing the "fuck" of it to "eff."

More than a decade later, my mother will tell me the rest of what Grace's mom said to her that night on the phone. "She would rather her daughter be raped than become a lesbian," she'll recall. My mom's voice cracks when she repeats it. "I'll never forget that she said that."

The grim fates of the gay kids in movies, the tragic love story I had started to write with Sam but couldn't finish because she lived too far away and I couldn't afford the gas—none of that prepared me for what happened to Grace, and how certain I was that it was my fault.

Grace never spoke to me again, but there were rumors about what happened to her after that night. Primary among them: that Grace's parents drove her to a mental hospital, tried to have her committed for being queer.

"Some *Girl, Interrupted*–type shit," or so churned the rumor mill.

I knew the place where they supposedly tried to take her. In an effort to avoid killing herself when I was eight or nine, my mom had checked herself in there. Dad took us to visit, and a nurse gave my sister and me little cardboard cups of vanilla ice cream swirled with chocolate syrup.

I will ask my mom, eventually, if she remembers the nurses, and the ice cream.

"Yes," she'll say, "I was there for ten days."

I'll ask if she was planning to kill herself.

"No," she'll say, and then the line will go quiet. "I just wanted to have a bad car wreck where I couldn't survive. Not kill myself."

I won't press her on the difference.

There was a silver lining to the *Girl, Interrupted*–type shit. The rumor mill also churned out this gem: when Grace's mom said she wanted to leave her at the hospital because she was gay, the staff told her to leave. That it was her who needed help, not Grace.

"Can you believe it?" one gossip or another asked me.

I couldn't.

But I always kind of knew that the ice cream cup nurses up there were all right.

7

. •

Life before Grace receded like a fast car down a dirt road, kicking up so much dust that I couldn't read the license plate. Basketball season ended, and with it, cheerleading. Some friends turned against me; others toward her. I didn't know how to be friends with boys anymore. When they got me alone, they'd ask about the kinds of sex I liked, something they never cared about when they were trying to have sex with me. They asked me questions like "When two girls fuck, who's the man?" and "When are you gonna let me watch?" They got too close when they asked, made sure I felt their breath on my skin. They placed an arm on a wall behind me, became a wall in front of me. I had taken something that didn't belong to me, and they were determined to get it back. If they couldn't get it back, they wanted to know how I managed to pull off the heist. The weight of guilt pressed down on me, and like an ascetic, I found meaning in the pain.

I started listening to metal bands on my drives to and from school and playing Grace's mom's voice on repeat in my head, a percussive whisper under the thrash and growl.

Faggot.

David, too, was a faggot, and acclimated to hurt. He took me in.

David's bedroom glowed orange with Christmas lights, a paradise fashioned from the sales racks at the craft store. Fake ivy hung tenderly from the lattice he'd affixed over his bed. Half-finished acrylic paintings of nymphs and faeries spread across a messy desk littered with bottles of black and purple nail polish and semipermanent blue hair dye. Clothes were strewn about in haphazard piles across the carpet, cleared out of a closet that hid something far more important: his altar, replete with candles, incense, an authentic-looking crystal ball, and the entire occult section of the public library a few towns over, which he had stolen, book by book.

Like wearing a parka to a pool party, I walked into David's bedroom for the first time in a logo T-shirt from Abercrombie & Fitch. My mom had bought the shirt for me only after explaining that it was exorbitantly priced and I should be ashamed of myself. Because the Fitch cologne they piped into the place lingered in the overpriced cotton, I didn't wash the shirt for weeks. I wanted to smell like the mall.

Under David's tutelage, even this most basic item of clothing could become totally punk rock. As a gay kid one year older and one year wiser, David would coach me in my first line of defense against boys and teachers and parents and those cheerleaders who were no longer on my side: how to look defiantly queer.

I pulled the Abercrombie shirt over my head and stood there in a bra with my arms unfolded, skin exposed for the first time to a boy who didn't notice. David used a Sharpie marker to change the *F* in *Fitch* to a *B*, then I pulled it back on so he could slide a pair of scissors against my skin, up my arm like a threat, and cut off the shirt's sleeves. He drew a necklace of pentagrams around the collar, and made one for himself to match.

In true punk fashion, I wore the shirt to school and got in trouble for it: a teacher ordered me to turn it inside out and wear it like that for the rest of the day, a punishment usually reserved for rednecks who stomped down the hallways in shirts advertising Bud Light, or stoners sporting bright green pot leaves. They never cracked down on kids wearing shirts emblazoned with Confederate flags—those were permitted.

I sat down at my new lunch table with David and the weird girls who fawned over him, wearing the inside-out T-shirt that showed only an inverted *B* where the ink had seeped through.

"Fascists," David said, acknowledging my humiliation, and we went on dipping our chicken fingers in ketchup and washing them down with school-issued skim milk, all of us allied in our oppression.

I wanted to drop cheerleading senior year—it wouldn't quite fit with my new punk rock persona—and my parents weren't happy about it. They didn't understand that all of my cheer friends had been older, had graduated the year before me, and the squad was being overtaken by a group of under-classmen who didn't drink after games and wished the skirts were longer. The younger girls made it clear that they didn't want me to base for their pyramids. They didn't want my gay hands all over their straight thighs.

I needed a concrete reason for my parents to let me quit, and looking like a lesbian was a good excuse to refuse any ac-tivity that involved wearing a skirt. A haircut would seal the deal. I went to the salon like my mother had just days before the pretty baby contest, but instead of asking to look like a *bitch*, I asked to look like a *butch*.

"How am I gonna wear a bow?" I asked my mom when I

got home. I ran my hands through my hair, just long enough then to tuck behind my ears. Pieces of it fell into my face, making me feel like a boy heartthrob. "The bow is part of the uniform, Mom. I have to quit."

"You could have been a lesbian without looking like a boy," she said, hushed, making sure my dad didn't overhear.

She had cut her hair to stand up to him, but I wore a beanie around the house for weeks. I wasn't ready to make him face the truth.

On the off chance that they tolerated my lesbian haircut, David came up with a foolproof idea to get me disqualified from cheerleading that fall.

"Let me pierce your lip."

David had a small spike pierced into the little dip between his bottom lip and the sharp point of his chin.

"They'll never let you cheer with facial piercings," he said. "Problem solved."

It was David's idea, but I didn't let him do it. I wanted it to be my own. I gathered my supplies—ice, a picture nail, a ring, borrowed from David—and waited until no one was home. I numbed my chin with the ice cube and started slow, let the metal tip bite, determined the surface tension of my own skin. The sharp heat of it washed over my face. I wedged a slice of potato between my flesh and bottom teeth so that I didn't accidentally stab it into my gum. Then, I pushed the nail through fast, a pop of relief before I removed it and, with shaking hands, slid the ring into its place. The high from it was the same as I felt kissing Sam for the first time. A forbidden feeling, carrying me straight up through the ceiling.

Like my mother before me, I wanted to look like what I was called, wear insult like injury. I had been studying armor all my life. I watched men plant their feet and lower their hats when anything that might hurt appeared on the horizon.

I watched classmates puff up their chests, call each other faggot after being forced to read poems aloud in English class. I watched Jess pull a blade out of her pocket, use it to eat an apple or pick at her fingernails, just so everyone would know that she had it. I toughened my hands. I ate every meal until I was so full my breath got short and my body got sturdier. I quit cheerleading. I pierced my lip. I got the lesbian haircut I swore I'd never get. It felt safer, somehow, to be unfuckable.

The boys' questions changed. "Why do you wanna look like that?" they asked. "Why do you wanna look like a man?"

That thing I had taken that didn't belong to me: it was myself.

At home, I had mastered the art of moving undetected. I walked softly, avoided the creaky stair, the third from the second-floor landing. I unlatched the living room's bay window and let myself out into the night. My parents were heading into a divorce that had been a long time coming, and they lost track of who I was and where I had been. I hid my queerness from my dad for over a year, but eventually, he saw it.

He saw me leave the house in a spiked dog collar and laughed when I was sent home from school because my English teacher insisted it was a weapon. He saw the pounds I'd gained and was no longer capable of hiding. He saw the spoils of the shopping trip my mother funded, where I replaced my entire wardrobe at Hot Topic.

"What in the hell were you thinking," I heard him ask, "letting her dress like that? And that haircut . . ."

The changes I was making, little by little, they wore him down. He started asking the questions in unison with the boys at school. "Why does my beautiful daughter want to make herself look ugly?"

When he came home from work one day to find the

silver ring hugging my bottom lip, he asked the question he had wanted to ask all along: "Why are you trying to look like a dyke?"

I don't remember my answer, just his face slick with the hot grease of anger. He pulled me up off the couch like a child who needed to be carried to her room past bedtime. But he didn't swaddle me. He dropped me to the floor, my shoulder pinned. He pushed my face down into the family room carpet. It would have been the first time in years that he touched my face, because when do fathers get the opportunity? It didn't hurt, but pain blossomed there anyway.

I scrambled up off the floor, and he put his hand on his belt. He must have realized, then, that I was too old for a spanking, because he stepped back, away from me. He loved me. He wanted what was best for me. He knew that being queer wasn't it. But what could he do? He turned away, stomped toward the back door, and left, slamming it behind him. I wanted to beg him not to hate me but knew that I couldn't talk him out of it. I knew that he was lost in his rage and he would be for a long time.

I screamed after him it wasn't my fault, that I wouldn't wish what was happening to me on my worst enemy. And saddest thing is, no matter how much I loved David and the spiked leather dog collar, the lip ring and my new gay haircut, in that moment, I meant it.

8

. •

David and I got our queer education in Huntington, a college town ninety minutes away from our hometown, near the place where Ohio, Kentucky, and West Virginia meet. David would make the drive to meet up with guys from gay.com, and he let me tag along. Some of the profiles he showed me were nerdy-looking guys in polo shirts, their skinny calves poking out of khaki cargo shorts. Some looked like dads, beer bellies just starting to spill over leather belts, tufts of silver hair shimmering at their temples. Some looked like former football players who no one would have suspected. While David was hooking up in public restrooms, I passed the time looking for lesbians in Barnes & Noble.

I started on the magazine rack with *Ms.* and *Bust* and *Bitch*, treasure maps laid out across my lap. They clued me in to Ani DiFranco and Tegan and Sara, and I pulled their albums from the adult alternative section and played them all the way through, listening on the store's headphone station where you were supposed to quickly scan a CD before buying it, but I didn't have the money for that. The LGBT bookshelves were stocked mostly with erotica, or advice books for how to deal with a gay child. I picked through them until

I found titles like *Odd Girl Out*, *Tipping the Velvet*, and my favorite, *Girl Walking Backwards*. In it, two high school girls fall in love. They do drugs. They go to raves. They practice Wicca. They hate posers, and their parents. It was yet another blueprint by which to live.

David had his own ideas for how to live a gay life. Ever since he dragged himself across the finish line of his eighteenth birthday, he had been desperate to take the official plunge into gay adulthood: True Colors, a bar fifty miles upriver from our hometown. I was only seventeen, but when the opportunity presented itself, David swiped a driver's license from a friend of his older sister. I memorized her address and her birthday until they felt like my own.

We pulled down the long gravel driveway, and the unlit bar looked a little too dark, a little too abandoned, across a set of railroad tracks well off the town's main drag. The parking lot only had a smattering of cars at ten o'clock on a Friday night. David parked and pulled a bottle of rum out from under his seat. He quizzed me one last time as we passed the bottle back and forth between us. Tara on my ID was twenty years old and a Capricorn. You only had to be eighteen to get inside, but I was seventeen and scared. I got out of the car anyway and rode the rum buzz across the parking lot.

Clear plastic butcher curtains hung over the bar's entrance, separating the night air outside from the night air inside, the bar a literal meat market. The door guy didn't ask me for my address or birthday. That must only happen in movies. Instead, he glanced at the photo of a brunette who wasn't even old enough to drink and marked the backs of my hands with thick black Xs in permanent marker. I tried not to panic about whether or not I would be able to scrub them off with nail polish remover. He did the same to David, and I watched him give David's hand a squeeze that he didn't give mine, letting him know that he'd be sitting there all night if he wanted to put that hand somewhere else. We walked up to the bar and ordered Diet Cokes, lit cigarettes, and pretended like we had seen it all before.

A busty drag queen hostess with a sharp tongue and nasty name ruled the scene, quieting down the crowd for the midnight showtime. She called out, "How many *faggots* we have in here tonight?" and the crowd erupted. David squealed, squeezed my arm. It was the first time either of us had heard that word used with affection.

She asked how many dykes were there, and a few women clapped or shouted in the affirmative. My eyes darted across the crowd, trying to see which of the women had whooped and hollered, but I was too nervous to make a sound of my own.

She asked how many bisexuals were present, and more women applauded for that. The queen consoled them, said, "Don't worry, my bisexual children. I know you're confused, but the queens here tonight will help you find your way straight into some titties!" I puzzled over her gender logics. A whole new world of sexuality seemed possible inside True Colors.

When she started her number, Chaka Khan, light reflected against disco ball and sequin, and the queen mesmerized, spinning on the dance floor in a whir of color. On the sidelines of that sticky dance floor, craning my neck to watch her twirl, I felt like she and I were two weird sorts of girls swimming in that sea of men.

The queen bantered with the DJ, a stocky lesbian with a haircut David and I called the dyke spike—long in the front, short and messy in the back. I watched her up in the booth, admired the ways she moved her body with confidence, just like the men. She wasn't sheepish like the butches who kept to the sides of the dance floor, watching themselves in the mirror, trying to move without rocking their hips. The DJ bounced her ass with abandon, her cargo shorts shaking around to the beat of the songs she queued up and danced to herself, returning to her booth every second or third track to line up the next ones. I learned to dance there beside her, imagining my own body like hers: strong, boyish, and sure of itself.

After months of watching, I would eventually go home with the DJ. She had no idea I was underage and couldn't understand why I didn't know the words to all her favorite songs, not realizing that most of them came out when I was in elementary school. I wanted to be her, but I settled for being her once-in-a-while fling.

I joined the dyke billiards league and celebrated my "twenty-first birthday" at True Colors when I was only eighteen—that's when Tara from my ID became legal. I spent my senior prom night there, the dress my mother co-erced me into soaked in floor beer and the stench of indoor smoking. When a bartender asked why I was all dressed up, I claimed that I wanted to audition to be a drag queen. He told me that wasn't how it worked, and I feigned disappointment. I had made True Colors my home, but just like all the other homes I'd known, I had to lie for a while to stay there, to stay safe.

On a summer night after high school graduation, I spotted a woman I'd never seen before across the bar. She was dancing with a woman who was there so often that David had given her a nickname: Salt-N-Pepa. Salt-N-Pepa hadn't updated her style since the early nineties: she wore white high-top sneakers; high-waisted, tight-rolled acid-wash jeans; a visor; and an oversize Starter jacket that she didn't ever take off. It some-how never made her break a sweat. She wasn't wearing the jacket on the night she danced with the woman I'd never seen before. They were glued together, grinding, skin on skin.

This stranger was the most feminine lesbian I had ever seen at True Colors. Every lesbian I'd met was butch, or was trying her best to be. I was trying my best to be. The stranger's hair was long, dyed jet-black, and she wore Doc Martens, ripped-up boot-cut jeans, and a silk shirt buttoned only halfway up her chest. She had big tits, a nose ring, buck-teeth, and confidence.

A couple of hours and several beers after I spotted her dancing, I saw the stranger at a high-top in the corner and got the courage to pull up a barstool next to her. Salt-N-Pepa hovered at her side, determined to be the one in the stranger's car at the end of the night. Patrons would drive two, even three hours to get to True Colors from whatever speck of a town they had never left. The parking lot was a place to fuck, or sleep off the liquor at closing time. Salt-N-Pepa held on to the stranger's arm when I sat down, made it clear that she would be the one steaming up her car windows.

I struck up a conversation with the stranger anyway, and she told me her name was Megan. We discovered that we both drove up that night from the same county. We hadn't gone to the same high school, but she lived with her aunt and uncle just a few miles down the highway from my parents' house, the place I would be leaving for college in a couple of months. That night at True Colors, I was eighteen and she was twenty-five.

I pulled my wallet from my jeans to order another round, and realized that Megan might know the girl from my ID. They would have gone to the same high school, been close to the same age. I slid the license out of my wallet, onto the high top, and over toward her.

"Does she look familiar?"

I said it with a smirk, wanting to be a girl who could get away with anything.

Salt-N-Pepa swiped the license off the table, stormed over to the bouncer, and handed him my ID. The bouncer dragged himself up off his perch and made a beeline for me as Salt-N-Pepa cast a shit-eating grin in my direction and sauntered outside to have a smoke.

The bouncer held the ID up next to my face. Two brunettes. Tara from the ID had long hair, and mine was short, but it wasn't unusual for women in that bar to shave their heads and call themselves M.J., while their licenses read Miranda or Melanie or Melissa. But Tara's eyes were brown. Mine are green. He asked me to step into the light.

"This isn't you," he said, bored to death with underage stupidity.

I told him to go ask the DJ. I told him she could vouch for me.

He walked over to the DJ booth, held up the ID, and pointed my way. I watched the DJ shake her head—"I don't know her"—like I hadn't been in her bed a few weekends back.

Megan stood by my side through the whole ordeal.

"Get out of here, kid," the bouncer said. "Shit like this could get our liquor license pulled."

I had witnessed cops barging into True Colors once before, looking like an old-school queer-bar police raid conducted under the auspices of checking for underage drinkers. Luckily, I had just left the bar to go smoke weed in the car when officers strode in to bust the likes of me.

The bouncer walked me over to the door and slid my stolen ID into the cashbox. "I'm doing you a favor," he said, "not calling the cops. I don't want to see you back in here."

Tears welling up, I retreated outside, where Salt-N-Pepa stomped out her cigarette like she'd just done to me.

Megan followed me to the parking lot and became my girlfriend.

• •

Megan and I had sex for the first time in my parents' house. It no longer housed my parents, who had both moved on to new relationships—into new homes—but they let me camp out for the summer while they waited for it to sell. In the bedroom I would soon abandon for a college dorm room, I ran my fingertips all over Megan's skin, pausing over the pink satin scar that made its way down her left thigh, a deep tear that looked like something had been dug out of her. She told me she had a metal rod in her leg, the result of an accident, her car smashed like a soda can into a concrete overpass on her way home from her shit job at a meat-packing facility. It gave her a limp that I hadn't noticed at the bar.

"It was that job that about killed me," she answered when I inquired. "I'm doing better now."

I bent down and kissed her scar with my open mouth.

I was still asleep when Megan left the next morning. I woke up and stretched out and patted down the spot where she'd been to find it empty. Where her body wasn't, I found a roll of cash: ten twenty-dollar bills. I stuffed it under my mattress.

Megan called me the next night and didn't ask about it. She didn't even sound relieved when I told her I'd found it. I knew then that she hadn't lost it. It hadn't fallen out of her pocket. She had wanted me to find it.

"I'm not a prostitute," I laughed, not sure if I should be flattered or offended. "You don't have to pay me to have sex with you."

She told me she hadn't meant to leave it, that she just hadn't noticed it was gone. I thought about being the kind of person who could lose $200 and not notice. Megan had a job and a car, but I knew that she wasn't that type.

"I *like* having sex with you!" I assured Megan, and told her that she could have sex with me anytime she wished, "for free!" I wanted her to fuck me, but more than that, I wanted her to pick up the money. I didn't know why Megan left that cash in my bed, but I did know better than to accept money from someone if I didn't know what they were paying me for.

It wasn't that I didn't need cash myself. The year I graduated high school, West Virginia was desperate to increase its number of college-educated citizens, so the state offered a full ride to a public university for any high school senior with a B average or higher. My dad hadn't said anything about sending me off with pocket money, and my mom had recently lost her job and couldn't afford it. I had my tuition covered, took out loans to cover room and board, and was determined to make it work. I didn't know what I wanted to do with a degree, but I hoped college would keep me out of the meat-packing facility.

I asked Megan why she hadn't gone and she said she wasn't interested in college. The state scholarship I was getting hadn't been available when she finished high school, and without it, I probably would have said the same.

After Megan recovered from her wreck, she started working as a janitor at a power plant a few towns over, a place where my dad sometimes worked construction.

"I know your daddy," Megan said.

She sucked her teeth before she said it, made it sound like, *I know something you don't know about your daddy.* I didn't ask her what it was. Within a month of dating, Megan had given me chlamydia and sold my fourteen-year-old sister's boyfriend a handful of Xanax. Still, I didn't ask many questions.

Megan followed me four hours north when I left for college. She carried my heaviest boxes into the dorms. Together we tacked a poster of two women kissing in white underwear to the concrete wall above my bed and managed to get my desktop computer logged on to the campus internet. On the first night of move-in weekend, she slept next to me in my twin-size dorm bed. When my roommate showed up on night two, Megan insisted we get a hotel room. I said nothing about wanting to go to the new students' welcome tailgate party.

The night before classes started, Megan kissed me goodbye and drove home. When she arrived, she called and woke me up, just to check that I had settled in okay and to tell me that she already missed me. I wanted to be missed. My parents didn't call. They had another daughter and a divorce to worry about. I took out an additional student loan for food and books and gas to drive home as often as I could, to see Megan. Megan sent me money for weed and cigarettes. That first month of college, I realized why she had left that roll of twenties in my bed that first night we slept together. She wanted me to know that she could take care of me. I needed an adult in my life, and Megan was it.

All semester, I sat alone in the cafeteria every morning and wandered around campus alone at night, let the streetlamps wash me orange, so I could trick my roommates into thinking I had somewhere else to be. At orientation, I'd spotted a girl across the packed auditorium wearing the same yellow Tegan and Sara T-shirt as me. Every time I left my dorm, I looked for her. I only saw her once, on my way to Anthropology 101—where I learned about human evolution for the first time, since my high school had decided to skip it—and cut class to follow her. Before I could work up the courage to say hello, she disappeared into a lecture hall, swallowed up by the crowd rushing in, the crowd pouring out.

I copied down information about the college gay club from a bulletin board littered with student group flyers. The building where they held their weekly meetings was nearly empty at 8:00 p.m. and quiet enough that the squeak of my sneakers echoed when I walked down the corridor, like I wasn't alone, like I had a phantom friend. I glanced through the small window in the door, behind which the meeting was just getting started, but I kept walking: a gay kid coincidentally strolling to that particular bathroom in that particularly deserted part of campus at 8:00 p.m. on a Tuesday. When you come from a place where everyone knows you, you get no practice introducing yourself.

On a few occasions, I drove to the town's dyke bar, where you had to be twenty-one to get inside, and hung around the parking lot pretending that I'd just stepped out to have a smoke. Once, a woman came out alone and took me home. We drank our way through a twelve-pack of Budweiser, tucked up to our necks in her bed because the gas at her apartment had been shut off. We took turns learning how the other needed to be touched. That was the only night I didn't spend at least an hour on the phone with Megan. I told her I'd left my phone in a classroom, and couldn't get it back until the next morning when they unlocked the building. She would have killed me if she'd found out I cheated, but I felt like I was going to die of loneliness anyway, so it didn't matter much to me.

When fall semester ended, I had passed most of my classes with the B average that meant I could keep my scholarship. I'd flunked only University 101, a one-unit course meant to help students integrate into college life. I didn't need the F on a report card to know I failed it. Megan never asked me to transfer and move closer to home, but I knew that I needed to. In January, after a month crashing on my grandmother's couch because my childhood home had sold, Megan moved me into the second dorm room of my freshman year.

Besides my clothes and desktop computer, all I had left was my black-and-white lesbian kiss poster, which Megan helped me rehang on a new white cinder-block wall, careful not to rip its fragile corners. She was happy to have me nearby—the new college where I had enrolled was just over an hour away from the little redneck town where she still lived. Unlike me, she never wanted to get too far away.

I called my mom after I was settled at my new college, and she made it clear to me that she was skeptical of Megan.

"You know," she said, "I heard that girlfriend of yours used to have sex with a lot of the men who worked up there at the plant."

When I asked her why she was gossiping about my girlfriend, she had only one explanation: *people talk*. I hung up the phone.

I got busy trying to forget about home, but home was all around me. I did my philosophy reading and Shakespeare homework at the same Barnes & Noble where I used to wait for David to hook up with men from the internet. I spent Friday nights at an eighteen-and-up gay club called Stonewall, where I'd been in high school with my fake ID, before Salt-N-Pepa had ruined everything at True Colors. Sometimes, I still ran into David there; but now we were grown and had nothing to hide.

At the new college, I worked up the courage to join the campus queer group. The radical one, not the gay-straight alliance, where the closeted kids went to talk about their feelings. I joined the one that infiltrated the Campus Christian Center and protested their *total brainwashing tactics for breeding homophobia*. I wasn't afraid to walk into the meetings; I'd met these kids first inside that gay club, pulling flasks full of warm vodka out of our waistbands in the gender-neutral bathrooms. We danced and dated and broke up and hung out in the newly opened LGBT office, sat among the flyers about coming out to your parents, and averted our eyes when straight guys wandered in to grab handfuls of free condoms, the only reason they'd be caught dead anywhere near a bunch of fags. I read angry poetry about them on open mic night at the coffee shop across the street from campus.

By sophomore year, Megan got a new job near my university and rented us a one-bedroom apartment a couple of miles away from campus. I should have been excited to leave the dorms. The fluorescent-lit hallways always smelled faintly of vomit and the sanitizer they sprinkled on top of the vomit, and I stepped on used tampons in the communal showers on more than one occasion. But there was something wonderful about sleeping alone in a bed I had paid for myself; or would pay for one day, when the student loan bills arrived. I liked leaving the late-night leftovers line in the cafeteria after midnight, walking along the foggy lamplit paths across campus. I liked reading with the lights on as late as I wanted because my roommate never came home. I fantasized about meeting a woman at the bar and bringing her back to my dorm to drink boxed wine. I concealed a bag of it inside a cereal box, just in case, until I cleared out my dorm room to move in with Megan.

I had already started to regret moving in together when I found the email that Megan left open on the shared desktop computer that sat in the corner of our dreary bedroom.

I want to do it bent over the hood of my car. Think of a safe place to park.

The email was signed *Tony*. The name was familiar. Her former supervisor, I remembered, from that warehouse job at the meat-packing facility. The job she left after second shift and hurled herself at eighty miles per hour into a highway overpass. I had never met him, but she would drive out to see him sometimes. They went to the movies, she said. Dinners at Applebee's. I didn't know much about him until I read his email and found out that Tony wanted to fuck Megan on the hood of his car the next time they met.

I didn't stop there. I searched for more emails from Tony and found prior meetings and dirty pet names and descriptions of his favorite sex positions. I found a request for a deep-throated blow job. Then I found an email from all the way back in August, the summer Megan helped me move into my freshman year dorm. It was a negotiation for price: $250. I printed the emails and drank my way through a six-pack. Megan got home from work to find me on the bedroom floor, undone by the booze and the weight of an ending. She yelled at me like a mother whose child couldn't understand the world of adults.

"I was fucking him for free anyways," she said, "a long time before I met you!"

"I fucked people before we met too," I screamed, "but I stopped fucking them when I met you!"

I kept my mouth shut about the woman I went home with from the parking lot outside the college dyke bar up north.

"And the money?" I asked.

Megan said that she had wanted to stop, but Tony didn't, so she'd told him she'd have to charge. She'd been half joking, she said, but he went for it. It became an offer she couldn't refuse.

"I did feel bad lying to you about it," she paused, "but you also *like* that I have money."

"Everyone likes fucking money!" I howled.

But Megan was right. She picked up bar tabs and regularly took me out to dinners at Red Lobster. She bought half ounces of weed that she rarely smoked, and rolled joints for my friends. She signed us up for premium cable. I wasn't suspicious that she did all of this on minimum wage. I just thought she was an adult, more adult than me at least, and adults had money. When she wasn't paying, I bought two-for-three-dollar hot dogs at the Speedway station and scavenged food from my part-time restaurant job.

"He was getting it anyway," Megan insisted. "He would have gotten it one way or another." It was the same excuse she used when I found out she'd sold pills to my sister's teenage boyfriend. I pushed Megan out of the bedroom and slammed the door in her face.

Megan had taken care of me, and now I knew that she could because Tony took care of her. She slept on the living room floor that night, and I woke up in our bed the following morning wanting to know what it would be like to take care of myself.

"I want in on it," I told her, while she was still rubbing the sleep from her eyes. "A threesome or something. For cash. Tell him I want in on it."

I didn't care that I looked like a dyke. Megan looked like a dyke herself, I thought, so he must like that. She gave me an *Attagirl* kind of grin, basking in what must have felt like absolution. She made a pot of coffee, sat down at the desk, and wrote back to Tony.

We planned to meet the following weekend. Beyond the most basic of details negotiated over Yahoo! email—yes, he wanted to meet both of us, when, where, and for how much—Megan and I didn't talk about it all week. I went to my classes, took an extra shift at work, and avoided spending time at home if she was there. Until the moment when Megan's disgrace became mine as well, it remained hers, and I wanted nothing to do with it.

When Saturday came, I called a coworker to cover my shift in the kitchen. I shaved my legs for the first time in months. I'd been experimenting with the feminist art of body hair and had been proud of the soft, dark filament growing in patches down my calves, up my shins. I thought I might miss the progress I'd made, but I told myself that hair grows back and dried myself in preparation for Tony. I dug a bottle of Clinique foundation out of a bag I'd stashed under the sink: a holdover from high school that had probably long since expired but would still do the job. I slathered the beige liquid over freckles and blemishes and the tiny scar under my lip where my piercing had been, before I took it out for a summer job at Taco Bell, for which I needed to look *professional*. I didn't bother with lipstick, figured it would get sucked off or licked off or smeared off anyway. The foundation and a little mascara went a long way, I thought, toward making me look woman enough to fuck a man for money.

In the car, I thought about a book from my philosophy of sexuality course, *The Straight Mind*. Monique Wittig, a radical French feminist, argued that what makes a woman *a woman* boils down to her relationship with men. Her physical and economic obligations to them. Lesbians escape being women, she wrote, because they refuse this relationship. I nodded along when my professor read Wittig's lines aloud from his copy of the book, and underlined them in my own. *I've escaped*, I wrote in the margin, and added three exclamation points for emphasis. I wondered what I would be after

Tony. Would I still be a lesbian, or would I become, once again, a woman? I was fulfilling a man's physical obligation and *my* economic one, but I didn't think that would matter to Monique Wittig.

I cried while Megan drove, silently at first, holding my breath, thinking of Wittig. I didn't want Megan to stop the car. But when I tried to start breathing again, there was no air. Little sobs drummed out from my chest, and Megan pulled off to the side of the highway to calm me down.

"You don't have to do this," she assured me, putting the car in park and rubbing the backs of my hands. Each time a truck sped past on the highway, a burst of wind jolted the car, made me flinch. I tried to breathe slowly through my nose, to open my mouth for tiny gulps.

"No," I choked out. "I want to do it." I was annoyed by my own fragility, annoyed that all the ways I'd tried to toughen up had failed.

"Why don't we go," Megan asked, "but we won't have sex?"

"Then do what?" I laughed. "Take him out for a movie?" Megan considered, said sure, we could put on a show.

She squeezed my hand: "Then it's just you and me."

Somehow, I thought that might be worse: taking what we did for each other and doing it for someone else. But I didn't want any further discussion, so I nodded instead. Megan pulled back onto the highway.

When we got to Tony's place, he was out in the driveway, revving his engine. His car was a souped-up Toyota Celica that sounded like a swarm of bees inside a soda can. When he'd asked to bend my girlfriend over it, I imagined it would be American muscle. I imagined *him* as American muscle. Something about the name *Tony*. But once he climbed out of the car to lead us inside, I saw that he was a skinny nerd, pale and furry, his chest hair climbing well above the collar of his polo shirt. My nerves dissipated with our awkward hellos in Tony's living room, and I knew that nothing about this experience was going to alter my lesbianism, though it would disqualify me from a fair number of prospective lesbian partners, should they find out. I didn't plan on telling anyone about this, and I never did.

Megan explained that we were just going to put on a show for him, but she used the word *mostly* when she relayed that information. "We're just going to put on a show for you. *Mostly*." I wondered why she kept it open-ended. I will eventually learn that the lure of *maybe* is a powerful tool for separating men from their money, but it's also a dangerous game.

"It's cool," he said, and dragged a kitchen chair into his bedroom. He placed it in the corner, sat down, and seemed relieved that he wasn't expected to take part in the performance.

Tony's squeaky double bed was adorned in NASCAR sheets, bright yellow 24s advertising his love for Jeff Gordon to every woman he paid or somehow otherwise convinced to lay down on them. Megan and I climbed atop those ugly sheets and started kissing. It felt different, like a TV kiss, all drama and attention to angles. Megan took off her shirt, and then mine, but I couldn't feel her hands on my skin. My body felt plastic, anesthetic, like the nerve endings had died after some tragic accident. We stopped to sit down, to pull off our jeans, and our underwear, then we got right back up into position and resumed kissing.

Tony sat in the kitchen chair, stroking himself through his pants. I tried not to look. Megan told him to stay put, but it sounded more like a challenge than an order. He didn't comply for long, and she didn't ask again. He moved to the bed, lay on his side, and propped his head up on his hand, made little grunts while his other hand pawed at his concealed erection. Megan pulled back from our kiss to ask me if I was okay, and I nodded, because I was. Then, she left me kneeling, lay down on her back, and Tony settled himself between her legs. I lay down beside her and stared up at the popcorn ceiling, wishing the fan were turned on.

Megan seemed to enjoy everything that was happening, but it must have been for show. When Tony rolled out from between her legs and nuzzled his face in between mine, the stab of his tongue was painful, but I didn't want to direct him on how to touch me. *He's paying for this*, I thought. *This is a job—you're not supposed to enjoy it.*

I let him go on like that for a few minutes, but he tired quickly. It was clear that Tony and I both wanted it to stop, for our own reasons, but I knew his orgasm was the only thing that could end it. I pulled Megan toward me and whispered, "Can you please get him off?"

Megan sat up, told Tony to lay down on his back, and he obeyed. She straddled him. I slid off the edge of the bed and put my underwear back on, then sat back down, up against the headboard, where I watched her pull his dick out of his pants and roll a condom down over it. I looked down, and he made eye contact with me while she rode him, a silent plea for my participation. When it became clear that all I could offer was an insincere but encouraging smile, he turned away, began to focus, to thrust up into her, and he came with an ease that drove home the sheer number of times they had done this before.

Tony took a shower without offering us the same and gave Megan the money. The next day, I took my half of the cash and bought a black futon sofa. In my lifetime of minimum-wage jobs, I'd only ever worked for seven dollars an hour. Tony lasted far less than that, and I made $250. What we had done with him wasn't pleasant, but neither was working the Taco Bell drive-thru. I lounged on my new futon, smoked a joint, and thought about leaving Megan. She had made things possible for me, but she was also the limit of possibility. She was a gateway out of my hometown, but she had never really left it herself.

A new friend from school helped me move my belongings from Megan's apartment back into the same dorm I had left. He helped me rehang my tattered posters, for a third time, on yet another concrete wall. I had to leave my new futon behind.

I made one last trip to Megan's place, gathering up anything I'd missed: unopened bills, dirty underwear I had to dig out of the laundry pile. When I finished, Megan offered to drive me back to campus. On the way there, we yelled at each other about everything that had gone wrong between us. We didn't mention anything that had gone right. We yelled about the time I cheated, and the fact that she'd known it all along. We yelled about the time she got jealous and ripped the phone line clean out of the wall. We yelled about the time I read her emails. We yelled about what we'd done with Tony.

I worked her apartment keys off my key ring with my chewed-up thumbnail and placed them into the cup holder between us. She dropped me off in front of the student center, and I slammed the car door behind me without a thank-you or a goodbye.

Before she drove away, Megan rolled down her window and tossed the discarded set of keys back at me—an invitation to return, if I needed it. The keys bounced off my backpack and hit the ground. I kept walking.

9

. .

Old Main was the grandest building on campus. The red-brick facade and stone archways looked the way college was supposed to look and made me feel the way college was supposed to make me feel. It housed the college bureaucracy, and I went there to register for classes or petition the financial aid office for the Pell Grant refund check I would cash to buy books and pay for food. Two floors below the financial aid office, a man could walk into the quietest restroom on campus where, if he was lucky, there would be another man sitting in the last stall, waiting for a penis to be shoved through a glory hole carved out of the wall between the stalls. A rumor spread through campus about a particular professor who, it had been said, frequented the sitting and waiting side.

I imagined the professor there, rolled the image of it around on my tongue. I fixated on the objectification of the thing—he waited for a penis, not a person. Anonymous: no name; a wedding ring, maybe. It might catch the light when a man shoved himself in to be taken. But no woman would be attached to that ring. No duties. No vows. He was nobody's dad; he was just a dick.

I became obsessed with the indiscrimination of the thing.

How hard you'd have to be to let just anyone relieve you of
it. It wasn't an itch to be scratched, it was running toward a
sink with your hair on fire. You don't need a lover for that
kind of thing, you just need a wet mouth. I thought about the
heaviness of footsteps on those stairs down to the Old Main
basement. I thought about the hesitation. The fear of being
caught and the courage to overcome it. Coming had become
more important to these men than ever going home.

"Is that actually a thing men do?" I asked my friend Ben,
who assured me that it definitely *was* a thing that men do
and he'd seen it for himself. He had *seen it*, but never *used
it*, he made sure to emphasize. It was for closet cases, he said,
and ugly people. He was young and out and beautiful. But
he would take me down there and show me, he said, since I
was so curious.

We descended the basement stairs late on a weekday afternoon, when the admissions officers and HR staff were likely
staring at the clock, counting the minutes until they could
turn off their computers, pack up their empty lunch boxes,
and leave for the day. Ben pushed open the door, dipped his
head to peer under the stalls. Then he dramatically kicked
each one of them open.

"Can't be too careful," he said. "Guys will hide with their
feet up, sit in the stalls for hours, waiting."

I started to question whether he'd really never been in
there for more than a piss.

I stepped into the last stall. The hole in the partition
wasn't small. I thought it would be the size of my fist, but it
was the size of my head. It looked like it had been knocked
through with a sledgehammer, and I wanted to interrogate
the man who did it. Glory holes don't just appear. Someone
put in work. A janitor, maybe. Or a student. A provost, or

a dean. A construction worker or a dentist who just liked college boys. Whoever made it had padded the jagged edges with duct tape, a small kindness to match the larger one.

I wanted to know what it was like to so easily extract pleasure from another body, like it was a vending machine, or one of those shiatsu massage chairs you fed five dollars for five minutes of vibration, out in the open where everyone can see you in the hallway of a shopping mall. Women may not have been welcome to take part in such perversions, but the Old Main glory hole would be the first place I refused a man's pleasure as a means of obtaining my own.

• •

Junior year of college, I was working a part-time job at a chain restaurant, in the kitchen with the men while the other college girls kept to the front, waiting tables. I had never been good at fake smiles and preferred the back of the house. My shift trainer had been a wiry old redneck called Pops. Management warned me that he would try to fuck any woman who came into his line of sight, even a woman like me, who didn't look like the kind of woman old men wanted to fuck. The kitchen manager laughed about it, like a joke and a warning would neutralize Pops's advances. I was bad at being a line cook but great at withstanding sexual harassment, and that was as good a kitchen skill as any.

I became friends with a coworker named Nick, a townie a couple of years older than me who frequented the college bars. He liked college girls and bragged about hooking up with them like a frat boy, sans tuition bill.

I hadn't befriended a straight guy since high school, but I found Nick innocuous. His bright orange hair and lisp that got worse when he laughed made me feel like I was talking to a cartoon who had come to life and pried himself off a TV screen. On a rare night when we both had the evening off work, Nick came over to the apartment I'd moved into on the outskirts of campus, our first time socializing without the heat of an industrial grill and fryer covering us in a slick layer of grease and sweat. When he walked through the door, he said, "You look different out of your work clothes."

I didn't know what he meant, since I wore dirty jeans, a stained steakhouse logo T-shirt, and my green Yankees baseball cap to work, and I was standing in the doorway wearing slightly cleaner jeans, a fresh T-shirt, and a black baseball cap. It wasn't as if I changed from butch to femme when I went from work to home.

"You don't," I replied, and shut the door behind him.

I introduced Nick to Stephanie, a girl I'd met through the campus gay group, and the three of us polished off half a bottle of Southern Comfort. From the moment Nick walked into my apartment, Stephanie made it clear that she didn't care for him. She rolled her eyes when he suggested we go to a dive bar in the shadow of the university, one that specialized in binge drinking. Bartenders there lured students inside by advertising on a sidewalk chalkboard drink specials with names like *the blackout*. They listed no ingredients, but the sign was effective. A few of my friends had woken up on a Sunday morning with no recollection of the night before. We all recognized the potential for sexual assault in the time and space between the dance floor and dorm room; we just accepted it as part of the price of admission to college.

"A straight guy shows up and suddenly we go to straight bars?" Stephanie asked me without bothering to lower her voice.

"It's an everyone bar," Nick replied.

"It's an everyone bar," Stephanie retorted, "says the

straight guy who definitely knows what *everyone* feels like when they walk into a straight bar."

Stephanie loved an argument. She wasn't afraid to take on older commuter students in our sociology classes, men who'd lost their jobs and enrolled in college for the first time because unemployment paid for it. They thought they were right about everything because they'd lived in ways we hadn't, and Stephanie knew how to show them exactly how she lived and why it mattered.

Stephanie's inclination toward debate always impressed me, until the moment she put Nick on the spot.

"He's right," I said. "We should be able to dance wherever we like."

"Fine," she conceded. "But watch our drinks. That place is rape central." And with that, we put on our coats and left.

I knew something had happened to Stephanie in her freshman year, but she wasn't forthcoming with the details. Maybe she had good reason to distrust this dive bar, and on the walk there, I felt bad for pushing it. It wasn't as if I didn't know that straight bars could be dangerous places.

The summer before, when the dorms closed, I'd had no choice but to drive back home. Crashed in my father's old bedroom at my grandmother's house, I no longer had a place where I belonged, but I thought I might be able to make one with my outcast hometown friends, those who'd stayed or had otherwise found themselves in their grandparents' spare bedrooms. One sticky July night, I went with David and his friend Julie to drink in the hillbilly watering hole off the side of the highway. It was a bar we had always sped past without notice, on the way to Walmart or to parties out in the strip mines and back home after curfew. It was called the Good Times, and we were sure it would be, or we told ourselves it would be because we had few other options within a twenty-mile radius. We told ourselves that the jukebox would rock Hank Williams and the bartender wouldn't care who we slept with, as long as we tipped her.

David idled the same busted Toyota Corolla he'd been driving since junior year of high school into the gravel parking lot, and I pulled my shamrock green Yankees cap down into my sightline for fortitude and good luck. I was afraid of rednecks, but this place was my birthright.

The Good Times didn't live up to its name. The jukebox blasted the same Lil Jon song that was playing on the Top 40 radio station, and the bartender gave us a look that told us we were in the wrong place as soon as she saw the easy way my shoulder pushed into Julie's. She splashed the pitcher of Killian's we'd ordered all over the bar and walked away without offering to wipe it up. She wasn't running a queer bar, and she wanted us to know it.

We took our pitcher and a clean ashtray to a corner table, and David snatched the safest seat, leaving me and Julie with our backs to the room, exposed. We already knew it was a mistake going there, but we'd paid for the beer and were broke enough to stay and get our money's worth. I craned my neck to scan the patrons from under the safety of my baseball cap, and saw two falling-down drunk girls in flip-flops, Daisy Dukes, and spaghetti straps, commandeering the jukebox, grinding on each other and glancing toward the bar's opposite corner, where two roughnecks were smoking cigarettes, playing video poker, and ignoring them.

No time passed before I turned back to our corner and David widened his eyes, drew a bit too hard on his cigarette. I didn't have to turn back around to know that the girls had given up on the rednecks and were walking toward us.

"Got a smoke?" they asked, practically in unison.

David tapped a Marlboro out of his pack and slid his lighter across the table without a word.

"Y'all from around here?" one girl asked, taking a seat and pulling another over for her friend.

"Workin' on the river?" the friend guessed.

Docked barge workers were some of the only out-of-towners who might end up in a bar like that, in a town like this. David and Julie said nothing. I smiled a tight-lipped smile.

The girl who asked looked straight at me.

"What's wrong with him?" she asked David. Then, she grabbed the bill of my ball cap: "Don't you got any manners?"

With her hands on me, I got a whiff of her cucumber-melon body lotion, slathered over vodka.

"Seriously, y'all are rude! I can see *he* don't like girls," she nodded to David, his black painted fingernails a dead giveaway, "but what's wrong with y'all?"

"Just trying to mind our own business," I finally answered, out of options.

The sound of my voice made the girl who asked jump backward, out of her seat, and her friend cracked up laughing.

"They're fucking dykes!" she squealed. "You thought they were hot, and they're fucking dykes!"

I winced, betrayed by my own voice.

"Don't y'all got your own bars?" the bartender yelled from across the room, watching it all go down.

David pulled his keys out of his pocket, and the three of us headed for the door. The girls followed, hurling insults but nothing else. We didn't hurl anything back. It could have gotten bloodier. It still hurt.

I wasn't sure if it took a lover or a fighter to survive being gay in the country, if you needed to take shit or give it to make it out alive. I did know that whatever it took to stay, I didn't have it. Jess had it. Megan had it. I wanted nothing to do with it. I wanted nothing more than a way out.

My college town was just over an hour away, but it felt like a world of difference. There was a record store, and an independent theater that played foreign films with subtitles. There was a bookstore and a coffee shop and a church with a gay pride flag hanging from an awning. It felt like the kind of place where you could go to an *everyone bar*, and as long as you avoided the blackout special, you'd be fine.

• •

Nick, Stephanie, and I stumbled back to my apartment after closing time, sliding in icy alleyways and trying not to bust our asses on the pavement.

"It's freezing in here!" Nick yelled when we got inside, stripping off his coat instead of zipping it tighter. My roommates complained about the gas bill whenever I turned the thermostat above sixty degrees, and we always turned the heat down to fifty, just enough to keep the pipes from freezing, when no one was home. Nick walked into my bedroom like he owned the place, and I was too drunk to notice that he was making himself comfortable to spend the night. When he plopped down on my bed, I realized for the first time what it would mean that he was too drunk to drive.

Stephanie wobbled from foot to foot, trying to kick off her shoes without falling, then she dived face-first into my bed with her coat on. I left them alone in the room while I brushed the beer scum off my teeth.

When I walked back into my bedroom, Nick had stripped down to his boxers and a T-shirt and declared that he was sleeping in the middle. Stephanie was already knocked out up against the wall, snoring softly, so I didn't argue with him.

I needed to be on the outside, to keep one foot on the floor, a trick I'd learned to stop the room from spinning.

Minutes after my head hit the pillow, I found out why my townie friend from work hung out at college bars with drink specials like the blackout. I faded and came to with Nick's dick pumping into the palm of my limp left hand. I jerked it away but said nothing, because nothing is what I wanted to pretend had happened. *If you sleep, he will sleep*, I told myself, and let the churn and sway of the booze in my gut carry me back out to sea. When I came to a second time, Nick's body was stiff and shaking, his own hand clasped tight around mine while he thrust, shallow like a pulse, into my fist under the covers. I could tell he was close and resigned to let him finish. Once he did, he got out of my bed and drove himself home, I assume, still drunk. I pulled Stephanie in tight and went to sleep, my face mashed into the back of her black wool peacoat.

Nick stopped being my work friend after that night. He joked with Pops and flirted with the waitresses, trying to catch their eyes when they popped their heads into the kitchen and asked for extra sides of ranch dressing. Once in a while, he'd make one of them laugh, look over at me, and wink. That was the extent of our interaction.

Not a month after Nick and the blackout special, the same manager who'd warned me about Pops's dirty mouth cornered me in the walk-in freezer at the end of a Friday night shift. He kissed me on my closed mouth, then on my neck, and pushed his erection into my stomach. I shoved him off and squeezed my way past him, through the freezer door and back out into the kitchen, where no one remained but the dish guys, who were outside, finally getting their smoke breaks when the night was all but over.

"What's wrong with you?" the manager asked, following me.

"I'm gay," I said, gesturing to my whole look. "Which is obvious."

"I was just joking," he said, "chill out," then threw up his hands and watched me leave.

I didn't go to my next shift, or any shift, until the owner agreed to meet with me to hear what had happened. After I'd missed two days of work and, with it, my rent, he invited me into his office to talk.

"He just wanted a date," the owner explained. If it happened again, I should take it as a compliment. He squinted at me when he said it, like he was trying to see what the kitchen manager could have seen in a boy-girl wearing a green baseball cap. But then again, the pretty waitresses rarely had to go into the walk-in.

He suspended the kitchen manager for a week without pay and moved me to a different restaurant, forty minutes away in Ashland, Kentucky. I quit after just a few weeks. I couldn't ever make it to work on time. I swore off friendships with straight men. I figured that men already had too much, and I should deny them even the smallest of kindnesses if I could.

• •

College overlapped with the twilight of gay chat rooms, before smartphones and apps made it more efficient than ever for gay men to facilitate a hookup.

Disembodied sexuality came easy to me. Like most of my friends, I had been having cybersex since seventh grade, the screen name BuffyGirl14 never deterring middle-aged men eager to tell me what they would do to my fourteen-year-old body. At twenty-one, I searched gay.com profiles in places like San Diego and downloaded photos of beautiful blond boys with tanned skin and puka shell necklaces. I became *Ryan* and signed in to the local West Virginia chat room, where I encountered the Old Main glory hole for the second time and learned that it wasn't simply a cruising spot for college boys and professors, but an infamous rendezvous point on the chats, drawing guys from across the state and into Kentucky and Ohio.

One of my first times logging on to waste time as Ryan, I talked to an admittedly married man from the southern part of the state who, when I shared my fake picture and told him I was a student, offered to drive hours to meet me at Old Main. I thought about saying yes and hiding behind some bushes, watching him walk in, expecting to walk out satisfied. But I had respect for a perfect stranger's time, so I told him no.

Eventually, I recognized one of the guys from the chat as a fellow student who lived in the red-brick dormitory next door to mine. He was closeted, I guessed, because all the openly queer kids knew and protected one another. I told him I'd never been to campus for any reason other than the glory hole, and we chatted late into the night about how often we beat off and what we thought about when we did it. It would be fine for me to trick him, I thought, as long as I didn't out him. He would lose an hour of his time, not a full day's work, or a job, or a wife.

On the day we planned to meet, I arrived at Old Main early and sat down on a bench outside, near the door closest to the infamous glory hole bathroom. Right on time, the boy showed up in the red hoodie he told me he would be wearing. I wasn't waiting for him, as promised, on my knees. I was just a girl sitting on a bench, pretending to do her homework.

Twenty minutes later, the boy in the red hoodie emerged from the same door, his face flushed and his fists shoved deep into his pockets. I wanted to run to him, to comfort him maybe, or to laugh in his face, but I did neither. I just watched him retreat across the quad and savored my first rush of control over a man, a pleasure that I wouldn't return to for years but would recognize immediately when I did.

10

• •

After college, I moved back and forth between cities in the Rust Belt and the Midwest. I learned how to ride a bicycle in traffic and politicized my body hair. In my first city apartment, I lived with a country boy. We hung a taxidermy deer head on our living room wall to remind ourselves that home was just a few hours and a missed rent check away. Because he moved to Pittsburgh and got citified a year before me, he was able to teach me how to ride a bus and eat with chopsticks.

I knew I wanted to go to graduate school, so I didn't bother trying to find a postgrad "career." Instead, I worked as a security guard in an office building downtown, watching late-night television and walking the floors once an hour, until I landed the job I wanted: as a receptionist in a university office. The job paid only a couple of dollars over minimum wage, but it came with a transit pass and an employee ID that gave me access to the university library. I no longer belonged in the library because I was no longer a student, but I spent a lot of my free time there anyway. When I wasn't working, I read Foucault and Lacan and Derrida and imagined my life as a professor. It didn't matter that my college life had been only a couple of hours from home: it was the life that was furthest away from where I'd been.

I wanted to someday live in a house like the ones where my professors lived; where I, a trusted student, fed their cats when they were away. The professor houses had wineglasses blown to accommodate the differences between red and white wine, refrigerators that spat out ice, and paintings purchased from artists' galleries in Spanish cities I'd read about in a Hemingway novel, assigned in class. I thought that if I could learn their elite languages—if I could come to understand both language and the elite—I would prove myself worthy of a life of the mind: a life that came with a house and bookshelves.

I should have spent less time worrying about French theory and more time worrying about the standardized tests that would determine the amount of money I would be paid each month if I did gain entrée into an elite institution. I didn't know that the school I chose used the scores to determine the distribution of funding. I didn't understand cost of living, for that matter. I figured the stipend that the school provided its graduate students must just be the amount you needed for a year of food and shelter. I wouldn't find out otherwise until after I'd packed up my things in the Midwest and drove them out to Los Angeles to start my PhD.

I moved into one dreary room in a run-down apartment just off the 101 freeway. My roommates were a gay man who left his room only to go to AA meetings down the street and a lesbian whom I hoped to befriend but who only asked me to feed her cats and change the litter box when she was sleeping in someone else's bed. I listened to the traffic move quickly each morning as the sun rose, then slow to the creep and honk of rush hour. I didn't have to look at the clock; I could tell the time from the sound. There was an orange tree outside my window, its Day-Glo orbs bobbing in the Santa Ana winds, blocking the morning sun from my pillow.

I had driven west in a cheap-but-reliable car that I bought with a student loan. As soon as I unpacked my boxes in California, I filled out a dating website profile and used the car to drive across the city, meeting women for beers and hikes and coffees. I didn't really want a relationship, but I did want friends and had no clue how else to make them. I hooked up with a woman from the dating website and tried to drive away at dawn before she woke up and offered me coffee. Blinded at sunrise on a freeway on-ramp, I crashed that car just a couple months into what I was starting to think might be a brief stint in California.

Covered in blood from my gushing nose, I sat outside a junkyard in the Valley and did the math. I needed to stretch the $2,000 monthly stipend the university gave me for nine months out of the year to cover a new car payment for all twelve. And I was in the process of paying off a dental bill that saved my teeth from rotting out of my mouth. Graduate students were expected to have decent teeth and fly them out to academic conferences where they could show them off with smiles and handshakes. That is, if we ever wanted to become professors. We had to act like we were professors already, even if we weren't paid like it. I put all of it—the teeth, the smiles, the conference travel—on credit cards. I took on more student loan debt to pay off the credit card debt, and I did buy a new car. A vehicle would be necessary if I wanted to keep working my way through the dating websites, if I wanted to find someone who would collect me from the side of the freeway should I find myself stranded there again. If not, it would be necessary to drive me away from California.

I had been chatting with Catherine on the dating website for weeks before we met, just a few days before my twenty-sixth birthday. I would spend that birthday in a mountain town with someone else: a woman I knew I shouldn't have been dating, not seriously enough to warrant a birthday weekend, anyway. I knew it when she reached under my shirt for the first time and felt the tight, nylon binder I was wearing to flatten my chest. In the dark, in her bedroom—a bedroom in which I was excited to sleep because she had central heating and the nights were dipping into the low fifties—she took her mouth off my neck, her hand out of my shirt, to ask me what it was.

"I want someone who isn't ashamed," she said about the binder, "of being a woman."

It wasn't the first time a lover had been disappointed by the shape of my body. In college, in secret, I slept with a curious girl whose boyfriend played in a Christian rock band. He was a pro-life activist who tabled in the student center, his chubby fingers pushing around those little plastic models of fetuses meant to show when it would be the size of a pea, then a lemon, as if knowing a fetus was big enough to eat would trigger enough guilt to change a woman's mind.

In a coffee shop a few days after the last time we hooked up—when she declared herself straight, once and for all, and I declared her an asshole—she asked if I'd heard of a procedure called a labiaplasty. Our women's studies class had been discussing whether it was anti-feminist to get plastic surgery.

"You know, you should consider getting one," she said, in front of our mutual friends, as if the asymmetry of my labia was what sent her running back into the arms of a guy who had picketed outside an abortion clinic. I thought that hooking up with women who promised they were straight made me special. It felt good to be an exception, exceptional. But that didn't make it hurt any less when they made good on those promises.

By the time I turned twenty-six, I knew how to make myself smaller to accommodate a lover. Some part of me liked becoming the object of desire, even if I had to sacrifice a great deal to be found desirable.

"I don't *need* the binder," I told the woman before Catherine. "I'm not, like, *trans*—I just like the way it looks."

Her disappointment hovered above me, the spent potential of the date she'd paid for at a decent sushi bar.

"I'll stop wearing it," I promised, "if you don't like it."

She unzipped the binder and put her mouth back onto my neck.

I did like it. I liked the way my body looked with a flat chest. With my tits zipped up tight, I was able to button men's shirts down over them without the awkward bunch and pull. I never felt like a boy, even if my chest did. I'd worn the binder on my first date with Catherine, just a few days prior to my birthday. She put her hands everywhere with no complaints. Fireside in the cabin with this other woman, I could still feel Catherine's hands on me. I zipped my tits back up in the binder and broke up with my birthday date before we got back to the city.

Earlier that week, I had arranged to meet Catherine at a cocktail bar by her house. It was obvious from our conversation that she wasn't the type of woman to go out of her way for a date, and it was also probably obvious that I was. I went straight over to her neighborhood after an evening class, wearing a cutoff T-shirt, yellow armpit stains removed, and skinny jeans rolled up at the ankle. I couldn't afford to replace my wardrobe with anything more grown-up, anything more LA.

I watched Catherine walk into the bar wearing a black sweater that dropped off each of her shoulders, tight blue jeans, and very-high-heeled boots. She sat down on a barstool next to me, next to the door, and I was soft next to her. I couldn't take my eyes off all her hard places: collarbones, stilettos, the winged tips of her eyeliner. She was tall and intense and had traveled to all the places I wanted to go. She was only twenty-eight, she said; but she felt much older than me, and I liked that.

Catherine told me that after her last serious relationship, she'd sworn off dating academics. *Grad students*, to be exact. They were too self-involved. She told me that she had followed a boy to LA. He was a grad student too, studying philosophy, and his friends treated her like a bimbo wife. I couldn't imagine anyone treating Catherine like either a bimbo or a wife. She said that she showed my OkCupid profile to a friend who knew her rules, and the friend said I was cute enough to make an exception. I chose not to focus on her disdain for my career path and to focus instead on being, once again, exceptional.

In my first semester of grad school, I hadn't been exceeding expectations. I felt outpaced by my peers, who I was sure had read more than me, who spoke multiple Romance languages and had no trouble answering difficult questions on the fly. So I accepted Catherine's compliment like a stellar report card. If I couldn't be the smartest, I could live with being the cutest.

Catherine wouldn't let me pay, not even for one round. On the phone before that first date, I'd asked her what she did for a living. She said she would tell me in person, and I thought that meant she must have a trust fund, as if a trust fund were a thing people wouldn't discuss with someone they'd never met. She waited until we were three drinks in and out on the sidewalk to tell me she was a professional dominatrix. She kept her tongue poised on her teeth after she said the word and waited for my reaction. I smiled and placed my hands behind my back like a submissive. I'd learned to play that game in college with a girl who got all her ideas about sex from reading erotica online, and in that moment, I was thankful for my education. Catherine took hold of my wrists, and we kissed until a guy across the street noticed and started begging for more. When she let me go, I got in my car but couldn't drive. It took ten minutes to defog my windshield, the heat of my body keeping me stuck still in place.

When I got home, I googled *Dominatrix, Los Angeles*, and Catherine wasn't hard to find. The next day, I called a friend from class and asked her to meet me out in the Valley, at one of the city's last remaining lesbian bars, to play pool. What I actually wanted was to show her Catherine's website. I felt interesting, all of a sudden, because Catherine was interested in me. On our second date, she asked if I had looked her up online, and I lied, said that I hadn't, that I wanted to get to know her as a person before I learned about her persona. She said that was sweet of me to say.

Catherine told me that she had just started doing sex work full-time when we met. She had been doing it part-time for years, on the side, she said, simply because she liked it. But she'd gotten laid off from her office job a few months prior to meeting me and took it as a sign that she should give pro-domming a real shot. She had been renting rooms at a commercial dungeon, but she dreamed of opening her own place. There were a couple of commercial spots in the city, places licensed for massage that had rules in place to keep it legal. No *jobs*: no blow jobs, hand jobs, foot jobs. If there was no nudity and no sex, the commercial dungeons could operate mostly out in the open, and it was in these spaces that many dommes in LA got their feet wet.

The dungeons required most employees to take their turn on the other side of the paddle before they earned the privilege of moving up to the position of domme. These were more-than-minor annoyances for women who wanted to get paid to beat men but weren't inclined to be beaten in return. It was a trade-off. Working at a commercial dungeon meant that the house booked and screened clients, and there were other people around if a guy got too handsy. There was a business license, even if it was shady, and you had coworkers who could help you figure out how to file your taxes. Catherine told me all of this over the course of our next few dates.

Until recently, Catherine had been sitting on shift with the other dommes, subs, and switches at the commercial dungeon. She handed over half of what she earned to the house. When she quit and started doing her own advertising, safety screenings, bookings, and website design—what those in the business refer to as "going independent"—she still had to pay the house $60 an hour just to use the rooms. She got fed up with the dungeon bleeding her bank account and vowed to open a private studio of her own, where she would be accountable only to herself and could bring in other independent dommes to pay her rent. I didn't know it at the time, but I would be one of them.

11

• •

Falling in love with Catherine meant spending days on end at her place, where I learned what full-time BDSM work entailed. Hers were not eight-hour days of bondage and discipline, and since she'd gone independent, she no longer spent them sitting around in the dungeon dressing room with other dommes, practicing hogties and complaining about what girls got the best shifts either. Catherine's days were filled with social media, website updates, SEO concerns, research, advertising, cardio, Pilates, manicures, client calls, and sales pitches. Mine were filled with readings—novels and histories and theoretical accounts of both—and trips to campus, a green oasis in the middle of the city, to talk about them. Nothing I was doing felt like work to me. Work was my parents leaving the house in hard hats and steel-toed boots, returning dirty, smelling of chemicals, holding fast to any hour spent off the clock.

Doing my reading and writing that didn't feel like work at Catherine's apartment, I listened for context clues that would give me a sense of what happened in the dungeon: if that part of her job were closer to mine, or to my parents'.

"What kind of session are you interested in?" Catherine would ask the clients who called.

Bondage.

Tease and denial.

Foot fetish.

Golden shower.

Feminization.

Humiliation.

Whipping, spanking, caning, paddling: corporal punishment.

I learned the profession's vocabulary from the lists of activities she repeated back to the clients on the phone.

"Tease and denial? I'm an expert," she cooed. "Tell me what you find humiliating." She demanded their secrets.

I also learned about the types of scenes that pushed her limits.

"No sex!" she scolded. "I don't do full service."

"I don't care if Mistress So-and-So did a session topless! Why are you contacting me if she was so thrilling?"

"Why don't you read my fucking website?" she asked them, kind of nicely.

She would tell the clients her rate per hour, calling it a *tribute* or *donation*, never *payment*, a linguistic sleight of hand meant to avoid entrapment by the police. She sometimes got intel from other sex workers that cops were doing raids at downtown hotels. They would set up in a suite and just call down the list of girls advertising for clients on Backpage or Eros, a site specifically designed for sex work advertising.

"Escorts though," Catherine said. "Not dommes. Nobody cares about dommes."

In California, she explained, it's illegal to offer or accept money for *sex*. The point being that sex wasn't what she was selling.

"Or lewd conduct," I added. I'd been doing my research.

Lewd conduct is vague. It's mostly defined as touching someone's genitals for sexual gratification.

"Cock torture doesn't exactly sound gratifying to most
cops," Catherine noted. "It's a gray area."

A gray area is neither black nor white, but it could be
made to seem like either. A sentence could carry six months
in jail for a first offense, but the whiteness of those operating
in the gray area would lighten it. Catherine is white.

Still, the idea that every phone call could be a cop trying
to darken the supposedly gray area of the law put me on
edge. When she left for work, I wondered if she would come
back. I lay in her bed and stared at the pages of the books I'd
hauled over there to study, but failed to read a word.

"I don't fuck my clients though." Catherine defended
herself as if I had called her to the stand.

"You *do* fuck your clients though." I couldn't see anything "gray" about fucking a man up the ass.

"Cops entrap escorts because they want to get laid,"
Catherine explained. "No cop is going to put something up
their butt just to bust a domme."

That did sound reasonable.

I never tried to talk Catherine out of her choices, but I
needed to decide for myself whether or not she would be safe
to love.

• •

It's hard to tell when the seasons change in California, but the
days got longer, spring semester seminar papers were coming
due, and I got an acute feeling of summer on the horizon. I
called the graduate school, just to be sure I'd gotten it right.
They confirmed that, yes, May was it, my last paycheck until
we returned in the fall. And it would be half a month's pay at
that, same as August. They weren't responsible for me in the

summer; I was on my own. I hung up the phone and calculated rent, car payment, and insurance—that was more than half my regular paycheck—not to mention my phone bill, internet, credit card payments, and food. I stopped bringing my course readings over to Catherine's and started applying for jobs instead.

In April I got one, at a fancy, new coffee shop in West Hollywood. The other baristas already knew what they were doing. One had trained with a man who'd competed in the World Barista Championship. I had no idea that coffee shops were cutthroat—I couldn't afford to hang out in the fancy ones—but the owner said that if I proved I could pour milk onto espresso with a hand steady enough to draw a heart, or a little leaf, after a month of training, I could stay. I wasted gallons of milk practicing. On my day off, after receiving my first paycheck, I stood in the line at the social services office downtown with a copy of my bank statement to prove myself eligible for food stamps. Somehow, I still felt upwardly mobile.

At semester's end, I took a bus from my place to the public university across town. I planned to do some research for an end-of-term paper, but fertility agencies had plastered advertisements all over the women's restrooms, knowing they could cash in on a crop of desperate students like me who needed to pay their summer rent. This was the difference between public and private school, I thought. I had never seen a single flyer for egg donation at the private university I attended, and I spent the day researching how to sell my genetic material instead.

I was twenty-six at the time—still young enough, but just barely. I may not have attended an Ivy League college—a big plus on donor applications—but I had somehow landed myself in a PhD program with other women who would have had no trouble selling their eggs. Maybe that's what they would put on my profile: *Donor pulled herself up by her bootstraps.* I left the library and made an appointment for a consultation.

Days later, I walked into a Beverly Hills office in business casual like it was a job interview. I filled out a form promising that I could forego drinking and smoking for months on end, and that I hadn't had a recent chlamydia infection. I lied and said that I hadn't engaged in prostitution in the past five years, since that day with Tony was apparently disqualifying. If I didn't have any active STIs, I wasn't sure why that last promise mattered. Maybe they thought whoring was genetic. They sent me home with a folder full of information and appointment cards for the medical screening, fertility screening, and psychological tests I'd booked on the spot. I had no feelings about egg donation, beyond annoyance at the prospect of a sober summer, but I got a parking ticket while I was doing the interview, and I cried about that for an hour afterward in my car.

I went over to Catherine's apartment the evening after my first medical screening, where I had been poked and prodded in another Beverly Hills office building, just down the street from the first. Catherine drew a bath for the two of us to share and asked me about my day. I sat on the toilet with my knees pulled in to my chest, watching Epsom salts dissolve as I lied: "I'm thinking about donating my eggs."

Catherine dipped her hand into the bath, tested the heat. She looked up at me and pulled her lips into a pained smile. She stripped off her clothes and stepped into the tub. I followed.

"Sell my eggs, I mean," I stuttered, once I'd settled into the water and her silence. "They just call it donation, but it's selling."

The way she looked at me, I thought, indicated that it was

bad form to bring up money when your lover has drawn a romantic bath, but Catherine talked about money constantly because she had plenty of it for the first time in her life and that was exciting. I ran my pinky finger over the blue bruise forming on my forearm, where a nurse had drawn my blood just hours before. I let little droplets of water sit on the tiny puncture wound, proof I was being proactive in trying to improve my financial situation.

"They said I could get around twelve grand after it's said and done," I bragged, "enough to pay off my credit card debt."

Catherine stood up from the bath and grabbed a towel.

"I don't want to know that you have babies out there in the world," she said, drying off faster than she'd gotten wet.

I hadn't thought about a baby. A baby with tiny hands that looked like mine, its small fingers latching on to a stranger's rough knuckles. I had only thought of the twelve thousand dollars. I had inherited my mother's hands.

Catherine and I had been dating only a few months. Long enough to say "I love you." Not long enough to know what loving each other would truly entail. Long enough to tell her about my mother and father. Not long enough to hear much about hers. Long enough to take a spanking so harsh it wiped all language from my brain. Not long enough to use my safe word, like I should have. I didn't know how to tell Catherine that I hadn't considered her in my decision. As I fumbled for the words that would convince her to sit back down in the bath, she took aim.

"Besides, with your family, their mental health . . ." She paused like a TV cop, hesitating, thinking about whether to let the bad guy have it in the chest or the leg. "How could you even consider bringing more of that into the world?"

My genes were not fit for the marketplace, but my body would be.

12

. .

My appointment with the fertility clinic was scheduled for the week following the blood draws. At that appointment, they would look inside me to determine if I was worth the psych test and the boxes of hormone injections that would stimulate my ovaries and make the eggs bloom. On the morning of the appointment, I stared at the date and time and address that I'd copied carefully into my academic planner. It was the final day of the semester. I'd turned my seminar papers in a day early to accommodate, but I called the fertility clinic to let them know I'd changed my mind. Catherine had changed my mind. They would have changed their mind about me anyway, I thought, if they took a long, hard look at my family tree.

A week later, I got a call for a job I'd applied to earlier in the spring. A self-described "genius camp" for gifted teens, it was to be held over the summer on yet another university campus: this one close to the ocean, overlooking the marina. I had applied to teach writing to the genius kids and never heard back, but the receptionist they hired backed out last minute and they were in dire need of office help. The job paid only minimum wage—less than the coffee shop, where I got tips—but it came with room and board, meaning I could sublet my apartment. My tips never would have covered rent. I was disappointed that the genius camp felt I was only qualified for the office, not the classroom, but I wanted to know what it would be like to live that close to the sunset. I packed up my clothes, handed over my apartment key to a subletter, and told my roommates I would see them in August.

In my first week of genius camp, I realized that the summer job would, technically, pay far fewer wages than the minimum, that the room and board came with strings attached. Required breakfasts and dinners supervising the little geniuses, in addition to nightly activities, meant the job worked out to nearly fifteen hours a day, five days a week. On weekends: excursions. A glorified babysitter, I would only get my eight dollars an hour for half the hours I was expected to work. I would have begged the coffee shop to take me back, but I no longer had an apartment.

After a week bemoaning my summer exploitation, Catherine suggested I quit the job and move in with her. I could cat-sit when she was away on domme trips, and I could supplement my coffee shop wages with a little sex work on the side. Catherine had just secured a lease in a building that would become her very own dungeon. I could help her set it up: paint the walls black, polish the concrete floors. I moved my suitcases for the second time in one week.

Catherine said that the part-time sex work would be simple. I could put up an ad on Backpage. I could do some training sessions, and her best friend, a fetish photographer, would take my photo. I wouldn't even have to show my face. I could obscure it with a crop, or a paddle, or if I wanted to allude to the whole intellectual thing, a copy of Marquis de Sade's *The 120 Days of Sodom*.

It wasn't like I hadn't considered domming before. Catherine had the kind of life I wanted, and there was no questioning how she got it. She dined with clients at restaurants with ten-course tasting menus and brought home leftovers she would scramble into eggs for me the following morning. She called it *hookers' breakfast*. The trick was to order too much—the client always paid—then you could continue the feast at home without him. Even the leftovers tasted better than anything I'd ever eaten, and I wondered what Dungeness crab tasted like hot, or how the vanilla bean whipped butter would have sat on my tongue before it melted. When I moved in with Catherine, I got to eat hookers' breakfast all the time.

Catherine also traveled. She flew to island destinations with a sixty-year-old insurance salesman who acted like a boy—a teasing, athletic, not-quite-handsome but not-bad-either former high school quarterback. He wanted the heaviest beatings she could give, his masochism a show of strength, and he rewarded Catherine's sadism with cash, bikinis, jewelry, and travel.

I had a hard time imagining that a sixty-year-old insurance salesman would find me similarly appealing. I hadn't worn women's clothing since I declared my queerness. I was comfortable in the men's section of Urban Outfitters, and had never stopped wearing the combat boots I'd picked up freshman year of college. I thought I had broken up with femininity for good. For the greater good, even. My masculinity invited insult from men, but I was convinced that it would also, somehow, be there to protect me if I needed it. The hurt made me sturdy.

Not too long before I moved in with her, I dropped in on one of Catherine's sessions, so I knew more or less what the work entailed. But it didn't matter whether or not I could command the client's desire: I had just been summoned there to watch. She was the femme fatale; I was the *vanilla girl*. The client was one of her regulars, and on this occasion, he had requested a cameo from a girl who wasn't accustomed to seeing men submit to women. The clients who want cameos from vanilla girls get a thrill from the shock that registers on a woman's face when she suddenly finds herself faced with them, in all their naked glory, groveling, preening, every secret on display. So said Catherine, anyway. She said that some of these men are would-be flashers. Some are just flashers, no would-be about it. Many have been playing with dommes for years, and the shine has worn off. A vanilla girl is meant to bring it back. She would kick me a hundred bucks to be the shiny, new thing for Bitch Vicky.

On the night of the session, Catherine outfitted me in one of her many black cocktail dresses and a pair of knee-high black leather riding boots: Bitch Vicky's favorite. She brought me to the dungeon, sat me down on the bondage bed, told me to cross my legs and wait, posed there like a doll in her dollhouse. I chewed my fingernails while she went out to greet Bitch Vicky, a small man who strutted into the dungeon behind her, wearing nothing but a tiny lavender thong and a purple feather boa wrapped around his shoulders. Catherine took a seat beside me and gave him orders: walk an imaginary catwalk like a high-fashion model, perform a cheer like a high school cheerleader, bark like a dog, moo like a cow, oink like a pig. I watched Bitch Vicky prance around in his kitten heels accomplishing ridiculous tasks until he tired out and wrapped himself around Catherine's legs like a cat, rubbing his face into her calves, cooing and smiling a slow stoner smile.

Despite the novelty of having me there, and the vigor of Bitch Vicky's performance, Catherine appeared bored. She kicked off her shoes and scrolled through her Twitter feed. I started to understand why clients request vanilla girls to watch. I wondered if they ever complained that she was on her phone at work. I got in trouble at plenty of jobs for being on my phone, and none of them had been paying me upwards of $200 an hour.

I'll ask her about it later, once he's gone, and she'll say that they like being ignored.

I couldn't ignore Bitch Vicky. Once he'd planted himself on the floor, we locked eyes and he stroked himself, flicking his tongue up and down on Catherine's toes. She kept her eyes on her phone; he kept his eyes on me. After fifteen minutes or so, his stroke hit a fever pitch and he finished in his hand with a jolt. Catherine stood up, slid her shoes back on, and walked over to grab a hand towel from a stack in the corner. She dropped it onto the floor next to Bitch Vicky, who wiped off, got dressed, and became Andrew, a black polo shirt replacing his purple feather boa.

He asked me if I liked to watch and I nodded affirmations. I told him that yes, he looked cute, that he was a good little boy and I had a great time watching. He grinned and thanked me for my time, and Catherine walked him out. She returned with a damp hundred-dollar bill for me. She'd been holding it in her cleavage until he was gone.

Bitch Vicky *was* good and I *did* like watching. I regretted the scene I had made, just a few weeks prior, when Catherine announced a client's request to see her in Dubai. He would pay her five thousand dollars, she said, on top of the flight and accommodations, for three days of play. I threw a fit when she told me, cried like she'd already been trafficked, like that was something that happened to white American women advertising themselves as masters, not slaves. All that fuss for nothing. Bitch Vicky was harmless. If they were all like that, Catherine's job was the safest in the world. I should have been more concerned about myself, teaching in college classrooms where you never knew what boy might hold a grudge and own a gun.

When Catherine secured my first real training session, I was more nervous about how I looked in high-femme drag than I was about dominating a stranger. I had abandoned makeup at sixteen, and even then had never attempted the level of femininity that the role of mistress would require. But the session was a double, meaning that Catherine would be there to guide me. Still, no more vanilla girl. This client expected me to participate, and she hadn't warned him that I was a novice. It was an omission I appreciated, but I would need to mask my anxiety under a full face of armor.

In the days leading up to the session, I watched YouTube tutorials and practiced my eye shadow. I cried when I failed to recognize the boyish girl underneath powder, color, and cream. When I tried to apply the false lashes, they stuck to my clumsy fingers, glued my eyelids together, or pulled off on one side like a drunk girl's on her way out of the club at 3:00 a.m. On the night of the session, I confessed to Catherine that I hadn't mastered the art and, like a patient big sister, she applied the lashes for me. It felt like a concession, but the drag was necessary. Domination is one of the only professions in which femininity is worth more than masculinity, and I was building my femininity to sell.

When we arrived at the dungeon for the session, Catherine revealed that the client had a specific wardrobe request: leather pants. I assumed I would be wearing another one of her little black cocktail dresses, another pair of her tall leather boots.

"But I don't have leather pants!" I said in a panic.

Unfazed, Catherine opened one of the armoires that lined the dungeon's common room like gym lockers and pulled out a pair of black leather chaps that I knew belonged to Rocky, one of the very few male doms who rented space in the dungeon. Rocky seemed to make most of his money selling GHB, but he moonlit as a sex worker, serving a mostly older male clientele who paid straight guys with frat-boy vibes to abuse them. He had leather chaps for just such an occasion.

Rocky was big, and I was swimming in his chaps. Whatever confidence I had mustered on the way to the dungeon diminished as soon as I examined myself in the full-length mirror, my legs lost in pants that looked more like the rubber waders my dad wore fly-fishing than any leather pants I'd ever seen or imagined. Catherine walked up behind me looking like pure sex in a tight black pair that laced up the sides of her longer-than-mine legs. I was her clueless kid sister, the Skipper to her Barbie. I wanted to throw a temper tantrum like I did as a child, desperate to get out of my dress after Sunday morning church service and not understanding why.

But there was no time to cry. The client knocked on the door, and Catherine told me to get away from the mirror and take my place. At least the session was pegging—the pornified word for a woman fucking a man with a strap-on—something I had never done before but was convinced I couldn't screw up.

My mom gave me my first strap-on when I was seventeen. After Dad moved out and Mom moved on, I came home from school to a brown paper bag on my bed, the contents of which would humiliate even the most open-minded teenager: a hot-pink strap-on with a vibrating butterfly at the base, a truck-stop novelty with flimsy elastic straps. Even though she was sporting an eight-inch phallus, the model on the package looked like the straightest woman I'd ever seen. I hid it under my bed and never acknowledged the gesture, nor did I answer the note she left in the bag: *I think lesbians need these. Love, Mom.*

When I showed my girlfriend, I pretended that I had bought it myself, and thus became a hero. Not only had I, a minor, gone into an adult novelty store, but I had made a purchase. This was something my friends and I often contemplated, perusing the cheap plastic vibrators in Spencer's, a cornerstone of shopping mall culture in the late nineties. We wondered who among us had the guts to attempt the $15 purchase. We walked down the aisle that sold strawberry and vanilla lubricant, vibrating tongue rings, and the long, plastic glow-in-the-dark phalluses that frenzied us. On a brave day, someone would put one into her basket, but it would inevitably end up back on the shelf, some nag champa incense purchased instead. Stealing a vibrator would have been a safer bet than facing the cashier, your impending orgasm like a secret pact binding the two of you together, while your parents browsed new dishwashers in Sears next door.

Needless to say, by the time I started training in professional domination, I had been having strap-on sex with women for nearly a decade. I foolishly assumed that it wouldn't be any different with a man.

Catherine went first.

"Let's get you warmed up," she said, patting the bondage bed where she wanted the client to lie down. He pulled off his shoes, folded his clothes neatly, and dropped them in the corner of the room nearest the door. He hoisted himself up onto the table, laid down on his back, and spread his legs, looping his arms behind his knees to hold them open. He appeared accustomed to the position.

I watched as Catherine slid her hand into a black latex glove. She let it snap around her wrist. We hadn't discussed the fact that I had never fucked anyone up the ass before and had no clue how this was supposed to go. I will tell her, afterward, that it had been my first time, and she'll look shocked, like I am the most dreadfully conventional woman in the world.

One finger, then two—I watched Catherine apply lube and work her way inside the client's body. He took in short breaths, his lips pursed like he awaited a kiss. Some moments passed between them, and his mouth started to relax. He grunted, and then moaned his approval.

"I think he's ready," Catherine said, pulling her hand from between the client's legs, peeling off her used gloves and thrusting the box of clean ones toward me. "Check and see for yourself."

I pulled on the gloves with less grace than Catherine, and squeezed some sticky lube onto my hand. Then, without looking where I was going, I poked my slippery fingers around between the client's legs. I immediately realized I had no sense of male anatomy. I was a boy who couldn't locate the clit. I stopped groping and instructed the client to spread his legs further and pull them up toward his head. Both he and Catherine gave me a look of approval, like I was a natural dominant, bossing him into the desired position. In reality, I was flying blind.

I got my finger in the client's ass just as Catherine pulled her strap-on up over her leather pants. He barely paid me any attention as I poked away at his backside, and I was sure it had everything to do with how ridiculous I looked in those oversized chaps. Catherine edged in, and I stepped to the

side, pulling off my gloves and fumbling with my own har-
ness. I watched Catherine thrust in and out of the client like
she was doing aerobics. She threw her head back and laughed
like life was one big joke and she was telling it; he was the
punch line. I wasn't in on it. I compulsively tugged up on
Rocky's sagging chaps and waited my turn.

When Catherine tapped me in, I got in between the
stranger's legs, once again poking around for the place to
penetrate. At least using my fingers, my body gave my brain
feedback; the dildo wasn't exactly teeming with nerve endings. As I floundered, the client rolled his eyes and looked
up at Catherine, who hovered just above him. With his legs
spread, hands around his thighs, he sighed an exasperated
sigh and asked: "Is this her first time?"

After he left, I cried the way I'd wanted to cry all day.
Catherine hugged me and told me not to worry about it.

"He was a prick," she said. "Most of them are sweet."
She kissed my cheeks and wiped my tears.

"You'll see," she said, "in time."

Catherine walked me out to my car. Another client was
on his way in, and she was ready to do it all over again,
without me, without a second thought. She shut my car door
and disappeared back inside the dungeon. Out of her sight,
I leaked a few more tears. The shame of the day was coming
out of me, but I couldn't pinpoint its source. It was in my
bank account, overdrawn enough times to make what I'd just
done seem like the right thing to do. It was in my sexuality,
gay enough to make what I'd just done seem like the wrong
thing to do. It was in my trembling hands, fumbling in front
of Catherine, whom I had spent the better part of a year
trying to impress. It was in the gulf separating me from my
grad school friends, the thought of them watching me do

something that they themselves would probably never do, would never have to do.

All that shame faded away once I put the car into drive.

I rolled the windows down to take the flush off my face, and Heart's "Barracuda" came on the radio. I decided it would be my whore song. I had just made $200 in forty-five minutes, and I hadn't even done a good job.

13

. •

Theoretically, all a domme needed to get started was an internet connection, a Backpage ad, and some photographs to post on it. Catherine's best friend the fetish photographer offered to shoot me for free. He offered to shoot my body, not my face—important because I was afraid that an endeavor into the dungeon might get me booted from graduate school. This was 2012, years before social media became ubiquitous in sex work, back when clients didn't expect 24/7 access to a domme's personal life, or the one she curated for them on Instagram and Twitter. In reality, there was a lot more to domming than a Backpage ad, more to it than skills in corporal punishment and bondage: you needed to know the logistics.

Catherine taught me. She taught me to make the client commit to a date and time in advance, and to make him call two hours prior to that agreed-upon time in order to be given the address. The confirmation call helped ensure that the client wasn't just going to masturbate to the thought of having a session but was actually going to have a session, during which he could masturbate if he so chose. She told me that I'd be doing well if more than half my inquiries turned into bookings and more than half of those turned into sessions. Men didn't mind booking a sex worker's time and wasting it. I would have to plan my afternoons around their erections, and they often came prematurely.

Catherine taught me the most important lesson in logistics: how to get the money. As soon as the client walks through the door, have him leave it on the table. Do not touch it while he's watching. Send him to the bathroom or to undress and count it while he's gone. Always count the money.

She told me to call the money a tribute for an hour of time. If a cop called to entrap me, he would have to prove that the money I asked for was an exchange for a sex act. Theoretically, you could be doing anything with the hour for which the client has paid. You could be playing Scrabble, or darning his socks.

Catherine also solved the biggest logistical problem facing me as a new domme: where to work. For sixty dollars an hour, I could rent a room in Catherine's new dungeon, one that came equipped with all the whips, chains, and handcuffs I would need to start working. By giving me access to her dungeon, Catherine made it so that I never had to *live in the dorms*, her euphemism for toiling on shifts with other dommes and subs at a commercial space. I would be independent from the start.

I knew how to book clients and where to bring them, but had no idea what to do with them once I had them at my mercy. Catherine's best friend, the fetish photographer, offered to rehearse with me.

"I'll teach you everything you need to know," he promised me over garlic knots at his favorite cheap Italian spot in Venice. He said it with an air of nonchalance, like I should recognize that I was being done a huge favor, but the man offering doesn't want too much praise for his generosity.

Catherine encouraged me to agree. He had good ideas about what men wanted, she said, what sex would sell. He had guided her, years before she met me, back when she first got her start.

It was decided, then. The fetish photographer would shoot photos of my legs, my feet, and my body stuffed into Catherine's outfits, and I would let him train me in what clients expected from a domme. I didn't realize until I agreed to both that the offer of the former relied on my acceptance of the latter.

"For starters," the fetish photographer said, mouth half full of pasta, "you can't brand yourself as a 'lesbian dominatrix.'"

"I *am* a lesbian dominatrix," I replied, firm in my decision. I wasn't yet a dominatrix at all, but I was already worried about what going straight-for-pay might do to my status as a lesbian, and I wasn't willing to risk it.

"Any man would look at that ad and think you only want to see women," he said. "And women, I don't think I need to explain this, don't pay for it."

I assured him that the word *lesbian* never stopped a man from trying. I would do what I wanted, and what I wanted was the illusion that all of this was happening on my terms.

After our strategy dinner, we went back to the fetish photographer's place, where he brought out an exquisite blond wig for me to try on. I pulled it down over my very cool, asymmetrical queer haircut, stared into the mirror, and felt like a Texas beauty queen. I took a sip of prosecco and loved the way I looked with that delicate glass in my hand, golden curls bouncing at my tits, just like Catherine's. No longer zipped up in a binder, they were swimming in a B-cup.

Before I had a chance to fully enjoy what I saw, the fetish

photographer came up behind me, put his hands on my hips, and gasped, "You need to be a blond!"

My hair was too boyish to domme; I knew that. I didn't need him to tell me. And I loved the wig, but it was hot and had already started to itch.

"A dominatrix should be the epitome of femininity, and that's always gonna be a blond."

I knew the type of woman the fetish photographer liked. He was the kind of guy who showed off pictures of his conquests, kept a whole folder full of them on his desktop, more on his phone. All skinny, big tits, blond. Hair-metal-video girls, long nails and tan skin. He used to be in a hair metal band himself. Now he was bald. He shaved his locks clean off when they started thinning, preserved the illusion that it was his choice as well.

I could definitely see the benefits of the wig, but even despite the heat and itch, I worried about it getting knocked off, the humiliation of being unmasked, a dyke in straight-girl clothing. I didn't want to be a bait-and-switch, the kind of domme Catherine complained about: women who were fatter in real life than their photographs suggested, or who didn't wear makeup when they showed up to the dungeon. She prided herself on looking exactly like the pictures promised. It would take more work for me, but I wanted to do the same.

A week after our photo shoot, I went alone to the photographer's house to train. When he opened the door, I saw that he had a large metal dog cage staged between the couch and the TV, waiting. He wore nothing but black boxer briefs and his prescription eyeglasses with transition lenses that had stopped working and never adjusted to clear, even inside, even at night. He told me he wanted to assist me in putting on makeup. I already had makeup on—Catherine helped me apply it before I left the house—but I acquiesced: I was training, after all. We went into the bathroom, and he dropped to his knees. He picked up a tray lined with orangey makeup, far too dark for my complexion, and held it out in front of him.

"I'm here to serve, mistress. To help you get ready," he whimpered. He wanted women to look perfect: perfect red lips, perfect cat-eyes. I wasn't surprised that this was his fetish.

I grabbed the foundation. He lowered the tray, pulled down his boxers, and placed his hard dick onto it. Its distinct curve to the right pointed directly at a cheap palette of shimmery eye shadows.

"You're so helpful," I said, resisting the urge to laugh. I realized that professional domination wouldn't be that different from other jobs I'd held in the service industry. That sex work, as they say, would be real work.

Beyond assuring that my makeup was applied to his tastes, the photographer's primary interests were in tease and denial and cock torture. We left the bathroom for the living room, where he produced a wooden step stool. He kneeled in front of me and placed his dick onto that as well. He told me that he wanted to demonstrate the amount of force you could exert with the toe and the heel of a pair of stiletto boots. He warned me not to scrape the skin as I applied pressure. It's impossible to stop the bleeding when the organ is engorged. With the blunt toe of my boot, I could smash, stomp, and even stand on it with my full weight. I tried it out, and delighted in the resiliency of the human body.

The stiletto was more difficult. I wobbled on my left heel with my right pressed into his flesh. I'd only learned to walk in them recently, for just this occasion. *I could turn my ankle and rip his dick off at any moment*, I thought. It wouldn't be the last time I worried about accidentally killing a client in session. I worried about killing far more often than I worried about being killed.

Catherine told me to use a pain scale with clients, to hurt them a bit and then ask how bad it was, like at a doctor's office: a scale of one to ten. If they said nine, you might ask if they want to stay at a nine or go to a ten. Or, if they want to stay at a nine or go down to a five. Then you could adjust the muscle you put into the torture based on their responses. A nine for me may not be a nine for you.

The fetish photographer didn't want to try Catherine's pain scale. It was a turnoff, he interrupted me to say, as soon as I'd started. He called it *contrived*. Nothing about stomping on a dick placed squarely atop a wooden step stool is natural, but I got what he meant. It's important to preserve the illusion of mutual desire, and the pain scale risked breaking the spell. If the submissive knows you are only hurting him according to his tastes, that taints the fantasy that you're hurting him according to your own. Never mind the fact that safe, sane, and consensual BDSM play demands adherence to these rules, the fetish photographer didn't want to play by them. So I calculated my movements, instead, by dialing in to sweat and scream.

Another crucial illusion to master: convincing a client that time stands still when you're together. Of course, it's also important to perfect this illusion within the hour or two for which he's actually paid so that he can get back home or to the office on time. I didn't yet know any of this—how to curate a playlist for the perfect hour or to pull out a blindfold before pulling out my phone—so I checked the time in front of the fetish photographer without ceremony and announced that we had five minutes left before I was out of those shoes that had tortured us both.

The fetish photographer stayed kneeling but started stroking himself, as most of them would at the session's close, an act that I had witnessed with Bitch Vicky and Catherine told me came standard. Just before I left our apartment, she had given me a tip: "Give him a countdown to come," she said. "Clients love that."

Something in her delivery told me that this was Catherine's favorite part. It hadn't occurred to me before that she would have a favorite part.

With the fetish photographer kneeling in front of me, pulling at his bruised dick with his right hand, a tissue in his left hand on the ready, I initiated the countdown: "You have ten seconds to finish."

Catherine told me to count him down slow, then to speed up and watch him get stressed, then to slow it down again.

"Ten . . . nine . . . eight . . ."

He pumped away at it, locked his eyes on me, waiting for my command.

"Seven six five four . . ." I spat the numbers out in rapid succession, watching him panic, wondering if he would be able to come on command or if he would embarrass himself, too fast or too slow. When I got to "one," the fetish photographer instantly came into the tissue and ran off to the bathroom to flush it down the toilet. This was the first of many free sessions I would give him in exchange for that first photo shoot, making me the latest domme-in-training he convinced into an unpaid arrangement.

The fetish photographer knew that I needed to obscure my identity in the photos I would use for advertising, but he told me that I should take a few with my face showing anyway, just in case I ever changed my mind. I thought that the only way I would change my mind would be if the university caught me doing sex work and kicked me out of my program, but that didn't seem entirely unlikely, so I agreed. I covered my tattoos with thick foundation, planted my feet in front of a white backdrop in his studio, and held a whip I couldn't yet wield up to my face as a prop. I fixed my gaze above it and stared into the blinding flash.

14

. .

My third year in the PhD program kicked off with an academic mixer like any other. I stood at the perimeter of the room, leaning against a bookshelf, and watched the new students make introductions. I had driven to campus straight from a morning session and was self-conscious about the kiss-proof lipstick I hadn't removed, the scent of sanitizer that lingered in my hair and made me smell like a hospital. When I left the dungeon to go home, I didn't notice the smell following me, but when I drove directly to campus, I swore I carried it with me, out of that dark warehouse and into the daylight. Into a cashless world where sex work was something that happened south of campus, in the neighborhoods beyond the university's gates, but within its gaze. Inside the gates, sex work only existed on a few shelves in the library: statistics in the sociology section, theories in criminology, or sad stories of lost women in cinema or literature.

After the introductions, students and faculty mingled, holding little plates of tasteless cheese cubes and room-temperature fruit at four o'clock in the afternoon on a Wednesday. I had loaded my plate with copious amounts of both. I was coming off yet another summer famine, and I was eager to be back on campus, where book talks and poetry readings and department mixers meant free cheese and halved deli sandwiches.

After a spring of abundance, aided by the fact that I was the new girl in town, Catherine warned me that domme work would slow in the summers. Clients go on vacations, she said, and pay for their kids' summer camps. I had been lucky. In May, I'd snagged my first regular client: a tech bro with a latex fetish. He liked dommes with expensive rubber wardrobes, something I personally lacked but could borrow from Catherine, who would lend me anything except her Louboutins.

My first sessions with the tech bro were tame. He was only particular about the outfits: short, shiny dresses and tall, shiny boots. I couldn't repeat the same color two sessions in a row or he would ask what dress I planned on wearing next time. He spent most of his hours with me on his knees, rubbing silicone lube into my dress—a practice rubber fetishists call *shining* the latex—admiring how soft the rubber felt in his hands. A year into the job, I'd learned to arrange playlists that would signal when there was fifteen minutes to go, and when the fifteen-minute song played, I ordered him to lay down on the bondage table where I would tie up his dick. I held on to the end of the rope while he thrusted and squirmed himself to orgasm, and I was proud of myself for picking his lock so soon after we'd started playing, a sign that I was getting better at domming. Afterward, he cleaned up and we exchanged pleasantries, then he got into his very nice car and drove away. He was cute, timid, and smelled good, and that's what we called easy money. There was certainly hard money to be made in the dungeon. The tech bro was easy.

On his fifth visit—a milestone because it officially marked his payment of my rent that month—I asked him to undress, and he just stood there, fully clothed, shielding his eyes from the overhead light.

"Why do you call it a dungeon if it's not dark?"

I assumed he asked because I looked like shit: I'd stumbled into some lighting that showed the cellulite on the backs of my thighs, or I had a false eyelash peeling. I didn't consider that he might be self-conscious about his own body. He was small, his brown skin smooth in places, pockmarked in others, a reminder of teenage acne. He had probably been humiliated more than once in his life, and he didn't see me for humiliation. I yanked a cord out of the wall to kill one of the spotlights. Then we proceeded, business as usual.

Except that when he knelt behind me to shine my skirt, he grabbed me rough, like a child desperate for a hug, holding on to his mother's legs and threatening to topple her over. I felt the scruff of his beard on my ass through the rubber, then his hard-on between my legs, just below my knees. It took me a minute to realize that he was humping my legs like a dog. Before I could decide whether or not this was a violation that warranted my safe word, I felt him shaking and realized he was about to come. And that would mean I had made two hundred dollars in fifteen minutes.

I let him finish.

After he cleaned up and left, he texted me to say he was disappointed I let the session end so early and asked for a free half hour the next time we played. What felt like a steady summer job was going downhill quick.

The weeks got hotter, and the tech bro got more demanding. He sensed my desperation and milked it. He stopped scheduling sessions in favor of asking me to meet him on a whim. He would send a text at ten o'clock, when I'd already washed off my makeup and sat wrapped in a blanket watching *Law & Order: Special Victims Unit* with Catherine and the cat.

Can you see me in thirty minutes?

I needed the money badly enough to bolt for the bathroom and shave the day off my legs. Not every client required perfection, but this one did, and thirty minutes' notice was not enough to achieve it. I started wearing full makeup until midnight in case he called. I shaved my legs every morning.

It went on like this through July, when, at a dungeon party, I found out he was seeing another domme. She was a friend of mine and, like me, a tattooed brunette. Most clients have a type, so we shared a lot of them. We commiserated over the annoying ones, laughed at the laughable ones, said nice things about the nice ones. She described the same attitude change in our tech bro: he started out sweet, then became demanding, sensing her need and his own power.

"But I fixed him," she told me, draining the whiskey from her glass. She said that a few weeks back, he made a rude comment about her dress, so she threw his ass over the spanking bench and paddled him until he cried.

"That fixed him," she shrugged. "Now he's a kitten."

After that, the tech bro remained loyal to her, and never saw me again.

In August, I made no money and ran up a credit card bill. I longed for the spring, when I'd had an envelope of cash in my sock drawer that I would pull out every morning, just to hold it, mesmerized by its heft. It never had more than three grand in it, but three grand in twenties is fat and sumptuous when your bank account has never had three grand in it ever, and even if it will someday, you won't be able to hold it.

Until business picked up again, I felt like an unwelcome

burden on Catherine, who had agreed to cover part of my rent. She paid it like a drug dealer, in cash or money orders. She had her own regulars to keep her afloat each summer. The new student mixer signaled the arrival of fall, and I should have been thinking more about my course list than my client list. And maybe I would have, but I was paranoid about the dungeon smell caught in my hair. I'd let it grow out. It hung down below my shoulders.

A professor approached me, with square teeth and a square jaw. He had been on the committee that recruited me to the university, just two years before. When I accepted, I had promised to be loyal to the school that had invested its good faith and money in me. I had promised not to work elsewhere, not to need or take more than I was given. I had promised not to sell sexuality to a man who humped my legs like a dog and kept me up at all hours of the night when I should have been cultivating a life of the mind.

I set my Diet Coke down on a chair and forced a smile at him.

"Hi," he said, his voice warm as he extended his hand. "I didn't catch your name . . ."

When I stood in front of the fetish photographer's camera, I made a promise to all the clients who would pay me to embody the lacquer and shine of my photographs. I promised them that I would give femininity a shot. When I stood in front of the fetish photographer's camera, I also broke my promise to school. I broke my promise to that professor with his outstretched hand. When I turned in my term papers in the fall of my second year, I still turned heads from time to time when I walked into women's restrooms. A year later, femininity had rendered me unrecognizable.

Masculinity had given me a way to say "fuck you" to men. It was my "fuck you" to redneck football players and

my friends' fathers, my own father, my high school principal, and the church pastor who told my mom she was going
to burn in hell if she didn't knock some sense into me.
When I found feminist theory in college, and queer theory
in graduate school, I found a political foundation for all of
the "fuck yous" I'd wanted my gender to express. Subvert-
ing hetero-patriarchal expectations: that's where the power
was, if you'd asked me. Once I started accepting money
from men who were paying me to not only meet but exceed
those expectations, I realized that money was more powerful than any "fuck you" my armpit hair might exude. The
hetero-patriarchy wasn't listening to my armpit hair anyway,
and men had money to burn.

I sold out.

I shaved my armpits. When that wasn't enough, I la-
sered all my body hair. I ran on a treadmill until the sweat
changed the shape of my waist. I learned to draw the perfect cat-eye and started wearing heels outside the dungeon.
Those four inches of power went a long way, wherever I was.
Except, perhaps, the academic mixer. I got a fresh manicure
and pedicure every other week. I bought perfume and called
it my *signature scent*. I put a *working vacation* to Europe
with Catherine on my credit card, and while I didn't work
enough on that vacation to pay it off, I had become the kind
of person who took vacations. It showed in my posture, my
skin, and the stories I had to tell over drinks. I exfoliated.
I didn't feel smaller, taking directions from the patriarchy.
I felt bigger than men, smarter even. I felt like I was taking
from them. I'd had enough of them taking from me.

I introduced my family to Catherine, and to my new
look, over the holidays. It was the last year we thought my
grandmother would be with us, and it felt important that I
make it home. My relationship to my dad had become easier.

He'd remarried and gotten more serious about Jesus, but he didn't drill down on the particulars, like men laying with men as they do with women being abominations. There were two thousand miles between us, and he had bad knees. They slowed his pace.

Dad never apologized for the ways he'd treated me in high school, but I got the feeling that he was sorry. I'd brought a woman home before—my last serious girlfriend after college, before Catherine—and I had to correct him when he called her my "friend." But he was kind to us and looked embarrassed, not angry, when I spelled it out: "*Girl*friend, Dad. She's not my friend; she's my girlfriend."

I borrowed Catherine's clothes for my family's Christmas Eve dinner, just like I borrowed them for work—a black sweater dress and spike-heeled boots.

"You're so fit," Dad complimented me, pinching at my diminished waist like he was administering a BMI exam.

"And your hair's getting so long." He said it while beaming at Catherine, the woman surely responsible for these positive changes.

"You should keep it like this," he said. "My beautiful daughter."

I had fashioned my femininity as an appeal to other women's fathers. It also appealed to my own. I had made my way back to him, his pretty baby.

Later that night, Catherine and I drove to my mom's house, twenty miles from the place where she'd raised me. It was her husband's house, really. He built it himself, way out in the country, so far out that you couldn't see light from a neighbor's window in any direction and the twilight echoed with coyotes howling themselves awake for their nightly kills. Every time I visited, it felt like the woods he'd cleared to build it crept closer and closer back toward the porch.

We took over the kitchen, baking late-night cookies, squinting to read the recipe in my mother's cursive. The cookies were the last item on Mom's holiday to-do list, and we wanted to help her get to bed before midnight. Catherine gave me a Hallmark Christmas movie kiss, our lips buttered from mixing bowl taste tests.

The man of the house, who had been keeping one eye on us, one on the Western he'd chosen to watch over the holiday movies that played on every other channel, bolted upright from his recliner and took off down the hallway. He didn't have the guts to say it to my face, so he found my mother and demanded that she make sure I knew that I was never to kiss a woman in his house again.

"I don't care what she does in her own house," I overheard him say, "but she's not gonna do it in mine."

Catherine and I left on the first flight we could get out of there. We made it to LA before our favorite Chinese place, where we would have Christmas dinners from there on out, closed for the evening.

One man in my life got less hateful and another picked up the torch. *Catherine is my family now*, I thought. And for a long time, she was.

15

• •

Every session began with an initial step into power exchange. Because dommes are women and clients are, for the most part, men, we both had to work to establish our new roles—dominant and submissive—inside the dungeon. As soon as the clients arrived, they were expected to hand over the money, and in order to enact the power exchange, we both pushed this act from our minds. If you kept thinking about the money, you wouldn't be able to forget that the man who paid is always, to some degree, in control of the woman who's working. After the cash changed hands, there were steps we took to forget.

I ordered the clients to undress, and I remained fully clothed. I asked them to kneel before me. Even the ones with bad knees did their best because they needed to forget that they paid. Then I leaned down to them, let them smell me. If they tried to meet my eyes, I made them drop their gaze to my feet. I ran my fingernails over their nipples, up through their hair, and whispered in their ears, "You're a big boy, so I'm sure you know the rules," even if I was sure that they didn't. I needed a sexy way to do what most find to be the least sexy part of the scene: boundary negotiations.

"You are to call me mistress, do you understand?"

"Yes, mistress," they would reply, 90 percent of the time. If they hadn't visited a mistress before, they'd seen one in porn and learned the conventions there. The other 10 percent would nod their heads or squeak out a yes, and when that happened, I would dig my nails into their nipples once more, harder then, and tell them I was wrong to have put my faith in their ability to take direction. I would ask again. They never got it wrong a second time.

Then, I would repeat the activities we'd discussed on the phone, making sure we were in agreement on what was about to go down. I would give them the safe word.

"If anything starts to feel like it's too much," I would say, "you can say the word *mercy*, and I will redirect my energies elsewhere. You won't hurt my feelings, and we won't have to stop the scene. I'll just stop doing whatever reached your limits and start doing something else." I would ask if they understood.

"Yes, mistress," they would reply.

"Good," I would say, then "get up!" or "stay down!"—it depended on the scene. Sometimes I would fasten a leash and collar around their neck and walk them on hands and knees around the dungeon, giving them a tour of the equipment, the whips and paddles and canes and clamps and some implements even I had no idea how to operate. If they were older, I would check in about the health of their knees and shoulders. If they were into bondage, I'd ask if they were able to be bound with their arms above their head, behind their back. Middle-aged men have old football injuries, slipped discs, tennis elbows. They came to me hurt and I made it worse, but only in the ways that they wanted.

I defied the fetish photographer's advice and posted ads calling myself "LA's Renowned Lesbian Dominatrix." When

I first started I was far from *renowned*, but by and large, the *lesbian* bit of this advertising worked: it attracted clients who sought me out for erotic humiliation. My clientele wanted a woman who would never want them in return, and at that, I excelled.

Those first years domming, I went to classes and workshops with BDSM community leaders who taught me that we are as likely to develop a spanking fetish if our parents traumatized us with corporal punishment as we are if we weren't spanked as kids and became curious about—even envious of—those who were. Those fetish workshops, held in sex-toy stores packed with grown-ups shifting uncomfortably in metal folding chairs, must have been full of men who were teased for having small dicks when they were younger. Small-penis humiliation was by far the most common fantasy to come across my newly repurposed desk. Not everyone seeks out BDSM to work through their trauma, but eroticizing rejection can be powerful, and we hurt each other in predictable ways.

True to the kink community wisdom, a lot of small-penis-humiliation clients, in fact, had big dicks. A client once opened a hotel room door for me with his penis flopped straight out over his zipper, wrapped up in the three hundred-dollar bills he owed me. He shook it back and forth and whined, "Mistress, isn't it so small? Can you even see it?" It was so big that I worried the room service guy collecting his tip ten doors down might have seen it, and the worse humiliation would be mine.

Passing through a hotel lobby while dressed to do sex work produces its own kind of erotic humiliation. I could feel the concierge clock the fishnet stockings peeking out from under my seasonally inappropriate trench coat. Once through the lobby and off the elevator, I would walk down the hall toward the client's room and feel myself getting wet for the cash that would be tucked into my boot on my way back out. I tried not to think about the fact that every client could be a cop. I knew that cops chose nice hotels for stings—it's harder for a worker to say no, even if she's spooked, if she thinks there's a lot of money on the line. Still, the more expensive the hotel, the more confident I felt moving through the lobby in my August trench coat. You can get away with a lot in a nice hotel; nobody wants to interrupt a rich man's good time.

Doing the same work at a Holiday Inn, where I might have to ride an elevator with a family on vacation, was stressful. I imagined moms and dads holding on to their daughters' hands a little tighter, hoping they wouldn't turn out like me. I once did a session at Disney's Grand Californian while the client's wife and kids were at the park. I didn't realize exactly where the address in my phone was taking me until I'd already driven over an hour into Orange County, and I wasn't about to drive back home empty-handed.

As with nearly everything else, I learned about hotel sessions from Catherine. She toured one week out of every month and returned home with thousands of dollars stuffed into her boots, her carry-on, and her luggage. She spent most of her time touring the South. The repressive regions produced plenty of men desperate to find an outlet for their fetishes. In Dallas, New Orleans, and Atlanta, I tagged along to learn the tricks of travel. Choose a hotel with elevators just inside the main lobby door, so clients can come and go without passing the front desk. Avoid hotels where you need a room key to access the elevator. Always get a room with two double beds and pick up a stack of disposable puppy pads to lay on the client bed so that you don't need to request too many extra towels—too many towels are a dead giveaway. Come to terms with the fact that on the last day of your trip, you'll be locked into a room with a strange man who can only assume you have thousands of dollars of cash in the safe. Vet the guys who request your last day harder than those who request your first. Take all these precautions while maintaining confidence that you're a badass fucking dominatrix.

Humiliation doesn't flow unilaterally from domme to sub. On some level, my clients understood that. Every so often, one would try to humiliate me by asking, "Does your father know you do this?" They would toss this question at me once I'd taken off my heels and started cleaning up, a task I already found humiliating enough, spraying the cum stains down with disinfectant and wiping them off the leather furniture. I wasn't supposed to ask them about their own daddy issues, but on bad days I snapped back, "No, does yours?"

These clients thought that the things I did in the dungeon and the things they had done in the dungeon were categorically different. They couldn't imagine my life beyond those walls, or they didn't want to—it would ruin their fantasies. A client might spend an hour parading around the room in pink ruffled underpants (cute) and then clean the bathroom floor with his tongue (disgusting). I might simply give orders, get my feet rubbed, and make my car payment from an app on my phone. But the real difference between my clients and me was that I saw us as equals once we were both out of our lingerie, and many of them did not. Even if they wanted me, they didn't always respect me.

Whether he was conscious of it or not, the big-dick client who waved his junk at me in the hotel hallway wanted to humiliate me as much as he wanted to be humiliated himself. But I was a badass fucking dominatrix.

"My mother was right," I said, pushing him inside. "Never put money in your mouth. You don't know where it's been." I shut the door behind me.

"Also, your dick is tiny."

Men paid me to make them feel: ugly, dirty, slutty, cheap, whorish, and feminine. All the insults that humiliate women at work, on public transportation, in schools and strip clubs, online, and in any other place they might go. I didn't have the stomach for the bloody side of BDSM: no cutting, piercing, or branding. Instead, I developed a specialty for making men feel worthless, and I found out the hard way that some of them believed me.

I had plenty of male clients whom I would have considered *fat*—perhaps the most common insult used to humiliate women. These men unbuckled their belts and emancipated their stomachs, spread wide their thighs that chafed on the inside, at the places where girls in my high school locker room complained of "chub rub" when gym class forced us into mesh shorts.

I was envious of the absolute ease with which men, fat or thin, would undress in front of a stranger. My rare female clients bought new lingerie for the occasion, kept their arms folded in front of their bellies when they were unbound, asked me to turn the lights down lower than dungeon low. I never had a female client who wanted me to humiliate her, and I would have said no had any woman asked. I didn't want to do anything in the dungeon I couldn't live with at home. I could live with humiliating men.

I only ever had one client ask me to use the size of his gut, not his dick, against him. Some traumas are easier to eroticize than others.

When he called my appointment line, I was walking on campus, to or from a class I was teaching or taking, and I couldn't risk the wrong person overhearing our conversation. He introduced himself and asked if I was available to play.

I told him that yes, I could meet that night, and asked what he wanted to do. I kept it vague enough that I could have been talking to a date, except that my date replied, "Erotic humiliation."

"Great, sounds good," I answered. I proposed that we meet at seven, ended the call, and texted him the dungeon address.

Catherine told me to always ask clients over the phone what they found humiliating. That way when they arrived, I could feign a natural reaction to the size of their dicks, or have the puppy gear ready to transform them into slobbery dogs. That was easy enough for Catherine to say; she didn't have to answer her work phone on a college campus.

When I opened the dungeon door at seven o'clock, I noticed the client's weight, his shirt buttons straining under the pressure of keeping him together. I wouldn't have mentioned it. As long as they were freshly showered, their bodies didn't make much of a difference to me. I had dressed men his size in XXL satin negligees and painted their lips. I had praised them for their beauty and meant it. These clients were my favorites. The moment when they gazed into the mirror and smiled: they looked like they felt the way I had felt when I tried on the fetish photographer's blond wig and saw myself as pretty for the first time in a long time. If we turned the lights down low, these clients became who they had been in their fantasies, and how many of us can say that we have seen ourselves as we wish to be seen? It felt good, sweet even, what we did together in the dungeon.

Not all clients who wanted to be dressed up as women were sweet. Some men put on wigs, slipped into tight dresses, and did to me whatever they thought they could get away with. They took more liberties with touch, slipped their fingers under my skirt, making me wiggle away and try to defuse their touch without killing the mood and ruining my chances of a tip. Embodying femininity gave them more latitude to act like men. Plenty of these clients found being dressed up as a woman degrading, meaning they found being a woman degrading, meaning they had no issue degrading me. When I didn't need the money, I didn't see these clients. When I needed the money, I put up with it.

Just inside the dungeon door, I asked this particular client what he found humiliating and he didn't list any of humiliation's greatest hits: wearing women's clothing, pretending to be my footstool, my Persian rug, my dog, my piglet, my naughty schoolboy, my pathetic husband. He didn't say having a small dick.

"I'm fat," was all he said. Anxious sweat beaded over his liver-spotted forehead when he said it, a slice of mortadella left out in the sun.

If I had listened to Catherine and asked him to specify his interests over the phone, I may have told him to call another mistress, someone with more experience. But he was already handing me the cash. Anyway, I figured, I knew as well as anyone how to inflict fat shame: I poked at my own stomach and pinched at my own thighs all the time. I insulted myself when I felt that I had eaten one too many slices of pizza. I watched the *calories burned* gauge on the rowing machine at the gym and accepted sweat as punishment for bad behavior. I tucked his cash into my boot and proceeded into not-quite-uncharted territory.

I led the client over to a seated cross, a bondage chair meant for ball busting, cock torture, and caning the tender white meat of the inner thighs. It allows a submissive to sit with his limbs bound open, vulnerable to attack from all angles. I asked the client to undress. He did it quickly, and folded his clothes into a neat little pile at the foot of the cross. I asked him to sit and chained his wrists and ankles, watched him struggle to perfect his posture against the vertical plank that ran up the length of his spine. The seated cross was not built to accommodate a body like his, and I could tell that he felt it, but I ignored his discomfort, lifted his stomach, and found his penis. I fastened the rope to the base of the cross and tied a little knot at the other end, looped around his dick so it wouldn't get lost again, so I could keep my eye on it. My plan was to tell him that every inch of his body was wrong, starting with that. I may have been uncomfortable, but I had taken the job and intended to do it well.

I swiped a leather riding crop from a hook in the toy closet and pushed it into the flesh of his belly. He swallowed it whole. I pulled it back out, pushed it in again, watched it disappear a second time.

"God only knows what's hiding between these rolls," I leaned in to say. He flinched.

"Yes, mistress. God only knows."

"What *are* you hiding in there?" I dropped the crop and grabbed a roll of flesh, dug into it. This time, his dick twitched in its little lasso, and I took that as my cue to go deeper.

"You're a fat fuck, you know that?" I let go of him and walked away, then turned back, leaned in to whisper: "I could barely find your dick under all that blubber."

I was surprised at how easy it was for me to hurt him. These felt like the worst things I'd ever said to another person, and I had a litany of bad things from which to choose.

"I wouldn't fuck you with a ten-foot pole," I declared, one of my favorite teenage insults, one I'd heard boys yell at girls at the skating rink and swimming down at the riverbank.

My disgust with the client's body was authentic, and authenticity is dangerous territory in the dungeon. When the line between fantasy and reality blurs, you're no longer role-playing, and we called it BDSM *play* for a reason.

I spit in the client's face. I didn't think of Grace's mom when I did it. Instead, I watched the slimy white bubbles burst and dribble down his chin, then puckered my lips as a warning that I intended to do it again, this time in his mouth. He knew the cue and opened, hungry for it. When he swallowed, I told him he should be on a saliva diet.

At the word *diet*, his dick went soft. We made it fifteen minutes into the hour for which he'd paid before I'd scared myself and he'd had enough.

A soft dick is a sex worker's worst enemy. If the hour is to move along as it should, the dick must stay hard. An hour-long erection practically guaranteed that the client could bring himself to orgasm right on time at the end of the scene. If women are typically expected to produce men's orgasms, sex work raises the stakes. My clients booked sessions to worship my feet, to accept a flogging, or, the trusted few, to clean my apartment; but what they were really paying for was the opportunity to jerk off when it was over. Their orgasms justified the expense.

Dommes weren't expected to produce client orgasms ourselves, but I prayed for them at the end of my scenes. The worst sessions were with guys who couldn't make themselves come. Nothing was more painful than having to stop their desperate pumping with, "Sorry, Steve, our time is up." Disappointment dripped out of them instead, and I was still the one standing there with a washcloth, waiting to clean it up.

When I decided on domming as a part-time enterprise, I sought out training from expert riggers in the art of bondage, but no amount of knot practice would prepare me to untie a man I'd met just an hour earlier, even if he *had* successfully gotten himself off.

For some, shame sets in after they come, and it's difficult to disassociate when the woman you paid to degrade you is still right there, herself degraded, panties soaked in urine from the golden shower that ended up running down her leg. They wished they could turn me off with a click like a porn video, but there I was, untying their wrists from their ankles, making small talk about traffic.

Some clients made it obvious that they regretted the money once they too were spent, and it's frightening to be alone in a warehouse with a man who's not afraid to show you his buyer's remorse. They opened their wallets, closed them, said things like, "I'd tip you, but you already cleaned me out!" huffing and puffing and buttoning their trousers. Contrary to stereotype, not all submissive clients are high-powered businessmen who need the tables turned on their day off, and when they are, they are even less likely to tip. The best clients weren't the rich ones but the ones who'd worked in the service industry.

I liked the clients who transformed upon orgasm back into themselves. They were usually dads who told me about their pretty wives, their smart kids. The older ones still had photos in their wallets: grandkids, family portraits complete with family pets. The younger ones flashed me kid pictures on their phones. They wanted to let me know that they were normal.

Even better were the ones who fell into slumbers after it was over, smiles on their faces like satisfied babies, asleep on the bottle. They laid there happy, in pools of their own sweat and jizz, and let me clean up around them before showering off and departing quietly, back into a world that couldn't guess where they had been. Whatever the aftermath, I came to see a man's orgasm as a way to diffuse a situation.

I would get none of that with the fat-shame client. His face changed when he went soft, like he'd awakened out of hypnosis, and I knew there was no chance we were coming back from where we had gone.

"Hey, it's cool," I said, dropping the act that wasn't one. I loosened the restraints on his right wrist, then his left ankle, right ankle, and left wrist.

His body slumped forward and he began to sob. He hadn't used his safe word, but if I'd given one to myself—as dommes should, but never do—I would have. I held him there on the cold dungeon floor until he stopped crying.

I got up to retrieve his clothes, and he laid down, a turtle on its back, in distress. I brought over his belongings, crouched down once again, and petted his head.

"I'm sorry, mistress," he said, still struggling to gain composure. "I've thought about this for years. I imagine it all the time."

"It's a perfectly fine thing to want," I said. I was careful never to shame clients for their desires, unless that's what they were seeking. This client had miscalculated his taste for shame.

"I see escorts sometimes," he went on, "a lot of the time."

I imagined letting him touch me, and my repulsion dilated. This was what we talked about in the sex worker support group I had recently joined. *The whore hierarchy.* Escorts deal with more stigma than dommes because they sometimes have intercourse with their clients. I tried to channel my feminist ethics and cast the disgust from my mind but failed. The client pulled up his underwear and fidgeted with the waistband.

"I know I disgust them," he whispered at the ground between his knees. "They don't say it, but I know."

"You're not disgusting," I argued, trying to keep him calm. I wondered if he was going to ask me to return the money. A month earlier, a client asked me to return the cash within five minutes of starting the scene, and I assumed it was because he expected me to be prettier. I pulled the three hundred-dollar bills he'd given me out of my bra, laid them on the bondage table, and immediately regretted it. It may have been dangerous to refuse the refund, but the session had started for me two hours prior to our meeting, when I straightened my hair and whitened my teeth. I sat in the dungeon alone for the hour, before returning home to Catherine. When she asked how it had gone, I told her it was fine, nothing out of the ordinary. I even paid her the $60 rental fee to avoid admitting what had happened.

"I've seen disgusting men," I told the client. "They're rude, entitled, late, inconsiderate. You were on time!"

He sniffled and forced a smile.

"Sometimes, we think we want something," I said, "and when we get it, it doesn't feel like what we thought it would."

Determined to keep the money, I asked what he would like to do with the time we had left. He suggested sushi.

We left the dungeon together and ordered tempura everything, hot grease slippery on our lips. We had nothing in common aside from the popcorn shrimp on the table between us. I ate until my stomach was so full it hurt and made a note to approach with caution anything that might cut too close to the bone.

• •

The year I started domming, I went to a book party in downtown LA with Catherine and a new friend from my feminist theory grad seminar. The place was packed, and it dwarfed a typical academic-lecture-size auditorium. The writers reading that night were very big deals. They presented work on failure, cruelty, and humiliation: the queer theory buzzwords of that season. Catherine loved the reading and bought books by all the writers, which was great for me and my new friend from school because we wanted to read them but couldn't afford them. We milled around the lobby after the reading, waiting for the writers to take their places at the signing tables so that Catherine could get each book inscribed. I leaned into her, hoping to get in on the conversation I couldn't afford.

When it was Catherine's turn, we approached the table and one of the big-deal writers reached for their book, took it from Catherine, and asked what brought her out that evening.

"I'm a professional dominatrix," Catherine answered. Failure, humiliation, cruelty: these were her buzzwords too.

The very-big-deal writer signed the book, looked up from the title page, and asked, with genuine curiosity and a tinge of condescension, "What are you doing *here?*"

Catherine never seemed ashamed of what she did for a living. More than that, she seemed proud, and I was proud of her in turn. She shared dungeon stories with friends over cocktails and then picked up the bar tab. She offered to send their delinquent parking tickets to her "financial slave" and had submissives chauffeur us to and from parties. She once ordered a client to drive an hour to our apartment to assist her with an undisclosed task. When he arrived, she asked him to hand her a pen from a table three feet away from where she was sitting and then told him to be on his way. She was the real deal—liked the work and was good at it.

But when the very-big-deal writer pointed out how implausible it was, meeting a sex worker in the company of academics on a Friday night, I watched Catherine change. She picked her signed copy up off the table before the ink had time to dry, and we left the reading. She never told me that it hurt, but it looked like it did, and I heeded her pain as a warning.

Catherine was always on the hunt for a *whale*: a big fish. That's what they call the guy in the strip club, or the casino, or in this case the dungeon, who stumbles in and stays for a long time: the guy who spends a great deal of money. Catherine didn't need a client on a one-time spending binge, manic or high. She needed a 401(k) client, a client without big regrets come Monday morning. I thought that Catherine was powerful. She traveled the world, threw extravagant parties, and paid her bills on time. I realized that night at the reading that I had a power of my own. If the big-deal writer had asked me what brought me out that night, I would have said that I was a graduate student. The big-deal writer would have signed the book and wished me well.

Catherine might find that 401(k) client, I thought, but I would have a 401(k) account of my own someday. Sex work was a means to an end for me—it wasn't *the* end. There it was, that *whore hierarchy* again, rearing its ugly head. Being a dominatrix was Catherine's life, and it was my dirty little secret. I knew that if I wanted to hold on to my power, my place at the top of that whore hierarchy, I had to keep it that way.

16

• •

The lines between work and pleasure blurred when Catherine and I took sessions together. We sold her client list on the concept of lesbian cuckolding, and once I had a client list of my own, we sold them on it too. For these scenes, we started the clients on their knees and hovered above them, kissing like porno lesbians, our tongues an inch out of our mouths, twirling, making sure we didn't smear lipstick all over our chins. We let the clients beg for more, then laughed at them, tied them up, threw blindfolds over their eyes, and turned on a vibrator for show. We faked over-the-top sex noises and watched them wiggle around in their bondage, pouting that they wanted to watch. Their pouting was as fake as our orgasms—the tease was what they were after.

I used to hate the ways that men fantasized about lesbians. I hated lesbian porn made for men. I hated the idea of girls making out for attention at frat parties. I hated Katy Perry's "I Kissed a Girl" because the girl who kissed a girl and liked it had a boyfriend who she hoped didn't mind it. My radical lesbian-feminist friends staged a kiss-in at a straight bar that, in honor of Katy Perry's sapphic adventure, held an "I Kissed a Girl" contest. Their septum piercings and faux-hawks, hairy legs and armpits, were a big "fuck you" to the male gaze. All of which is to say: I thought kissing my girlfriend for money was something I'd done once in college and would never do again. But there I was with Catherine, lesbian cuckolding our biggest moneymaker.

After our sessions, Catherine would take me out to toast the genius of our dog and pony show. I felt like both the dog and the pony. Sometimes, Catherine wanted to be fucked for real while the clients were tied up, listening. I was afraid their blindfolds might slip, but it wasn't worth the hushed negotiation within earshot of the client, so I just went along with it. Pleasing her was more important to me than articulating my own boundaries.

I would leave these sessions feeling bitter, but the bitterness would sweeten under the heat of bourbon. Catherine inspired obedience in me, and in almost everyone she met. This quality made her great at her job. It also made her difficult to love in an honest way. When she told me that I was a good domme, I glowed in the light of her praise. I had to earn it, but when I did—when I told her about the diabolical things that I too had dreamed up for my submissives—she would squeeze my hand and tell me that I was a *good girl*. And for a time, I was.

Academia had its own power dynamics. In my first year of graduate school, a respected scholar visited our program to give a talk and run a seminar. The work they were there to discuss was part of a forthcoming book project, and the program circulated their writing before they arrived. I read the chapter twice. I was convinced that my reading comprehension was worse than everyone else's, and I didn't suspect that any of my classmates shared the same insecurities. A few probably did, but a few more made it clear that they did not, and I envied their confidence.

In a stuffy, windowless room, we introduced ourselves as we always did: by first name, year of program, and area of research. I was *Chris, first year, queer studies.* I had been reading about the ways that those in power use sexuality as a means by which to manage populations, to cow all of us into submission, and made it my area of research: my grad school last name. I was theoretically interested in sex and power, but I didn't yet know much about BDSM. I hadn't yet met or googled Catherine.

Someone asked a question that I didn't understand. The respected scholar turned to me—*Chris, first year, queer studies*—to answer it. When I said that I didn't know the answer, they asked me if I'd read a book that I hadn't read. When I admitted that I hadn't, they asked me how it was that my grad school last name was *queer studies* but I hadn't read that book. Clearly, they had dismissed the *first year* part of my name, or it didn't matter to them. I should do better, know better, know more. The humiliation of the scene was almost unbearable, and I didn't eroticize humiliation like so many of the men I would come to know.

Two years later, I planned to attend a conference where the same respected scholar would give the plenary speech. They would run another seminar in another stuffy room full of nervous grad students. I read the materials four times. I read every footnote. I read most of the source material that they referenced in the footnotes. When it was time to talk with them about their work, I not only knew it, I challenged it. I asked a question that they called *fantastic*, a question they couldn't answer on the spot but appreciated, promised to keep thinking about. *Good girl*, I imagined them saying, just like Catherine. I saw two clients for foot-worship sessions in my hotel between conference talks and used their tributes to pay for the room. I thought I had both worlds figured out.

It was easy, then, for me to separate sex work from academia, business from pleasure. I was still a devout lesbian. I studied 1970s lesbian separatism and critiqued its racism but secretly fantasized about leaving the city for a queer commune in the woods. I went to Bikini Kill revival shows and screamed, *"Rebel girl! Rebel girl!"* from the pit, as loud as Kathleen Hanna. I got a second line of Anne Sexton's poetry tattooed on my rib cage. I shaved the lower left quadrant of my head like all the other queers in LA were doing at the time. I had to ask my hairstylist to leave enough remaining on top that I could cover up the shaved bits for sessions. When that failed and a client noticed, he tapped me on the shoulder and said, "Honey, your wig is crooked." I pretended I didn't hear him, intent on frantically scraping up the candle wax that I'd poured onto him off the rug before Catherine came in and scolded me for the mess I'd made.

On Twitter, on my website, and in sessions, I talked about being a lesbian like it was a choice I made to make men suffer. Those men wanted to suffer, so they saw me as a gift with their names on it. I didn't need those men to know the real me. A session lasted on average an hour or two, and when the role-play ended, I could go back to my feminist poetry, riot grrrl albums, and cool friends with queer haircuts.

When I told people that Catherine and I had promised each other monogamy, they looked at me like I was crazy, like sex workers were by default non-monogamous, just by the nature of our jobs. If they'd ever done sex work themselves, they would know that most of the time, you're not turned on by your clients, and if you are, being turned on is part of the job you'd otherwise have to fake, so a little reality just made the time pass faster.

I did see domming as just a job, and I wanted Catherine to see it the same way: labor that she wouldn't do for free.

But she loved it. And because she loved it, I resented every moment she spent with a man when it wasn't for money.

Years into our relationship, Catherine started spending more time with one particular man: the fetish photographer. She had all the photographs she would need for a decade's worth of advertising, and plenty of money to pay another professional for more. Still, she told me, she needed to play with him for services rendered: he had helped her out with a business plan, or a graphic design project, or a play party at the dungeon. The fetish photographer wanted to be with Catherine all of the time, and I fought with her about it for nearly as many hours as they spent together. But he was useful to her, she said, and she needed to keep him happy.

I thought back to those early days, when the fetish photographer had helped to train me. I remembered the countdown to come: Catherine's favorite part. I realized that it wasn't Catherine's favorite part. It was his. That was precisely where he wanted her, and he'd gotten her there. He'd gotten me there too. All those nights that Catherine and I had argued because she didn't come home from his place when she said she'd come home—those nights when I found paddles and canes stashed in her car, when she told me she was just going over to his place for frozen yogurt—I realized that this had been what they were doing the whole time: mistress and slave, the real deal, no money on the table.

I had neither the time nor the money to follow Catherine out of town, but I started doing it anyway. On the weekend before my unfinished dissertation prospectus was due, we flew to Vegas for a porn convention. I tagged along for no reason other than I couldn't stand the thought of her and the fetish photographer alone in a hotel suite, in the place where things happen and don't make it home. She promised me monogamy and I intended to enforce it. She had sunk thousands of dollars into sponsoring an after-party that the fetish photographer pitched as a great way for her to network with porn performers and production companies that might rent the dungeon for shoots. I saw his pitch as nothing more than a way to get her alone, and I wanted to ruin his plan.

In a penthouse full of beautiful people with fake tits and big dicks, I knelt at Catherine's feet and trailed my tongue down the length of her inner thigh. When I reached the top of her leather boot, I followed its zipper all the way down to the floor, where the Vegas strip ground into her stiletto. I was a domme, but not yet domme enough to care if people watched me worship my girlfriend's thigh-high leather boots. I sucked her heel clean and gazed up at her with saucer eyes while the porn stars gazed at me. Catherine cooed, "Good girl," and stroked my hair. I watched the fetish photographer watching us. He wasn't taking any pictures.

As much as I would have liked it to have been, Vegas wasn't our last trip to the desert. A client offered Catherine his vacation house in Palm Springs, empty that off-season week when the temperatures topped 115 degrees, back when that wasn't a common occurrence. The fact that she and I had been fighting about the fetish photographer for months didn't stop Catherine from inviting him along.

"I'm not playing with him out there," I told her before we left. I didn't owe him anything.

She did owe him, she said, as she always did, and asked me to reconsider, just for the first night of the trip.

"Friday night only. Let's just get it out of the way." She kissed me, and I softened. "The rest of the time will be for us."

I agreed, as I always did. I even wrote him an email telling him what we planned to do to him. It may have been easy for me to keep business separate from pleasure, but it was becoming more and more difficult to keep business separate from my relationship with Catherine. I no longer knew where our personas ended and personhood began. We called each other by our fake names all weekend long.

On Sunday, Catherine sucked down skinny margaritas that the sun had warmed to the temperature of breakfast tea. I pretended to read poolside but slid into the water every five minutes to avoid heat stroke.

"Get the canes!" I heard Catherine shout from her shaded perch in the backyard hammock.

I didn't know who she was commanding, me or him, but the fetish photographer shot up from his lounge chair, bolted inside the house, and was back outside to kneel before her, two rattan canes poised on his outstretched palms, before I could pull myself out of the water.

In even less time than it took him to retrieve the implements, the fetish photographer had pulled his crooked dick out of his swim shorts and Catherine had gestured for me to join them. I ignored her, dropped instead onto the lounge chair that the fetish photographer had left damp and empty. Catherine climbed out of her hammock and stumbled toward me, sat on my lap, and pushed her tongue into my mouth, the citrus on her lips stinging mine, chapped from the desert heat. Whomever I had been moments earlier, floating weightless and blue, staring up at the San Jacinto mountains that waited each day to blot out the sun, she was gone.

"I don't want to play," I whispered, pulling away from Catherine's embrace. She ignored me. I wondered if *mercy* would have worked, but I was the domme, I reminded myself—no one needed to take mercy on me.

• •

I traveled with Catherine for a long time before I booked my first domme trip alone. In the first year of my dissertation research, the university gave me a small fund to cover a cross-country flight to Washington, DC, and a cheap hotel. My clients there would give me a much larger research fund to cover a much nicer hotel, room service, champagne, and oysters in the hotel bar. I boarded the plane with a copy of the book everyone was reading that summer: the one about all the sex worker skulls and torsos scattered on a beach. Those girls visited me when I dozed off above the clouds and they told me to go back home.

I heeded no warnings. No Catherine. No safety check to call. I would prove that I could keep myself alive.

I had never been to Long Island, but I learned its geography from that book. *Jones Beach. Oak Beach. Gilgo Beach.* I learned the names of the sex workers whose skulls and torsos had been scattered there. *Shannan Gilbert. Maureen Brainard-Barnes. Melissa Barthelemy. Megan Waterman. Amber Lynn Costello.* If I were found dead on a beach, the police would call me a Craigslist prostitute. They wouldn't respect the whore hierarchy—dommes above escorts—the gray area of the law, or the fact that by that point, all the sex ads were on Backpage, not Craigslist. *Craigslist prostitute* just has a nice ring to it.

When I returned from a long day of research at the Library of Congress to start a long night of domming at the hotel, I asked the bartender in the lobby restaurant to recommend a glass of wine, and I didn't ask the price before I ordered it. I watched the cook manning the raw bar slide his oyster knife into the slit of a shell and work to pry it open. I thought about how easy it would be for a man to do the same to me: slip, pry, twist. I ordered two dozen oysters and ate them all by myself.

I knew as much as any woman knows that men can be unpredictable. BDSM, however, is nothing if not predictable.

Good BDSM is a flirtation with danger, never dangerous. It's an unloaded gun, with the safety on. The safety is in its scripts, its rule books. I was here to do BDSM, not to be killed. I told the girls from the beach to shut their hot-pink glossy mouths.

I told myself what Catherine told me: submissives are kittens. I am not destined to become a true-crime special. I defied Catherine's orders and asked housekeeping to refresh the towels in my room three times on the first day—a telltale sign of a hotel hooker—and let the dirty ones overflow the bathtub while I ventured out to do my research.

Nothing terrible happened in DC. The kittens were kittens. I didn't get caught. I proved what I needed to prove: that with or without Catherine, I was a dominatrix. I could keep myself alive.

On my last day in the city, my dad drove six hours east from my hometown to meet me for lunch and to see the Lincoln Memorial. We read placards instead of talking about my research, our past, or how I'd been able to afford the scallops we'd eaten back at the restaurant. Dad hugged my shoulder into the snug of his arm while we walked. He loved me like he had before he knew me, before I knew me, before I went and ruined what we had.

"Don't you have two beds in your room?" Dad asked. We had walked too far in too much heat, and he was too tired to tackle the six-hour drive home.

I wanted to be alone in my room, to peel off my sweat-stained T-shirt and shower, sit naked on the bed reading my dead-hooker book and let my hair dry in the air-conditioning, asking for a cold.

Instead, a mighty, powerful dominatrix, I laid myself down on the cum-stained client bed and let my dad take the clean one.

17

• •

Most people don't know what it feels like to beat another person bloody. To hit and hit and hit and hit until bruises form before your eyes, until the skin breaks over those bruises and blood flies. But I do. And I can tell you that if you so much as raise your hand to someone's face, they will flinch. Even if they expect it, even if they paid you for it, they will recoil. You'll recoil too, at first. You'll mirror their fear. You'll expect a return on the violence you're about to inflict, even if you know no return is due.

But if you hit, over and over and over again, and there is no return on the violence, something might change in you. You might stop flinching. You might not recoil. Your reflexes will soften. Your fight will waver. Your flight will walk out on the job. If you hurt enough men, you might, for a time, forget to fear them.

They will remind you.

Back when I was still the boyish girl in skinny jeans and a skinny tie working at a coffee shop, Catherine went on a trip to the Caribbean with a divorced insurance salesman. I hadn't met him, but in her bedroom a week before they left, she modeled the arsenal of bikinis he bought her to wear on the beach. It was clear that he wanted to see her in as little clothing as possible, and I was jealous, but I hadn't known her long enough to admit it. Instead, I agreed to stay over at her place while she was gone: to sleep in her bed, curled up with a dirty T-shirt that smelled like her shampoo, and feed her cat.

It wasn't Catherine's first trip with the insurance salesman. A group of pro dommes organized an annual trip to an anything-goes swingers' resort where wealthy Americans and Europeans paid the local hospitality staff well enough to look the other way. She'd gone on the same trip with the same client the year prior, and the year before that she'd shared a villa with the fetish photographer. She told me about ocean-view bondage and dommes floating their submissives around the pool in latex gimp suits. It was 24/7 kink, she said, and hot tub flirtations with fetish models. I simmered with a jealousy that I didn't let boil over. It wasn't that I didn't want Catherine to do those things, it was that I wanted to do those things with her.

A year later, when I had traded in my skinny jeans and skinny tie for a skinnier body—and leather corsets and latex dresses to show it off—I would get the chance. Catherine returned home from the dungeon one night to tell me about an eager new client who had been following her on social media for years, and wondered if this could be the year—his year—he accompanied her on the infamous Caribbean kink vacation. She had already committed to the insurance salesman, she said, so she referred the new client to me. The three of us went out to dinner, to see how we got along, and at the end of the night I agreed to the trip. I knew the new client was only taking me to get closer to her, but I didn't mind: he seemed harmless, and I'd never been to the Caribbean. I emailed my students an excuse and packed my dissertation reading into my luggage, as if I were going to read a stack of critical theory while sipping watered-down resort cocktails and watching men in rubber gimp suits bobbing in the pool.

The fetish photographer was going, and I was grateful that the event organizers hired him to take photographs of everyone's fetishes. It left him little time to insist on playing with Catherine. Instead, we hung out with him in the sunshine while he set up to shoot the daily activities: a perverse slip-and-slide where giddy mistresses forced their submissives to slide headfirst down a soapy tarp, crashing into each other's crotches, one tied spread-eagle at the tarp's end like a single, petrified bowling pin. Or a game of Marco Polo where the players are gagged and blindfolded, splashing around aimlessly in search of dommes who won't respond to their muffled calls.

All week long at breakfast, the fetish photographer plopped down next to Catherine and me and moaned over tepid coffee that the organizers were working him like a dog. I considered my labor that week far more exhausting. There were the tedious nightly dinners, held on an outdoor terrace in the Caribbean humidity, and the tropical weather didn't deter anyone from fetish formal-wear. To fit in with the other mistresses, I followed suit and suffered through three courses in a tightly cinched leather corset. After dinner each evening, I was tasked with tormenting my client in a manner inventive enough to warrant the trip's hefty price tag.

On the final morning of the trip, I sat on the terrace with Catherine and our two paying clients. I watched the fetish photographer walk in, pick over the warm pineapple and congealed eggs on the buffet table, and take a seat as far as he could from where we waited for him to initiate our morning ritual. Catherine sat for a moment, mumbled curiosities about what she'd done wrong, before she ordered the clients to clean up our plates and get back to the rooms, where they could pack all the leather and latex back into our suitcases. We finished our coffee alone.

When we loaded into the airport shuttle, the fetish photographer took the front seat and shot the shit with the driver. Catherine and I piled into the only remaining seats in the back row. At the airport, he didn't speak, and once we were on the ground, he got his own taxi back to the Eastside of Los Angeles. Something was wrong, Catherine said, but she knew what he was like when he was angry. She knew that he would grow angrier still if she pushed him to talk when he wasn't ready. I too was about to find out what the fetish photographer was like when he didn't get his way.

Before our sunburns had time to heal, the fetish photographer purchased some domain names. He bought the URL of my fake name—my sex work name—and directed it to my real name and university grad student profile. There I was, smiling in front of a bookcase, wearing my glasses and the blazer I bought for academic conferences, trying my best to look the part of the young professor. He bought the URL of my legal name and directed it to my dominatrix website, potentially outing me to my students, my professors, my parents—anyone who happened to google me.

Anxiety about my image was not a new feeling. I spent a lot of time worrying about who had taken my picture at what kink event, and where it might end up online. I turned my head anytime I saw someone raise a phone, wondered if my tattoos would be visible in whatever they had managed to capture. *Revenge porn* wasn't yet a term we used, but I knew better than to let clients record videos in session, a request I had to repeatedly deny. The entire week in the Caribbean, I wore a little blue wristband meant to signal to the photographers and guests that they didn't have permission to take my picture. I was the only domme wearing the wristband. I was in the client club, the client closet: hiding.

All of those worries suddenly seemed trivial. The fetish photographer sat on a stockpile of incriminating photographs. I clicked through a folder of our first photo shoot on my laptop and remembered when he told me he would take some shots that showed my face, just in case: just in case I wanted them, just in case he needed them.

I was in my fourth year of graduate school—the first one dedicated to writing my dissertation—when the fetish photographer went on his digital warpath. It was the first semester I'd been given the chance to design and teach a course of my own, a moment I had been looking forward to since I enrolled. It was a contemporary literature course, and I titled it Coming Home: Narratives of Exile and Return. The irony wasn't lost on me. I had always been more frightened of being exiled from academia than of being hurt by a dangerous submissive. The former seemed more likely. It turned out that they could be one and the same.

The fetish photographer's power over my career gnawed at me for more than a month before I gave in and decided to do something about it. By the time I made an appointment to speak with my department's director of graduate studies, I'd rehearsed my story a dozen times.

"He's a jealous ex . . . ," I muttered to myself on my way to campus. "I don't think he's dangerous." Never mind that I hadn't had a boyfriend since I lost my virginity in a cemetery and the fetish photographer was, without a doubt, dangerous. I hadn't asked for the meeting to come clean. I had asked for the meeting to lie.

I usually took the stairs up to the English department, but I was already sweating, so I rode the elevator. I walked down the familiar fourth-floor corridor, where flyers for scholarly events and poetry readings hung from doors, where old-school professors left file boxes sitting outside their offices for undergrads to drop off seminar papers when they came due. At the end of the hallway, I saw that the director's door was cracked, warm lamplight spilling out into the otherwise fluorescent-lit hallway. A student was inside, so I waited in the hall. I heard him say something about *King Lear*, something you would want to speak to your professor about in the soft light of her office on a late campus afternoon.

When they finished, I counted thirty seconds before knocking. I wanted to give the director a chance to catch her breath, to make a move for the door if she needed to leave for the bathroom, or if she'd forgotten that I'd requested a meeting and had somewhere else to be. She didn't, so I knocked, stepped inside, and took a seat.

Going into as little detail as possible, I told her that a man was harassing me online and possibly stalking me and definitely trying to ruin my reputation. I cried when I said it, and took a strange comfort in the idea that, as a woman, she'd probably been blackmailed, or threatened, or stalked herself, so she would take my word for it. I didn't use the words *sex worker* or *dominatrix* because I figured that she'd been neither of those, and if she knew that I was, her sympathy for my situation might wane. I did tell her that he had taken my photograph. He'd taken many photographs. She looked more confused than concerned, but assured me that if he got in contact with her, she would keep it to herself and let me know. I thanked her and left, feeling no better than I had when I arrived.

We think of closets as safe places. Hide in there from a home invader. From your parents' screaming. Huddle through a tornado, or a hurricane. But when you're in that closet, you're trapped. I knew that coming clean about sex work would free me from the power that the fetish photographer had over me, but I also knew it could have just as easily left me powerless, and that wasn't a risk I was willing to run.

Eventually, the client who took me on the kinky Caribbean vacation hired an attorney. The fetish photographer had also purchased the URL of *his* legal name and redirected it to the California sex offenders' registry. He was a high school teacher. The attorney wrote a few threatening letters, and everything stopped, but nothing was ever the same. The fetish photographer never spoke to us again, never told us why he had done what he had done. He didn't have to, it was clear: Catherine was his, she owed him everything, and he would hurt everyone in her life to remind her.

I stayed with Catherine after the fetish photographer was out of our lives, but his absence didn't bring me the relief I imagined that it might. Once he was gone, I wanted to know how she could have let all of it happen to her *good girl*, how she could have let it happen to me.

18

. .

"When did you do your first session?"

The client closed his eyes and smiled, remembering. He wet his lips, said it real slow: "Nineteen . . . eighty . . . three."

That was two years before I was born, but I didn't say so. Although if I had, it wouldn't have made a difference to him. Clients have no problem growing older while the sex workers they hire stay the same age. It's why we're afraid of aging out and they aren't bothered in the slightest about being men in their sixties and seventies, stripping naked in front of women in their twenties and thirties. That's precisely the service for which they're paying.

Professional dominants, at least, can transition from mistress to "mommy" around fifty, when the time is right. They can swap out their catsuits and whips for pencil skirts and canes, play the role of the strict school marm or sadistic nun. I imagined that escorts and strippers had fewer options, that their careers had expiration dates. I once took a bondage class from a domme in her sixties who ran the room with the authority of a PTA mother, breaking the class up into groups, checking on the girls and disciplining the boys, making sure everyone had refreshments. Catherine told me that the teacher was a crazy old lady with a parrot who would ride around on her shoulder. I never saw a parrot. Catherine didn't say as much, but I suspected she was afraid of becoming a fifty-year-old dominatrix, overly fond of a pet bird.

The client was fat, with a bushy white beard. The kind of man I associated with motorcycle gangs: leather vests, big-haired blond wives, and Harley-Davidsons. He was shorter than me, even out of my stilettos, and despite his tough demeanor, I thought that he posed no threat. He wore a white T-shirt, neatly tucked in, but with a stain down the front that looked like Kool-Aid. He didn't seem ashamed of it, didn't apologize. I thought, *This is not the type of guy who can afford $500 amusements on a Tuesday afternoon.* When that guy walked in, I knew it. He would be glued to his phone, remaining on the line with a client as he entered the dungeon and slipped off his ugly sneakers that cost more than my rent. He would take off his watch, but never his wedding band. He would bark out his fetishes while fishing through his wallet for the exact tribute amount. He rarely tipped.

This guy was not that guy. He handed me fifty dollars more than I asked for and apologized that he couldn't find an envelope to tastefully conceal it. I didn't need to count the money. I had been domming long enough by that point to know what $500 in twenty-dollar bills felt like between my index finger and thumb. The only reason I ever wanted to conceal the money was when I imagined the client feeling remorse for spending that much on an orgasm.

I tucked the cash into my empty bra cup. I'd tried a few times to fill them up with breast forms, to give myself real-looking tits for sessions, but my clients weren't permitted to touch them anyway, so it seemed like a waste of time. I was also worried one would flop out of my bra and hit the concrete floor like I'd seen happen one too many times with my feminization clients. They were never wearing bras that fit them, since the bras at the dungeon were not designed to fit adult men. There are companies that cater to people with larger torsos, but we were cheap and collected client bras as hand-me-downs from clothing swaps. The sound of a breast form slapping the floor was humiliating enough for me to embrace the worth of my small tits instead.

After the client paid me, I led him to a bar we had set up in the back of the dungeon. Once in a while, we used it for parties, but mostly for these scene negotiations. The client huffed, trying to climb up onto the barstool, his short legs pressing into his large gut, convinced it was the stool's fault that he couldn't climb it. I squirmed, watching him fumble, and started my line of questions to avoid acknowledging the tragedy of his climb.

"What's on your *no* list?" I asked.

He got himself settled.

"Bad feet," he replied. "Can't stand for a long time."

I assumed gout or diabetes, conditions with which I was familiar. I had family members marching toward death by country cooking.

The client was not nervous. He was self-assured about his kinks in a way that proved he had been talking about them since 1983. He told me he liked pain—whipping, caning, scratching, paddles—and he smiled a big toothless grin. My expression must have changed, shocked by the sight of his slimy gums. He noticed and chuckled, "Yep, no teeth." He smiled wide and ran his tongue along the exposed pink flesh. He no longer looked to me like a Hells Angels biker. More like a sad shopping mall Santa Claus on December 26.

"I'm gonna call you Santa," I said, petting at his beard

and pinching his nipples through the sugary stain on his shirt, hoping he would be amused and not offended.

"You can call me whatever you like, sweetheart."

And so, I did.

Santa had a taut belly. His navel pushed outward in an unnatural way, like his insides were desperate to break through the skin. I wondered if I touched it, would his navel be sensitive like mine, or had the years of brushing against his T-shirts and pinching into his waistband dulled it. I was curious, but not enough to find out. A long, silvery scar cut down the center of his gut, parting the hair, and I thought about the surgeries he must have had to keep himself alive. I had gotten used to seeing men's bodies in all the ways they had been stitched together. I saw all the ways they could have died.

I told Santa to get on the bed, on all fours, and I was shocked by the arch of his back. I thought of my grandmother in her final years, standing up from her armchair where she sat piled under heating pads and blankets. She teetered and creaked, rubbed her knees and complained: out of sincerity, out of habit, or just because having someone acknowledge our pain abates it a little bit. Nothing like my arthritic grandmother, Santa was more flexible than me, pushing his hips back like a satisfied cat so I could get started with the caning. He was speckled with liver spots, and patches of white hair sprouted in unexpected places, like the tops of his shoulders. He told me he was into shaving, if I wanted to make him smooth. I passed. I didn't want to make a mess.

Santa took a hard beating. He was the kind of seasoned submissive who barely flinched. Years of cane strokes and paddle bruises had chapped his ass into leather. He kept interrupting the beating to tell some story or another about some other dominatrix, some other caning, and I wondered if he was bored. Bored clients don't make repeat appointments.

But I decided that he'd just done this so many times it had become banal and that was not my fault.

Between cane strokes, Santa told me he was a *switch*. He liked to play as either a submissive *or* a dominant. The name itself is a turn: switch. A turn-on that might turn on you.

This was a rare admission, especially by a man. Technically, I was a switch, and I knew plenty of other women who were switches, but men are more likely to pick a side and stick to it. They settle on their fantasies and fetishes early in life and don't shift and grow as much as women, who might not even feel comfortable masturbating until they're much older. It's not as if shame and stigma don't affect boys, but what they do with that shame and stigma is different. Most of them don't abstain from masturbation. The forty-year-old man who fantasizes about being walked on by a woman in high heels can usually recall the first time he masturbated to the thought of it. Maybe the neighbor girl stepped on his foot on the school bus and apologized. He wished she hadn't because he liked it: it was the first time she noticed him, all he ever wanted. Or a cruel older sister made a sweet little brother pretend to be a footstool during a birthday sleepover and all her friends laughed at him. Oblivious girls everywhere are giving boys their future fetishes, each and every day. I asked most of my regular clients how they got to be the ways that they were and many of them remembered. A lot of it was Wonder Woman. Even more of it was Catwoman. Rarely was it Mom. Never was it Dad.

Santa said he first satisfied his itch to dominate back when he used to play all the time. When he drove long-haul, he stopped into dungeons all across the country. You could find their ads in a magazine called *DDI: Domination Directory International*.

"Do you know it?" he asked.

"Yes," I said. "It's still around." Catherine sometimes submitted ads to bring in the old-timers who never caught on to the whole internet thing.

"You could find it in dirty bookstores back then," Santa went on, without listening to my answer. "The nicer ones anyway, the ones with good selections."

Not the truck-stop variety, I thought. *Not the ones built for a trucker like you.*

"When I had lots of money," Santa said, "I visited you ladies all the time. Every chance I got."

Considering that he had paid me $500 for a beating he didn't stop talking long enough to enjoy, I would have said he had lots of money still, but I also knew that I could get someone to do it for free and he could not. Women don't have to pay to relinquish power. We don't have to pay to be told we are worthless. We don't have to pay to be scared out of our wits.

I wondered if Santa still got the itch to switch. I wondered if he was itching at that moment and inching his way toward a request to turn the tables on me. The only time I had played the role of submissive for a client was when a pro sub who was scheduled to costar with Catherine canceled last-minute and she was desperate for a warm body to lie over the client's lap while she supervised the spanking he'd paid for in advance. She asked me to fill in, and I said I'd try it. I didn't realize until undressing in the client's hotel bathroom that I had a bad flare-up of folliculitis, causing red-welted bumps to rise all across my ass cheeks and thighs. When Catherine pulled my underwear down and pushed me over the client's lap to take the spanking, I felt like a piece of spoiled meat in a pricey steakhouse, served to a paying customer who deserved better.

Santa referred to the place in Hollywood where he saw

his first submissive as *the old ball and chain*. I wasn't sure if it was a euphemism, like he was once married to this bitch of a dungeon, his *old ball and chain*, or if there really was a BDSM dungeon in Hollywood called the Ball and Chain. Regardless, there was one dominatrix and one submissive on staff that night at the old ball and chain, and he wanted to play with the submissive.

He said the girl was blond, looked more like a young Hollywood starlet than the kind of girl you expected to find at a dungeon. I wondered which I looked like. The girl probably moved out to LA to become a Hollywood starlet, but there she was, in the old Ball and Chain with some middle-aged trucker, getting gagged and spanked for $50 an hour. Decades later, in a warehouse district five miles south of Hollywood, where luxury condos and Equinox gyms have replaced all the sleazy old joints like the Ball and Chain, Santa would tell me that her hair smelled like mangoes and she looked just perfect in her pink satin negligee.

"Usually, these places would have a few girls working," he explained, as if I'd never heard of a commercial dungeon nor knew how they operated.

"They'd parade them out and you'd pick one, then she would grab you by the hand, or the shirt, or the belt if you were lucky, and she'd drag you back to a room to have her way with you."

"Mmm," I hummed, half listening, running my fingertips over the bruises finally starting to reveal themselves through his thick skin. He looked back at me to make sure I was paying attention. He was paying me, after all, for my attention.

"This submissive though," he said, meeting my gaze, "they had a collar on her. And a leash. And the domme there with her, she put the leash right in *my* hand and told *me* to drag *her* back to a room and have my way with her." He raised his bushy eyebrows, smiled that toothless smile.

"Tell me what you did," I demanded, knowing that was what he wanted. I shouldn't have asked.

Santa said that he tied the starlet to a chair. He secured her arms and ankles with rope that the dungeon provided, and then tipped the chair backward, holding it at a slant, sneering and teasing her as she begged to be let back down. This was probably part of her act, the begging she had done dozens of times. I only knew one pro sub—an older woman who brought a hot young bodyguard boyfriend with her when she rented the dungeon—but I figured they had their standard lines, just like we did.

"Please, sir, please stop!" was probably her equivalent to my "You like that, don't you?" It was the part she was scripted to play, even if she had hoped for a better role.

Santa tipped back her chair, he explained, because he wanted to know if she thought she could trust him. Like those team-building exercises people do on company retreats. He sucked at the place where his teeth would have been, and I got the sense that he wanted my disapproval, so I gave him some.

"Bad boy!" I exclaimed. "You shouldn't try to scare innocent girls like that. Maybe I should get revenge for my sister at the old Ball and Chain."

Santa sat upright then, swung his feet over the side of the bed, planted them, and put his hands up—*mea culpa*. He grinned and got back up onto all fours. I understood, then, why he was more interested in telling stories than taking cane strokes. He was looking for punishment, the real deal, and if you want real punishment you have to commit a real infraction. That's the true mark of the switch.

Around the time I met Santa, I took a motorcycle safety course. The instructor told us this: never ride high. Don't ride on drugs, don't ride drunk, sure; but that's not what she meant. Don't ride if you've been hurt. Don't ride when you're falling in love. Don't even ride if you're a little too horny. Powerful feelings don't mix with dangerous machinery.

I tried not to ride high in the dungeon, and that meant I tried to avoid clients who liked to push my buttons, to see me angry. I agreed to fantasy, not reality. I was afraid I would hit someone and like it for the wrong reasons.

"Nobody told me the rules," Santa said, laughing at how I'd taken offense. And with that, I knew the story about the starlet was about to take a turn for the worse.

In BDSM, players negotiate scenes from the outset, before anything gets underway or out of hand. Players discuss their likes and dislikes, what they're open to doing, what they want to avoid, their safe words, plans for aftercare, descriptions of the ways their bodies process pain and pleasure. Zones of the body are marked with yellow caution tape. Santa didn't tell me anything about his negotiation with the starlet. He only mentioned that he didn't yet know the rules, and so I knew the rules were about to be broken.

"I brought her chair back down to the floor," he continued, "and I reached into my backpack."

I thought about the overstuffed backpack he carried into the dungeon an hour earlier. I tried to spot it in the room, to gauge whether it was within his reach.

"I pulled out the hunting knife that I always carried with me."

Where's the backpack where's the backpack where's the backpack?

I'm not in bondage, I thought, *I can outrun him.*

I wiggled my feet out of my six-inch stiletto heels, hung them casually over the edge of the bed. I tried to make a plan for my survival without breaking character. Even when

I thought I might get my throat slit, I didn't want to cause unnecessary offense.

I'd noticed the backpack when Santa walked through the door. I had even asked him what was inside. He pulled out a pair of vampire gloves—leather gloves with rows of tiny metal teeth that can be used to grind into and chew up a submissive's flesh. Dungeons can't keep them on hand because they are too difficult to sterilize, and the clients who are into them know that and bring their own. He set the backpack to the side: "Everything else in there is vanilla."

He grinned and I accepted the grin as good enough. I put on the gloves, tested them out on his hairy forearm. I remembered my friend Lena telling me about how she made clients strip as soon as they got inside the dungeon, a Taser hidden behind her back, in case one of them had a weapon.

"You don't think that's overkill?" I asked.

"Maybe," she answered, "but better to be overkill than get fucking killed."

I never did buy myself a Taser.

I pushed Lena from my mind, pointed at Santa, curled my index finger, and beckoned him farther into the warehouse-turned-dungeon.

Santa told me that he'd flashed the hunting knife in front of the starlet's face, passing it back and forth between his left hand and right, running the flat surface of the blade down her arm, secured tight to the chair. I imagined the goose bumps rising on her flesh, the fine blond hairs on her arm being sliced off and landing on the rancid carpet of the old Ball and Chain.

"She went crazy!" he said with an incredulous laugh. Santa jumped up then, and I followed, but he just stretched and settled back into position, poised like a cat, ass in the air like it was the most natural thing in the world to tell a woman you just met about once holding another woman you'd just met at knifepoint.

"But then," Santa said, "she turned into a real bitch. Screaming her fucking head off."

I walked to the toy closet to retrieve another implement, but I never took my eyes off Santa, or his backpack.

"It killed my mood," he continued, his deflated erection suddenly the victim of the story. "And the dominatrix, she burst through the door like an action movie! I couldn't believe it!"

I wondered if the starlet and the domme were lovers, or if they became lovers after that night. I imagined the two of them trauma bonded like I had trauma bonded with so many women, talking about the ways our fathers hit or touched or refused touch or refused entirely. The domme grabbed the hunting knife from his hand, Santa said, and used it to cut the ropes that bound the starlet to the chair.

"She carried her out into the lobby like a fucking baby," Santa laughed. He said he could hear when the starlet stopped crying—just a few moments later—and he was pissed that she left the Ball and Chain without finishing the session he'd paid for in advance.

"What's the big deal?" he asked. "Every man carries a hunting knife."

• •

When I was ten, my father handed me his hunting knife. He came home with nearly a dozen grouse, brown-speckled game birds with fat breasts and tiny, gnarled talons that I opened and closed with my small hands, working the joints and letting the sharp bits bite into my fingertips. I had eaten these birds on a few occasions, chewing carefully so as to not chomp my milk teeth into birdshot. I had learned the hard way, biting with abandon through the dry, overcooked flesh into unforgiving lead composite that had exploded inside the bird before my father's dog gathered her, dropped her with pride at his boots.

Here they were, nearly a dozen grouse: a fantastic haul, they would line the huge freezer in our garage, full of game meat. My dad was in galoshes and Carhartt overalls, excited to show me what the inside of a bird looked like. When his knife broke through its flesh, the sounds of breaking bone and torn skin startled me, and I grabbed at a new kind of hot pain in my throat. A tenderhearted thing, I wasn't cut out for the country. He removed her esophagus and held out a pink pouch, pierced like an uncooked meatball on the tip of his blade.

"Go ahead, open it," he encouraged.

I took the knife in the way he'd shown me before, grabbing by the handle, never by the blade. I pointed it down, poised to puncture the bird's insides, readying myself for the blood that would surely pour out from the wound.

Cutting through the tight, cold stretch of skin, there was no blood. When I saw what was inside, tears rolled hot and easy down my cheeks. The blade dug into a burrow of leaves and berries, intact. She had just eaten breakfast, and then she died. I returned my father's knife and ran inside. Threw a fit, as my parents described it. I was a silly child. Tenderhearted, a favored insult. From my bedroom, I heard my dad stomp inside, slam the sliding glass door, a loud sigh summoning my mother to ask him what was wrong.

"Ridiculous!" he spat.

I didn't appreciate anything he did for me.

It would be a few years yet before Dad taught me to shoot a gun. He wanted to teach his girls like he would have taught his sons. His father taught him, and he would teach my sister, a stronger child already, readying herself for a life rougher than mine. His failure wasn't his desire to teach me how to live in the country. His was a failure of empathy. It's difficult for men to see past the outer edges of themselves.

• •

The domme at the Ball and Chain didn't make Santa leave. He still had the better part of his hour remaining. She returned his knife but made him zip it up into the backpack and set it way across the room.

"She took revenge for her friend," Santa said, through that now omnipresent grin. I imagined the domme securing his arms and legs to the same chair he used to threaten the starlet. I imagined her dumping all his belongings onto the floor, finding that hunting knife, and running it up and down his swollen gut, the same gut I pawed at with vampire gloves, a cat sharpening its claws, listening to his story and giving him his money's worth. I dug the spikes in harder than I knew I should, but he barely flinched. I imagined her slicing that knife into him, opening him like an oyster. I ran my finger down the silvery scar on his abdomen once more.

"Did she threaten you with your own knife?" I asked. At the very least, I wanted the story to work as a story, to come full circle.

"No," he said. "She pulled out some crazy device and electrocuted my balls. After that, my cock dripped for a week."

Justice, I thought.

I asked if he had to wear diapers, imagining the girls at the next dungeon down the highway laughing at the too-young-for-incontinence trucker.

"Not piss," he answered, "it was cum!" He scoffed at the implication. "I still think about her sometimes. She was so mad at me!"

If she was still alive, the starlet would have probably been my mother's age. She worked at the Ball and Chain in 1983, two years before I was born. I imagined her drinking decent red wine at a dinner party, laughing about the time she thought she was going to lose her life to a psychopath trucker who tried to gut her with a hunting knife when she was a naive twentysomething professional submissive. Her friends would shift in their seats, a little uncomfortable, but they would chuckle with her, happy she made it, happy she had done these crazy things and lived to tell the tale.

Then I imagine her in her therapist's office, admitting that she pissed herself, blacked out, knocked the chair she was tied to backward, bashing her head on the concrete floor before her coworker, whom she'd known for no more than a week, broke through the door to stop him from killing her. I wonder what else the starlet survived, before and after the hunting knife at the old Ball and Chain.

Women are afraid that men will kill them. Afraid that they will slice us open to see what's inside, like a grouse leaping forward into flight, sensing the presence of the hunting dog suddenly directing his attention right at her, trying to alert the man who will shoot, her wings unfolding for the last time. Maybe Santa would have killed the starlet if, instead of begging for her life, she had laughed at him. If she had given him a different reaction than what the script called for, the one that made him hard. He must have wondered what it sounded like, a woman begging for her life. What else could a man be after, tying a woman to a chair and pulling a hunting knife from his bag? I imagine the starlet laughing at the sight of the blade, the laughter burrowing deep inside him like the kind of insult we play back to ourselves on bad nights when we can't sleep. I imagine him fed up with women who refuse to cower.

Men make excuses for their bad behavior: it's the madness

of youth, or no one told them the rules, or they simply can't understand their tenderhearted daughters. When men scare women, the fault lies elsewhere, and we all go looking for it like a lost set of house keys.

I cried when I saw a bird's belly, bursting with a good morning's haul of berries. The starlet screamed when she saw the light hit the blade of a knife. I never took my eyes off Santa's backpack for more than a few seconds, and after he came, he tipped me another eighty dollars. He pulled his stained T-shirt back on, and we showed each other pictures of our pets.

I told Santa that when I was a little girl, it was my dream to drive a truck. I liked to watch them barrel past from the back seat of my mom's minivan and make faces at the drivers, or pump my fist in the air, a gesture my dad taught me, to see if I could get them to honk their mighty horns. I thought that when I grew up, I would be the driver, not the hot femme silhouette featured on the mud flaps. "But here we are," I laughed.

Santa laughed too and told me the same thing my parents told me when I said I wanted to be a trucker when I grew up: "Truckin' ain't women's work."

He said it like a dad, and patted me on the knee. "You'd run into too many weirdos out there on the road."

19

• •

On the rare occasion that I had a female client, she typically walked into the dungeon a step behind her husband or boyfriend. It had taken months, I would learn, even years of his begging to get her through that door. No matter which one of them was the dominant and which one was the submissive, the men always did the knocking and the paying. The women dressed up for the occasion like they were going out for a nice dinner. Underneath, they wore their best lingerie— no sagging elastic or snagged lace. Men wore whatever was clean and easy enough to take off.

These couples were typically made up of a submissive husband who wanted a wife who would attack him like a home intruder, and a submissive wife who no longer felt she had a husband who could protect her if someone were to intrude upon their home. He didn't tell her he was submissive until five years and two kids into the marriage, and now he had to beg her to let him beg.

I sympathized with them both—heterosexuality doesn't make it easy for men to ask for submission or for women to imagine much else. I did my best to guide these women into finding their own pleasure in domination, since I knew that their husbands would never stop asking them for it.

Women also made it into the dungeon as submissives. Their husbands fastened leashes to their collars as soon as they stepped inside, and they waited patiently to hear what he would like to have done to them. Male dom–female sub couples bored me. If I wanted to see men telling women what to do, I could spend my evening eavesdropping on couples at the Olive Garden in Burbank. The husbands usually wanted me to dominate their wives while they watched, then they would dominate their wives while I watched. At the end of the session, the two of them would have sex while I hid behind a room divider in the front of the dungeon and scrolled through Twitter.

Most of the time, these dominant men booked sessions because they wanted tips on their own technique. Straight men think that the secret to domination is all about equipment: the *best* flogger, the *best* cuffs. Or the perfect technique, like the *best* flick of the wrist, as if throwing a whip were the same as pitching a baseball.

Throwing a whip isn't easy. Every whip is different, its length and its weight affecting the way it travels through space into flesh. It requires poise and concentration for accuracy. I tied these men's submissive wives up tight, upright, facing the St. Andrew's cross, and ran the length of a whip up both of their legs, across their lips, under their noses so they could smell the leather. I made a mark on the wall beside them and practiced hitting it first, watched them flinch, anticipating the bite and bleed of their own flesh. The instigation of fear was the secret of domination, not the equipment. I could have produced the same feeling with my twenty-dollar belt as I did with a five-hundred-dollar hand-plaited leather single-tail whip. Try telling that to a dominant straight guy.

Once in a while, hiring a dominatrix was the submissive woman's idea. This was rare. If a woman asks her male partner to hurt her, he's likely had more than a few sadistic experiences to mine for content. Nothing much will break in a man if he calls a woman a *slut*.

I can remember nearly every woman who ever walked into the dungeon alone. The queer filmmaker I met at a party. She flirted with me until a friend told her I was a sex worker; then she decided to pay me rather than ask me out on a date, a decision I resented at first, but then preferred once I had her money in my hand. The straight woman who wanted to be dominated by a man, but men are too scary. The closeted lesbian whose husband I heard playing video games down the hall while I spanked his wife in their bed. The pocket-size butch who got handsy with me at a party where I was hired to tie up the guests and get the juices flowing. When she booked a session, I was happy to put her in her place. The bisexual clothing designer who wanted to role-play a gynecological exam. The hedge fund manager who ordered a double helping of caviar at one of the best restaurants in town just because she didn't want us to dip out of the same jar. And Jenny, my first and only female regular.

Jenny was younger than me and fresh out of rehab. She told me as much on the afternoon of her first session. From her cheap rainbow flip-flops to her cargo shorts, white wife-beater, and messy bun piled on top of her head, she looked like so many gay women I had known, I would have sworn we'd met before. If we had, it would have been in the Midwest. She told me she was from Florida, and looked out of place in LA. Like me, before I became a domme.

No "Hello, mistress," when I opened the dungeon door

and beckoned her inside, Jenny just stared straight down at her feet and muttered, "'Sup?" Then, she glanced up at me, smiled, smacked her gum, and looked back down to her feet. I knew that if she couldn't make eye contact, she would have a hard time expressing her desires. I expected as much from most women: we have no culture to support us in asking for what we want.

Even I got to try things in the dungeon I would never have asked for at home. It was a relief to worry so little about my own desires, since I wasn't there to have them fulfilled in the first place. I'd thought of paying for sex myself. I wanted to understand what it felt like to take, after all that giving. But each time I found someone who seemed interesting and started to write her an email, I got nervous and deleted the draft, afraid I'd ask for something wrong, afraid that what I wanted wasn't right.

It would take some coaxing to figure out what Jenny wanted, and so I prepared to coax her. The bed at the back of the dungeon was used primarily by the couples who rented the space overnight. I'd learned the hard way that playing with clients back in the bed was an invitation for pushed boundaries. They felt at home there, with themselves and with my body. I sat Jenny down on the bed for just that reason. The main play space in the dungeon was home to shiny, intimidating objects: glass cases full of heavy metal bondage gear, anal hooks, speculums. I thought a familiar setting might put her at ease: not with my body, but with her own.

"I want to be dominated," Jenny squeaked out once I got her situated on the bed.

I told her that *dominated* means something different to everyone, and took a deep breath to keep her nervous energy from overtaking my calm.

"Why don't you take off some of your clothes?" I asked. "Whatever you're comfortable with, nothing more."

Jenny stood and pulled off her tank top, unbuttoned her cargo shorts and let them fall to the floor. She peeled off her sports bra and crossed her arms awkwardly over her chest. Standing in her underwear, Jenny shifted her weight from hip to hip, still looking down at her feet. Then, she looked up at me, smiled again, smacked her gum, and looked back down. She performed bashfulness like a ritual.

"Tell me what you picture when you masturbate?" I coaxed from my seat at the foot of the bed.

The word *masturbate* sent Jenny into a fit of giggles, and her skin flushed red from head to toe. She looked more naked, somehow, blushing in her underwear, than any of the men who had ever stood before me. I didn't want to have sex with her, but I could have, and that made what we were doing feel natural in a way that made me uncomfortable. To me, professional domination was about artifice. This was something closer to real. I was worried that what Jenny actually wanted was not BDSM but rough sex, and that wasn't something I was offering, certainly not for $200.

"Look, we can just try a few things I think might feel good," I said, getting impatient. "You can use your safe word if I guess wrong."

This was not the way I wanted to start the scene, but I thought that the awkwardness of the negotiation was worse than any unwanted spanking could be.

I rarely accepted requests for over-the-knee spankings. After a few clients in my first year requested them and left trails of pre-cum across my thighs, I realized that the spanking was no more than a convenient position to get their dicks pressed into my lap. The trails of fluid on my skin threw me into a panic, like a middle schooler convinced I could get pregnant from a hot tub or toilet seat. Catherine teased me for my sensitivity to whatever fluids may have lingered on dungeon surfaces. If I walked in unassuming and sat down on the bondage table or spanking horse, Catherine would squeal—"Client babies!"—as if the whole place were covered in ejaculate and conception imminent.

Doused in antibacterial sprays all day long, the place was probably cleaner than most, but I never grew out of my teenage paranoia, and I hated the warm *thump* of dick on my thigh. I only acquiesced to an over-the-knee spanking if the client showed authentic interest—a mommy role-play or sadistic schoolmarm—and let me know well in advance so I could come prepared, wearing latex pants. Or better yet, a full rubber catsuit. I wanted to be inside a condom if there was a chance a client would bust even half a nut on my lap.

I didn't have to worry about client babies with Jenny, so I decided to put her over my knees. I planted my feet on the floor and instructed her: "Come here," I said. "Lay down over my lap."

Jenny did as I asked, and her stomach was warm and soft on my thighs. I imagined that if I'd missed any spots shaving my legs, she would feel them.

I grabbed her by the hips and pulled her panties up her ass crack to expose her skin. I pulled my hand back and then let it slap down onto her, hard. She didn't so much as flinch under my palm, so I proceeded to warm her up with light taps that got progressively harder, building up her tolerance. I spanked until her cheeks were warm and red and my hand throbbed. When I paused to shake it out, she turned to face me, face flushed, and asked, "Is that all you got?"

Then, she smiled, smacked her gum, and looked back down at the bed, like a teenage boy asking for detention.

Her attitude caught me off guard. The whole bashful routine suddenly felt like an act.

"What's next?" Jenny asked. "You got a strap-on? You gonna fuck me?"

I knew it. I forced a smile and repeated the disclaimer from my website: *BDSM only. No sex.*

It had always been a relief to utter those words, like calling up a witness to corroborate my alibi. The disclaimer was on my website for cops, or clients who might ask me for a hand job that I didn't really know how to administer because I hadn't given a hand job in a decade. Jenny wasn't a cop, and I knew how to fuck her if I had wanted to fuck her, so it felt different to administer the rejection. When I said those words to Jenny, guilt washed over me, having dashed her hopes to take what we were doing to the next level. The narrative I'd been writing in the dungeon was *lesbian dominatrix, keen on rejecting men*. Rejecting Jenny was another story.

Then she asked the question that I should have asked Catherine; that Catherine should have asked me: "What's sex?"

Jenny looked up to meet my gaze directly for the first time. She didn't wink at me, but that was the sentiment.

Years had passed since Catherine and I had promised each other *no sex* in sessions, but we never got around to defining what *sex* meant.

Fucking a man with a strap-on was *pegging*, and pegging, to me, was not sex. For plenty of people, it is—probably even some of the men I pegged—but I couldn't consider anything that involved a financial transaction to be *sex*. It would have made my relationships, to other women and to myself, far more complicated. Sex work was work, as we wrote on our protest signs every time a law was passed to make our labor more difficult, more dangerous. It was sexy—sometimes even for me—but it was not sex. If I'd met a woman in a bar and brought her home to tie her up, I would have considered it sex. But if the same woman paid me to tie her up, that was work.

Jenny knew what the men who showed up at the dungeon did not: that as queer women, we have a hard time defining sex, and since I would have a hard time defining it, she might be able to talk me into it.

As soon as Jenny asked, I knew that fucking her with a strap-on would have been sex, even with her money tucked into my bra. Not because she was a woman, although the lines between work and pleasure did blur for me, more often, when I played with women and feminine men. My acquiescence to her desire in that moment—letting her see the holes in the fibers of my boundaries—saying yes when I should have said no: that is what would have made fucking Jenny feel like sex. I'd had enough sex that I hadn't been sure I wanted to have. I knew it was worth more than the money on the table.

I told Jenny to shut up or I would graduate her from a spanking to the cane. She nodded her enthusiasm for the cane, and my sudden cruelty, and so she left me that day with welts bursting purple and red across her ass like thatch work.

• •

"You're useless to me," I snarled.

Jenny didn't make much money as a hostess at a strip club up in Ventura County, but she had been visiting me a couple of times a month for the better part of a year. She'd pushed my boundaries on our first session together, but I answered her entitlement with a discount. *Family discount*, I called it. I was no stranger to letting family treat me like shit.

"I'm sorry, mistress," Jenny cried. "I'm sorry I'm sorry I'm sorry I'm useless!"

Jenny hadn't gotten any further with me, but every session

ended with an invite to dinner or a movie. She believed she could wear me down. I believed I could string her along with a coy *maybe*: a word that doesn't belong in the dungeon.

"I want to be useful to you, mistress," Jenny whispered, her back heaving, face mashed into the mattress, sweating through her beating.

"Please, mistress," she begged. "Please tell me how to be of use."

Calling Jenny "useless" was *session talk*—words exchanged as part of a fantasy scene. Full of lies and bullshit. There was no real way for Jenny to be of use. I wouldn't have let her into my house to clean it, or into my car to wash it, and the dungeon was already spotless. She didn't have extra money, or any useful skills, as far as I could tell. But I was as adept at improv as any aspiring comedic talent who was also not making it in LA.

"I want you to start hustling for me," I said, stroking her hair. She whimpered under my touch, suddenly turned tender.

"Why should I be giving you a discount when there are men coming in and out of your club every night?" I stopped, gave myself a moment to imagine it: "You could rob them."

Catherine and I had recently rewatched *Thelma and Louise*, and domming sometimes made me feel like a woman on the run. Sometimes, it made me feel like a woman strung out, high on revenge. Sometimes, like a cowboy con man. The cowboy con man was my favorite feeling. That's who I felt like when I suggested that Jenny rob the patrons of her sleazy Ventura County strip club.

"Take from the rich and give to your mistress." I hit Jenny harder, then. She cried out but didn't move to stop me.

"I should turn . . . you . . . out!" I inflicted each word like a blow from my paddle.

This was a dangerous phrase—*I should turn you out.* Sex trafficking is a very real crime that people get into very real trouble for committing. Domming may have been a gray area; pimping was not.

"You're going to be my calling card," I continued, in the face of danger. "There must be guys in the club who like to get beat up. You're going to find the submissive ones and bring them to me."

"Yes, mistress!" Jenny panted. "Thank you for putting me to work for you!"

Jenny begged for my business cards, and I kept a straight face through all of it. Once our session ended—and with it, our session talk—I saw her out like I always did, into the disorienting afternoon sunshine that wiped away the hour that had just passed between us.

"I got a guy for you," Jenny's voice chirped into my voice mail a week later. Someone she met at the club, she said, a military guy. She told me he was a former Marine and that I was gonna love him. She would bring him to meet me on Saturday night. The line went silent with no goodbye.

It was Monday, and Jenny sounded manic, but I put the session in my calendar, just in case. I didn't think it was real, but I also didn't want her showing up with him, alone, to my place of business.

The next day, Jenny left a second voice mail. I tossed my phone from palm to palm, stared at the two-minute recording while I rode the train home from campus. The manic text messages, the former Marine she met at the club: I had a bad feeling about the whole thing and wanted to be alone when I confirmed it.

When I got home, Catherine was sitting at the kitchen table on her laptop, where she always was when she wasn't at the dungeon. I dropped my backpack inside the front door and beelined to the bathroom. I wanted to hear Jenny's voice, out of Catherine's earshot.

"Wow, the Grand Canyon," Jenny said on the recording, talking to someone else, sounding far away. "I've never seen the Grand Canyon." The recording crackled like she was speaking into a paper bag.

A man grunted in the background. I looked into the bathroom mirror.

"I-40 . . . it's a pretty drive," Jenny rambled. "Exit 160 . . ."

I stopped the recording, opened the bathroom door, and walked back down the hall. I handed Catherine my phone.

"What do you think this is?" I asked, and pressed the button to play the voice mail.

Catherine put the phone up to her ear.

"It's from that client Jenny," I interrupted. I had told Catherine everything there was to tell about Jenny, except all the times that she tried to convince me to fuck her, or go out with her, or run away with her.

"She told me she'd met some dude, and that the dude wanted to session with me on Saturday, but then she left me this weird voice mail."

Catherine shushed me, started the recording over again from the top.

Grand Canyon. I-40. Exit 160.

"She's giving you her location," Catherine said, handing back my phone. "Dropping clues: highways, exit numbers."

"It just sounds like she butt-dialed me." I didn't go to Catherine to reinforce my fears; I went to her to dispel them.

"You should call her back," Catherine said, turning back to her laptop. "That's like some *CSI* shit. She's trying to solve her own murder."

I went into the bedroom and texted Jenny.

Hours later, she texted me back. The night before, she explained, she had met a man at the club and asked him if he wanted to meet her dominatrix. He wouldn't be taking a beating, he said, but he would buy one for her and he would watch. First, he said, he needed to drive to Colorado to pick up a car. He asked her to join him, to drive his car back to California. They would be back in two days, with plenty of time to meet her dominatrix. They got on the road that night, as soon as she got off work.

Catherine had apparently seen one too many episodes of *CSI* because she was right: Jenny had tested the temperature of a strange man's anger and found it way too fucking hot.

The Marine threatened to gut her with the machete that she'd seen in the trunk of his car before they got on the road. She called me and let her phone fall between the door and the seat, and dropped clues to her location, or her body's whereabouts, in case I was the last person to ever hear her voice. By Flagstaff, when I returned her call, he had abandoned her on the side of the highway with $6 and no phone charger.

Why? wasn't the right question to ask, but I asked it, and Jenny texted back, *He's got a problem letting someone tell him what to do.*

Sounds like a great client for a dominatrix, I sent in response.

She told me that she had no money in her bank account, and I believed it because she sounded like she'd been using again.

I had been domming for five years. I had seen well over a hundred clients. This was the closest I'd come to getting someone killed. I promised to help Jenny get home safe—it was the least I could do. I called the Greyhound station in Flagstaff and bought her a one-way ticket back to LA. My dissertation defense was seven days away.

I wouldn't block Jenny's number for another year. She

had moved to California for rehab, started using again, then moved back to Florida to clean herself up after California. I defended my dissertation and started the even more economically precarious job of an adjunct professor. On a domme trip to Atlanta with Catherine, the last we would take together, Jenny asked if she could drive up to see me. Atlanta was five hours from where she'd been living, in north Florida with her parents. I said yes, and she showed up unwashed and shoeless in the lobby of the Hilton hotel where Catherine and I were trying to keep a low profile. There were rumors of law enforcement stings in the city, and Georgia cops weren't taking the time to differentiate between escorts and dommes. I didn't session with Jenny—she had no money— but she did ask me for $50 to get her car out of a downtown parking garage where she had slept and now owed to exit.

I'd heard Catherine read clients a list of her boundaries like Miranda rights. It would be easy to say that if you cannot do as Catherine did, you should not do sex work. But then, who would do it? There are far more women like me out there than there are women like Catherine.

Jenny confessed that she loved me after I got her back from Flagstaff, and she threatened to kill herself when I stopped responding to her texts. All those years I'd spent learning how to protect myself from potentially dangerous men, I didn't think for a second that I might need to protect myself from a woman.

After all that, it still took an hour of encouragement from my sex worker support group to finally block her number. We had gathered there—after hours in a queer coffee shop with a disco ball throwing no shimmer on the ceiling—to skill-share self-defense techniques. I knew exactly how to break free from a choke hold, but I still hadn't gotten the hang of saying no.

20

• •

Most pro dommes don't fuck their clients. Or if they do, they don't talk about it. There's a hierarchy among sex workers—imposed from the outside and enforced on the inside—our morality judged by acts engaged: their legality, their intimacy, their risk.

That hierarchy got inside me. I understood the relationship between myself and my clients as one of sadist to masochist, dominant to submissive—pain, not pleasure, connecting us—no matter the scene. Never mind that masochists derive pleasure from pain. There is no room for nuance in the whore hierarchy.

There is no room for logic either, for that matter. Most pro dommes I knew could be wrist-deep in client asses, feeling superior to other sex workers because they don't *fuck* their clients. It's fine if there's no nuance—it's fine if there's no logic—when you can imagine yourself on top.

It's hot that you're a domme . . .

Nearly every woman I will date after Catherine will make some form of this statement.

But, if you were an escort, I couldn't do it.

Even Catherine made some form of that statement.

The corners of their mouths got tight when they said it, like they'd swallowed a bite of yogurt that had gone off. They imagined me sullied by cock.

Cock is front and center in almost all forms of sex work, and no one—not me or my past lovers—should kid themselves about that. Even my friends who made feminist porn did it for reasons that could be traced back to cock. All those butch dyke fisting scenes were motivated by cock in their absolute refusal to center it. It was still the raison d'être, *otherwise*.

At the dungeon, the masochists came for pain and the fetishists came for feet. The cross-dressers came to feel dumb and slutty dressed as women, because that's how they saw women when they were dressed as men. They came for the power exchange, masculinity for femininity, with femininity always assuming its place on the bottom. I avoided these clients when I could. I often couldn't. Their money was as green as anyone's.

No matter what desire drove men to the dungeon, sloshing around underneath the vernacular of kink burned the white-hot flame of sex. There had been few clients over the years who had come to me for sessions that didn't start with their sexual desire and end with their sexual gratification. It was sex work, after all. Years of scenes stretched out behind me, and no matter how transgressive they had otherwise been, nearly all of them had ended in the way that the most conventional sex between men and women ended: when the man comes. The only difference being that my clients came into their own hands, not into mine.

The risk I would have run by letting a stranger come in my palm was criminal. It would have been fairly low on a scale of intimacy, but lower too on the whore hierarchy: all that degrading, largely racist talk of *happy endings* and the girls who give them. The difference between my hand on a client's hip and my hand on a client's penis was, to me, immense. Not because it was criminal—because it would have knocked me down one rung lower on that whore hierarchy ladder.

I did occasionally work with a particular type of client who came to me mostly absent the intoxicating pull of sex. These were the clients on whom I focused when I wanted to justify the real human value of my work, since our culture finds little value in the real human need for sex. These clients lived their lives as men but understood themselves as women, and they sought out dommes whom they could trust to see them, at least for the span of an hour, in the ways they saw themselves. I would have called these clients *trans*, but that wasn't a word they used to describe themselves. Some did tell me they would have sought medical transition—a *sex change*, they called it—if they were younger today. Back when they were younger, it had been too hard, they said. Most of them didn't know any trans women, so they didn't know that it was still hard, but I never took the time to make them face that. We only had an hour or two together, and that was barely enough time to fantasize about a different kind of world inside the dungeon, much less the one outside.

Most of these clients told me that they couldn't transition now because they were too old. They felt they'd missed their windows of opportunity to be pretty, to be desired, to be like me. They thought they would be ugly, and they knew that being an ugly woman was difficult. While I did have something they wanted, their submission was rarely to me. It was submission to femininity itself, and the dungeon was a safe place to hide the fact that they wanted it. It was submission to the parts of themselves that they buried at work, at home, in their bedrooms with their wives and girlfriends who didn't understand them, or were never given the chance.

I met my first of these clients early in my career. We exchanged cash and pleasantries in a Mid-City strip mall parking lot, just outside a cheap nail salon. His hands shook when he handed over the money. I ran my thumbs across his swollen knuckles to calm him. His fingers were arthritic and reminded me of my mother's. Until they saw that he brought his own nail polish—fire-engine red—the women working in the salon would think he was my father. When they saw it, they would think he was a pervert, and me a pervert by association. That was why he hired me. He'd flown in from Indianapolis for safety in numbers.

After our mani-pedis—and a makeup session at a Sephora location I chose because it wasn't in a mall and he could make a beeline to the car in his red lipstick—we drove to the dungeon, where he told me that he only let himself dress up with dommes. He never dressed up alone, he said. He told me that when he dressed up alone, it made him sad. Edge-of-a-cliff kind of sad. Dommes kept him from tumbling over.

I walked over to the dungeon's sissy closet and pulled out the hairbrush we used to brush out the wigs that the typical cross-dressing clients, *the sissies*, tossed on the floor after they jerked off into their trashy fishnets. I asked him to sit down between my legs and I started to brush his hair. His real hair, not a wig. It was long and thick, prettier than mine. He risked being called a fag when he grew it out, he said. He needed to look into the mirror and see something, even if it was just this one thing, that felt right. I ran the brush from his scalp to his shoulders. He sat there quietly, watching us both in the mirror.

"No one has ever brushed my hair," he said. "Not like this."

When I finished, he turned to me, pulled my hands to his lips, and kissed them, over and over and over again.

As the years ticked by, more of these clients found me, but they remained few and far between. So I kept doing the work, with cock its main objective, telling myself that one day I'd probably write about it and that would turn it all into art. If you can convince someone that sex is art, it loses its film of filth. I learned that in grad school, when I read the 1973 US Supreme Court decision *Miller v. California* for a seminar paper. Obscenity is utterly without socially redeeming value. Art, on the other hand, is at least open to debate.

The few times I worked alongside trans women, they were expected to offer their bodies in ways the clients did not expect of me. Sometimes, we got paid the same rate. Often, I got paid more. My rate was based on the fact that the client couldn't touch me, and their rates were based on the expectation of touch. The ability to mitigate risk—criminal or physical—like the ability to refuse touch, is dependent upon racial, class, gender, and sexual privilege. Not everyone can make money saying *no*. I made more money from the act of refusal than from acquiescence. That's the very definition of privilege in a sexual economy.

Refusal may have been lucrative, but it was also exhausting. The longer I did the work, the more men I encountered who didn't want to take no for an answer.

Can I?

Don't you want to?

No, really, how much?

Don't be like that.

Clients begged me to make exceptions, believing they were exceptional. This was fun for me when it was pre-negotiated. Most of the time, it wasn't. Pushy clients considered my no to be part of a kinky game: rules that were made to be broken

because they were made in a dungeon. Years into the hustle,
I saw these men differently than I did when I started. They
told me heroic tales of persistence, how never taking no for
an answer helped them succeed in business. I once thought
that they were telling me because they wanted to help me
succeed in business. I started to wonder how often refusing
to take no for an answer helped them succeed elsewhere.

There's a stereotype that submissive men are harmless.
Kittens, we called them. One night, a kitten reached around
my waist, pulled my panties to the side, and shoved two fingers inside me. He fastened them into me like a fishhook. My
limbs grew heavy, and it was him who kept me from falling.
He held me still from the inside. I tried to say no, but it
caught like an insect, stinging at the back of my throat.

A kitten once recalled to me with great excitement the
weekends he used to spend traveling to far-flung queer bars,
waiting in parking lots and drinking vodka in his car, on the
lookout for lesbians. When a group of women emerged after
last call, he would stumble out and call them dykes, man-
haters, hoping one of them would give him the beatdown he
played in his head when he jerked off. Years later, he called
me—a self-identified lesbian dominatrix—and paid me to
kick him in the balls. Was I the safety valve our culture required, protecting other women from homophobic attacks?
The emotional toll the word *dyke* took on me was probably no different from the toll it took on other queer women
who'd been on the receiving end of the insult since coming
out. I no longer felt the hurt bubbling into my throat each
time I heard it, but on the lips of a straight man, it still ignited
something deep in me, and I channeled the pain toward the
task at hand. I counted my money, and the money always
outweighed the consequences.

Over dinner, a kitten I'd been seeing for years told me

the story of his most memorable sexual adventure: when he walked down the Vegas Strip in nothing but thigh-high boots and a trench coat, opening it to reveal his erect penis to a mother and her daughter. The shock on their faces, and the way the mother covered her daughter's eyes, is still the material to which he masturbates, decades later. He claimed that the daughter looked of age, as if that exonerated him. I listened to his story and said nothing. I chewed and swallowed, chewed and swallowed. I told myself that he was baiting me, waiting for a reaction that I refused to provide. The truth was that I couldn't afford to lose him as a client. I was no safety valve.

21

. •

Years into the hustle, I started going back to my old ways, lying to men on the internet. Some nights, when Catherine worked late, I would make myself a cup of tea and get in bed with my laptop to write Craigslist ads seeking men for casual encounters. The replies inevitably rolled in: emails I knew I would never answer. I imagined these men hiding their phones from their wives or bosses—refreshing their inboxes, disappointed that I wasn't coming through with a response. I remembered the college boy in the red hoodie, hands buried deep in his pockets, on his frustrated ascent from the basement glory hole restroom. Unlike that college boy, the men who sent replies to my Craigslist ad were probably just as unlikely to make good on their offers to meet me as I was to answer them. It was the spent potential we were after.

When I started playing the game again, I was having a hard time living with Catherine. Even if the apartment was haunted by our late-night arguments and the growing distance between us, it wasn't a place where I would have ever made good on my promises to fuck a stranger. It was the place where I kept my grandmother's lamps, my box of childhood photographs, and the books I'd read to finish my dissertation. I wasn't going to give a stranger the address to the place where I kept my baby pictures. I didn't want a stranger petting Catherine's cat. Playing the game at home was playing it safe. Playing it at the dungeon—a place for pretending to be someone else, where nothing would have stopped me from hitting reply and giving out the address— would have been too tempting. I kept nothing of the real me there, nothing of mine. I worked at the dungeon. I never played the game there.

Until I did.

On a Saturday with a long break in between sessions, I pulled out my phone and downloaded Tinder. I tapped "women seeking men." I made a profile with the tagline "Looking for a quick afternoon fling, no strings attached." I used my real photos.

Playing the game reminded me of all the things I'd forgotten along the way. I'd answered so many times, I'd forgotten what it felt like to ask. I'd said no so many times, I'd forgotten what it felt like to say yes. But in the game, my yesses were lies. I'd also forgotten how to tell the truth. I wanted to know what it would feel like: to ask, to say yes, to be honest. What it would feel like to take, after all that giving. I wondered what it would feel like to play the game and lose.

Right swipe. Match. Right swipe. Match. *Dick is cheap*, I thought. This would be like shooting fish in a barrel. I increased my standards for a right swipe, unmatching the first few as the messages rolled in. Could I really have sex with a guy holding a can of spray paint in front of a canvas, wearing a Supreme hoodie? Maybe I needed an older man, who might be slower, more deliberate. Or a younger guy, who would be able to get and stay harder, faster. I wondered what it would feel like to kiss someone with a beard. I left-swiped all beards.

I matched with a man I liked for certain, if only for his abs. *Are you available right now?* I typed. *I'm a lesbian . . . but I feel like fucking a guy.* No *Hello*; no *How are you?* Right down to business.

Gonna have to pass, he replied. *Call me old-fashioned, but I like to get to know someone first.*

He unmatched me. He was afraid of me. Or he was afraid for me. I became more invested in the game than ever.

I immediately matched with another guy I thought was cute: a blond boy, younger than me by a couple of years, wearing a short-sleeved floral shirt, who reminded me of a young Leonardo DiCaprio in *Romeo + Juliet*. I was gentler in my approach, told him that I was gay but I liked to have sex with a man every once in a while. I asked if he was on the app to date, or if he might be interested in something totally casual. I didn't want him to know it would be my first time since high school. I didn't want him to think he was special. I told him it had to be now.

All he asked was *Are you a murderer?* And a simple *nope* was enough for him to risk it. I gave him the address.

When Romeo knocked, I jumped up to answer the door, and when I did, I downplayed the fact that we stood at the threshold of a sex dungeon, as if I hadn't noticed the leather swing or St. Andrew's cross behind me.

"What's this place?" he croaked, craning his neck to look back into the room, wondering if this was the day his dick would finally get him killed. I liked that he seemed nervous.

"I just rented this place to meet up with you," I lied. At least to me, that wasn't unheard of. I had once opened the dungeon for renters who admitted that they were just using the place to cheat on their spouses, so they didn't need the informational rundown of BDSM equipment. The dungeon was cheaper than a hotel, they said; you could rent it by the hour without raising any eyebrows and we accepted cash.

I told Romeo that it was a BDSM studio, but we didn't have to do anything kinky. That convinced him to step farther inside.

"Actually," I added, "I prefer if we don't."

I was conscious of the way I had just smiled at his discomfort and tried to relax the amusement out of my face. I wasn't afraid of him. The way he kept his eyes on the bathroom door at the back of the dungeon when he stepped inside and slipped off his shoes told me that he was afraid of me. His vanilla cheeks had flushed red, but they drained, slowly, back to vanilla.

Without further discussion, just inside the door we kissed clumsily like two people who had just met, because we were. I wanted the kiss to turn me on, but I was only able to focus on the novelty of a man's face on mine. It felt giant, and I worried I was doing a bad job with the kissing, my hands palming at Romeo's huge head like a basketball.

He hadn't shown up in his pretty floral shirt but in a black hoodie and board shorts. We stopped kissing, and I asked if he wanted to get out of his clothes. The truth was that they were a turnoff, and I didn't want to look at them, but I made sure to keep the reason to myself: he was not a client, I was not there to humiliate him. Instead, I too pulled off my T-shirt and jeans, stripped down to my underwear, and hoisted myself up onto the bondage bed where he could climb up on top of me.

He did, and I noticed that he smelled nice, at least, like teakwood and lavender laundry detergent. It had stayed on his skin after his clothes were on the floor. I tried to get lost in that smell but started to wonder if he had a girlfriend who did his laundry for him. I sat up and took off my bra.

"Go down on me?" I suggested, and without a word, Romeo pushed himself off and settled between my knees, peeling off my underwear. I enjoyed my boyfriend's mouth in high school, but this was a man, and he was rough—his stubbled chin dug into my skin. I started to panic, thinking that Catherine would notice if he rubbed me raw. She had been gone on a work trip, but she would be back the next day. Until that moment, I hadn't considered what I was doing to be cheating. It felt anthropological. My fear of chafing lasted only as long as his aborted efforts at oral, because just like you see in porn, he stopped after a couple of minutes, not considering that if I were going to come, that would have been how it happened.

Romeo jumped up off the bondage bed, grabbed a condom from his pile of crumpled clothes on the floor, and rolled it over his dick. It was the first time I'd gotten a good look at it. He was big. Too big for my first foray into adult heterosexuality, I thought. But I tried to relax and let him do his thing. No requests, no orders. The whole point was to give in, to say yes, to see what it was like. I wanted to experience sex with a grown man for what it was. As far as I could tell, it had little to do with my pleasure. I didn't mind, because I wasn't looking for pleasure: I was looking for sex with a man.

After a few minutes on top of me, missionary-style pounding between my legs, Romeo moved me to another position, then another, like the cuts between scenes in a porno. In each position, I tried to touch myself, to make the stretching and the pounding more bearable. Each time, he grabbed my hand and said, "Just relax."

I decided to keep still and wait for him to finish. Hoping it would get him closer, I started moaning, soft at first, then faster and louder, until I'd worked myself up to a fake orgasm. It worked and he came, pulled out and away from me. He tied a little knot around the open end of the condom, showing it to me so I could see that he kept it on. He wanted me to say thank you. I covered my tits with one hand and gave him a thumbs-up with the other.

Romeo pulled his clothes back on as fast as he'd stripped. I did the same and showed him to the door. The whole endeavor—from my impulse to see what all the heterosexual fuss was about, to shooing Romeo out—took little more than an hour, which is incredible considering Los Angeles traffic. I had ordered a man off the internet as if to be delivered by Amazon Prime, dropped heavily at the dungeon doorstep where we couldn't accept packages because it was in a shitty part of town and they would be stolen.

On his way out, Romeo thanked me and told me he had never seen a woman ask for anonymous sex online. It was all men, he said, pretending to be women. *Or women*, I thought, *like me, pretending to want men.*

"Nobody's real," he said. And he thanked me again, for being real.

I faked a smile like my orgasm and shut the door behind him.

Afterward, I didn't feel bad about anything but the faked orgasm. I imagined Romeo thinking his dick was magic. I imagined myself unafraid to tell him that it wasn't. I realized I had been afraid of Romeo the whole time.

I took a shower, did my last domme session of the day, and drove home. When I got there, I opened Tinder to find Romeo's message and tell him that I'd faked it. He had unmatched me. The message was gone.

It came as no surprise that, until me, Romeo had never encountered a woman looking for anonymous sex online. Men can be fearless in their desires in ways that women simply cannot. They can wander through labyrinthine hallways in sleazy leather bars. They can push themselves through holes in bathroom stalls in the basements of college administration buildings. They can wait on their knees. They can fuck strangers from the internet and no one tells them to meet first in public and make sure a friend knows where they're going. They can pay three hundred dollars an hour to explore their kinky fantasies with a professional dominatrix.

I hadn't been turned on by the ways that Romeo touched me. Saying yes, it turned out, ruined the game. But I liked that I had scared him, even just a little. I liked knowing that I had shown him what it felt like to be a girl, afraid.

22

• •

Paul had been submitting his body to professional dommes for twenty years, he said, before he found his way to me. Before he *would* find his way to me, if I could make myself available at ten o'clock the following Tuesday night. He wanted to play until six on Wednesday morning, when he would need to leave for LAX to catch a connecting flight and I would need to pull myself together for a long day in the classroom.

I had finished my degree. I chose Dr. as the prefix before my name when I purchased airline tickets. My parents were proud of me. They were proud, at least, of the parts of me they knew. Otherwise, not much had changed. I didn't leave Los Angeles for a postdoctoral fellowship on a beautiful new campus, creeping ivy and changing seasons that differentiated spring semester from fall.

I thought that BDSM would be a temporary occupation, akin to stripping through college, but like most strippers when they finish their degrees, I had student loans to pay. Adjuncting was a lot more work than teaching as a graduate student, but the monthly paychecks were nearly the same. I sessioned more after I completed my degree than I had since my first months domming. I came and went from the dungeon wearing a tweed blazer that was too hot for the California fire season, but it made me look the part of the professor I wanted to be.

I applied for tenure-track jobs. Hundreds of qualified candidates applied. I interviewed for a few positions, but I spent more time googling combinations of my real and fake names and *dominatrix*—unearthing incriminating photos that hiring committees might find—than I did preparing to answer questions about my research.

Over the years, social media had increased clients' expectations; they wanted access to sex workers' private lives. My boundaries softened like my thighs—once clamped shut, they cramped under pressure and opened. I unblurred my face and increased my demand. Showing my smile, my green eyes, my tattoos meant that clients like Paul would be just as likely to email me as they were to email the dozens of other women advertising as pro dommes in LA, those who seemed to have no problem attaching person to persona, or like me, were pressured into it by the demands of the marketplace. The more unlikely it became that I would find stable employment at a university, the more important it became to excel in the dungeon.

The email from Paul arrived at the same time as one from Catherine, and I wanted the good news before the bad. Catherine and I had broken up. We never recovered from the fetish photographer's betrayal, and I blamed her for letting a dangerous man into our lives, like she'd left the front door unlocked to an intruder. I couldn't see past my own hurt to see hers, right there, throbbing red on the other end of the line. Before we broke up, we opened our relationship and I invited in anyone who wanted to spend the night. A year passed before I realized that there was no going back to who we were before the big arguments, new lovers, and separate vacations. I forced my own hand and signed a sublease on a new apartment before I even told her I was leaving. When I did, we sent a mass text to our friends, announcing our *conscious uncoupling*. We had already argued about everything there was to argue about, and when we walked away from each other, we did so quietly. I didn't have much to move because everything that was mine had always really been hers.

Now I was waking up alone to read my morning emails in a new bedroom, a sublet, in a new bed, on a stranger's sheets that I didn't bother changing. They were heavy with patchouli and bergamot. They kept me from smelling like myself. In the weeks that passed since we'd established our separate lives and good intentions, I'd had plenty of time to sit alone and examine my heart like a small wound. Suddenly, staring at the hurt that was only visible in the bright white light of my new bathroom, good intentions were stripped from all our interactions. Her emailed request to avoid shared space at a mutual friend's birthday brunch felt like banishment. Her insistence that I pay up on the utility bills that were about to go delinquent felt like bankruptcy.

So I opened Paul's email first.

It was lengthy. He wrote of uninspired, pointless flogging sessions he had received from inexperienced dommes and recklessly brutal beatings he'd also received from inexperienced dommes. He wrote of a disappointingly robotic session he'd recently had with a legendary domme he referred to as a "bucket lister." It was unlikely that anyone would put me on a bucket list—I didn't do porn, and I hadn't been around for decades, as the dommes with legends attached to their names had been—but he did say that he had read reviews online that suggested I might be the right person to push his limits. I worried about what that meant, whose boundaries

I'd pushed and if the push had been welcome; or, if I'd done something fucked up and hadn't realized it, and *fucked up* was what Paul wanted. I knew that was a thing. Clients had told me about seeking out dommes they felt might be careless with them, and I didn't think I'd been one of them. I hoped I wasn't one of them.

I knew about the review boards, places where clients rated sex workers like restaurants they'd tried once on vacation. Yelp, but for kink. I was tempted to go searching online for those glowing reviews he might have read, but I was afraid I would encounter at least some that would make me feel like a cheap buffet, serving lukewarm soup and syrupy house wine in water-spotted glasses.

The email described Paul's primary interests: strict, inescapable bondage, serious gags, predicaments, betrayal, objectification, degradation, and something he referred to as *cathartic suffering*. Not pain. He was clear that pain wasn't the objective, but he didn't describe the difference. *Take that as you wish*, he wrote, leaving me room to get it right or wrong. Professional domination is an interpretive exercise on par with those I learned in school. Submissives presented me with physical cues—sweat, blood, flushed cheeks, and skin bruised to plum. They presented me with verbal cues as well—moans and screams and lists of turnoffs and turn-ons— and I deciphered them like images on the page. I wondered what *cathartic suffering* would look like if I figured out how to help Paul achieve it.

Clients like Paul, those who read the review boards and drew distinctions between things like pain and cathartic suffering, had often refined their interests and disinterests to the point that it was difficult for them to disappear into sensation—what you hope will happen once the negotiation ends and the scene begins. I could see the work of analysis furrowed into their brows, the cool demeanor of those who knew what came next. They were usually teeming with expectation, and burdened their dommes with evaluation, making the power exchange difficult at best and impossible at worst.

It wasn't that I preferred men who came in with their underwear soaked in pre-cum, eager to get off and leave. I preferred clients like Paul. But the ways they performed submission made me keenly aware of the ways I performed dominance. I knew that if I delivered my performance well enough, I could make my clients forget it was a performance altogether. I assured myself that my six years in the dungeon outpaced Paul's twenty. He did it on business trips. I did it as a business. I knew that if I could make a guy like Paul forget, I could make anyone forget, even myself.

After that first year of rejection on the job market, my enthusiasm for the performance had started to eclipse my enthusiasm for academia, so I was pleased to hear about the good reviews. My adjunct professorship at a state college paid me $800 per month. Thirty students, sixteen weeks. Studies in Popular Culture, a popular elective. Hours commuting; hours more reading to prepare tests, lectures, discussion questions; hours grading; hours each week in the classroom with those thirty students, themselves falling asleep at their desks because, like me, they worked two jobs to make ends meet. Paul would pay me $1,200 for four hours of *cathartic suffering*—as long as I could figure out what that meant—and then sleep in a cage for another four.

I gave Paul instructions on when to meet me, where to show up, and how much it cost. Then, *I'll make you wish you'd never sent this.* Like a film critic who walks into a theater, notepad in hand, and walks out wiping tears, nothing scribbled onto her page: I wanted to get him lost in the show.

I heard Paul's knock on the door at ten o'clock sharp,

his fist thumping over the music—dark, cliché, Portishead-adjacent. I paused it on my way to open the door. For the first hour, at least, I needed to hear only Paul. Pace of breath, wince, moan: a set of clues about where I was taking him, and how excited or afraid he was to be my passenger.

Just inside the door was a monitor, its corners soft under a layer of dust. It streamed video from a security camera that had been watching Paul on the doorstep. Catherine installed the camera to deter bad client behavior. They were confronted by their own surveillance when they walked into the dungeon, before they passed through the heavy black satin drapes that kept the depths of the warehouse from the prying eyes of the drug dealers circling the block on stolen BMX bikes, or the homeowners who'd moved into what their real estate agents told them was a neighborhood on the up-and-up, making their ways home from work. The camera was a ruse. Catherine never set it up to save the recordings.

I paused to watch Paul on the monitor, moving in and out of focus like a news anchor in a hurricane. The way he shifted his weight from one foot to the other made him look nervous, like he might not be the seasoned veteran he claimed to be, like his composure might weaken at the click and clack of my heels on the polished concrete. We stood there together, no more than a foot apart, one poised inside the dungeon, the other monitored on the step.

I flipped the dead bolt, piercing the silence between us like a balloon. The heavy metal door creaked open, and a man stepped inside, much larger in the flesh than he appeared through the fish-eye lens. I ushered him beyond the threshold and shut the door behind him, the sound of lock and bolt echoing back through the warehouse and its wooden bones, cavernous and exposed. I usually asked clients to kneel the moment they walked inside, especially the tall ones. I resisted the urge and instead let myself feel intimidated by Paul's height. If I truly wanted to exchange power with Paul, an exchange I thought necessary to ensure his cathartic suffering, I would have to accept that he had it. When he walked through the door, I knew that he did.

I didn't lead with any of the other usual rituals either. I didn't ask Paul to strip off his clothes. I didn't ask him to refer to me as mistress or to repeat his yes-and-no list from our email exchange. I didn't even ask him for the money. If we wanted the power exchange to work, we both had to forget about the money. The money was proof that I was doing a service, and no fantasy, no desire to move beyond those empty rites, could change that.

I pressed my hands into Paul's chest and backed him up against the door. I took inventory, pushed my elbows, my forearms, my palms and knuckles into every part of Paul that he might use to hurt me: his thick shoulders, his rough hands—large enough to wrap all the way around my throat—and his cock. I drew my thigh up toward my navel, got my balance on a single stiletto and dug my knee hard into his crotch. I felt him stiffen beneath his jeans. I planted both feet again, leaned in, and pressed my hip into his sex, shifted all my weight there and felt his hot breath shorten into little puffs that he exhaled right onto the crown of my head.

"Does it hurt?" I asked.

He didn't answer, but I knew that it did. His breath expanded: he was trying to calm himself through the pain. When I was with Catherine, I hated the smell of clients' breath all over me, all over her. I could rinse their spit off my feet in the dungeon shower, but there was nothing to be done about their breath, the way it lingered on my clothes and in my hair. Now there was no one at home to smell me, so I let it stink.

Paul's lips trembled against my scalp, his inclination to

kiss his tormentor evident. His desire for me diminished him, no matter how big he had been when he walked through the door. His desire for me, paired with my lack of desire for him, was an easy power dynamic within which to play. I had grown accustomed to it and had become bored. And I suspected that after twenty years of play, Paul might have been bored of it too.

I pried myself off him, and the dungeon door creaked, then I took a breath and pushed him backward, into it, hard. He bent at the knees, then at the waist, and crumbled downward to avoid injury. In that moment, curled into a loose fetal position, Paul looked like a man who would have been encouraged to play football, if only he had the stomach for locker room talk. The ease with which he softened a blow told me that he didn't. He brought his forearms to his face—his instinct, self-defense—and I knew my tactics were working on him. He was afraid.

I crouched down and reached for his cock, grabbed it roughly through his jeans, and a small croak came out of his throat, like the bullfrogs that used to jump into my childhood swimming pool, which Dad had to fish out with a net. Fingernails dug in there, I imagined any strength Paul had draining deeper and deeper down into parts of him I could easily diminish. I planned on doing things to Paul that would make him want to hurt me, and I knew that he had the power to do it. If this was going to work the way we both wanted it to work, he would have to hand all of it over to me.

I'd come to the door prepared, a leather hood waiting on a table in the foyer. I picked it up and pulled it down over Paul's face, shoving my fingers into the hole at the mouth to make sure it aligned with his lips, that he had access to an airway. Holes over the mouth and nostrils were the hood's only openings. It blinded him and rendered him anonymous.

I tightened the hood's leather laces over his skull, down the back of his neck like a boot, careful not to catch his ashy brown curls when I cinched it shut. I took his hands, one at a time, and zipped them into thick black leather mitts that balled them into involuntary fists. He heaved a sigh of what sounded like resignation, though it must have been resignation to some battle he was fighting inside himself because outside, with me, he mounted no resistance.

With Paul secure in the hood and mitts, I pulled him, by the arm, up off the floor. Once there, poised on his knees, I ripped Paul's shirt up over his head, over the leather mittens, and then locked his wrists together with a carabiner behind the small of his back. I pushed him back down onto his side with the toe of my boot, unbuckled his belt, and pulled it fast from around his hips.

The submissive has to help along the process of undressing, a practical necessity that interrupts the fantasy of having one's clothes ripped off—unless you've pre-negotiated that it's fine to actually rip them off and the client has brought an extra shirt and pair of pants, which ruins the element of surprise that makes having one's clothes ripped off worth the trouble. I dreaded having to ask, and sensing that dread—Paul had likely seen it on the faces of dozens of dommes before me—he hoisted his hips up into the air. I unbuttoned his jeans and started to yank them down, towing the cotton briefs as well, but I'd forgotten his shoes and fumbled with the laces, dropping each with a thump for dramatic effect. I felt the envelope of cash he'd prepared for me in his jeans pocket and left the money there uncounted, certain that Paul had brought it all and that I would remember to claim it before morning. I dropped the clothes into a pile at the dungeon's threshold, where he could pick them up on his way out the next morning.

Paul's dick was out of his pants for the first time, bubble-gum pink and throbbing hard.

"This represents something, and I don't like it," I said, prodding at it with my toe. "It represents power."

His dick and balls were cradled between his belly and thighs, but he acquiesced with a whimper and shifted his weight onto his hip so that more of his sex was exposed to my boot.

"Some power," I scoffed, stepping on it, with nowhere near my full weight. He accepted the punishment with nothing more than a grimace.

"Here you are, helpless on a cold concrete floor, at the threshold of a dungeon, at the mercy of a perfect stranger. And it's all because of this thing between your legs."

I kicked at it then, catching his balls too, and he croaked his bullfrog croak again. I crouched down.

"I'm going to neutralize it."

I stood again and kicked it harder.

"Yes, mistress," Paul choked out. He couldn't have known what I meant, since I hadn't yet decided what to do with him, but the words had been sitting right on the tip of his tongue. All I knew was that his cock was hard, impossible to cage, and Paul had come to me for a cathartic release, not an orgasm. For once, I didn't want the client to have an erection.

Anal was on neither Paul's yes nor no list, so I left his mouth ungagged as I pulled latex gloves down over my hands. I wanted to give him the opportunity to *mercy* if he needed, but was pleased when I ran my finger around his asshole and he didn't. I had been domming long enough to know that most men go limp when you penetrate them, no matter how much they like it. Paul curled his knees up to his chest, pulled his wrists in behind them, and lay still while I lubed a finger and pushed it inside. He sucked me in and I stayed there until his hips started bucking for more. Then I gave him another, then another, until half of my hand was inside him.

I was rarely jealous of the experiences I gave my clients, but when I saw Paul's skin go slick with sweat as he rolled through waves of pleasure, I felt the sting of envy. I thought I knew the feelings Paul must have been feeling within the contours of my own body, but my body was so different from Paul's, imagining was as close as I could get. Still, I had to convince myself that I knew something about what Paul was feeling if I wanted to take him to places that I had never been in the dungeon—places like catharsis—where I too desperately wanted to go. I fucked Paul harder, sensing we were close to passing pleasure like an exit ramp on a long drive out into the desert—last gas station for a hundred miles.

I was right. Paul stopped rutting into me and his ass clenched, then his cock went soft. I pulled my hand out of him and peeled off my glove. I left Paul in a pool of sweat on the floor, walked to the toy closet, and picked out a hard plastic chastity cage. I walked back and fastened Paul's penis inside it. He thanked me, knowing the session would be directed a little less by his desires, a little more by mine. I unlaced Paul's hood and pulled it off. His pretty curls had matted into a sweaty halo around his head. His eyes were wet and far away. He had gotten lost at sea, just like I wanted. But he had left me on the shore.

I unlocked Paul's fists from behind his back. His hands were free enough then to pull himself up onto all fours, but he needed me for everything else. He asked me to scratch his nose. I had always thought that would be the worst part of inescapable bondage—getting an itch you couldn't scratch. The thought of it made me shudder, but I ignored Paul's request.

He grimaced, resisting the urge to break character and scratch himself, and it was clear that my refusal made Paul despise me. But he didn't give in. He posed there like an obedient dog, tormented by the sight of a rotisserie chicken. He let me cup his head in my hands, but he winced when I ran them over his cheekbones, his chin, his brow. Nobody, especially not Paul, expected me to touch them like that. Not even the women I met in bars, or online, who knew what I did for a living, expected me to touch them like that. Tenderness had become transgressive. I put it out of my mind.

"Follow me," I demanded.

Paul crawled behind me, on all fours, toward the center of the dungeon.

"Up."

He rose to stand, backed himself up to the front of the St. Andrew's cross.

"Spread."

He widened his stance and reached his arms above his head. He'd been in the position many times before—I didn't have to ask. I locked his leather mitts—left wrist, right wrist—to the cross and crossed the room. I pulled an industrial roll of Saran Wrap from one of the toy closets that lined the play space and began the monotonous work of wrapping his legs, from ankle to inner thigh, then his thick torso, and arms, wrist to shoulder.

Paul made a half-hearted attempt to struggle against me, manufacturing a reason for me to reach for a rubber ball gag. He opened his mouth, hungry for punishment, then shook his head back and forth and moaned when he realized it was too big, latched too tight. I wanted it to be more uncomfortable than it had been in his fantasies. I'd told him that he would regret emailing me, and in that moment, I was right and he knew it. I picked up the Saran Wrap and continued the task at hand. Affixed to the cross, he looked like a bug pinned to wood, me the entomologist, studying.

Saran Wrap isn't pretty like rope, but it is just as unforgiving. The first time I saw another mistress perform bondage in this way, I wasn't surprised by its alternate use. I remembered the senior pranksters in our last week of high school who Saran Wrapped all the cars in the faculty parking lot so that the teachers would hear the final bell, try to go home, and find that they couldn't open their doors to leave.

Over my years in the dungeon, I found that Saran Wrap could also be used to inflict shame. Stretched carefully over the face, it contorted submissives into blank canvases, like whole dead fish, wrapped to be sold in the Japanese market down the street from the dungeon. Applied roughly, it could render submissives monstrous, their features scrambled: lips stretched, teeth bared. If I held up a mirror and told them to look, they often disobeyed, jerked their heads away, begged me to stop. They chose not to recognize themselves like that, unrecognizable.

Even my tamest of sessions flirted with shame. I forbade my submissives from making eye contact with me, an intense form of denial. Or I demanded that they look, forced them to dwell on the differences between us—*I am clothed; you are naked. I am clean; you are filthy. I am cold; you burn for my touch.*

But humiliation and degradation are different in scale. I learned that years ago, from the client who wanted to be fat-shamed, when I was oblivious and conflated the terms. If I put a pink rubber piglet nose on a submissive and made him *oink*, we both knew that he was still a man, not a piglet. *Oink* was a humiliating thing that he did, rooting around on a tarp, covered in pudding cups and Little Debbie cakes. A pig is not what he was.

Scrambling a submissive's face until it's unrecognizable is something else entirely. Stripping him down to his ugliest form and saying, "this is who you are," that's degradation: the infliction of shame.

Paul's email asked for degradation. *Strict, inescapable bondage, serious gags, predicaments, betrayal, objectification, degradation, and cathartic suffering.* So I wrapped his face. I pulled his eyelids back like a dog riding shotgun, head in the wind. Gag in place, I smashed his nose to the side. Breath obstructed, I let him panic for a moment before I unhooked the gag from the nape of his neck. He coughed, and a long, thick rope of snot and drool spilled out of him. I smeared it across his cheeks and wrapped him again, this time over the mouth. I let him panic, poked an air hole, wrapped him again, let him panic, waited longer to poke a second air hole, let him panic, ripped it off. I reached my hand down into his throat, deep past his molars, past the back of his tongue and choked him. He gagged with a violence that suggested his dinner might end up on the floor, and while the idea tempted me, I didn't want the stench of his vomit in the dungeon. I had to sleep there too.

I continued on like this for nearly an hour. When I finished, I walked over to the vanity that sat just behind the cross and took out the pink handheld mirror we kept for the sissies and their makeup tutorials. I rolled the plastic ever so slightly down under Paul's eyes, ever so slightly up over his lips. I held the mirror up to his eyeline, and Paul turned his head, like they all did, at first.

"Look at you," I hissed, "covered in your own filth."

Paul hesitated, like they all did, then he obeyed.

Hanging from the cross, he looked straight into the mirror. Nose smashed brutally to the side, chin slick with mucus and spit, face flushed hot like a sunburn, Paul smiled at himself like he'd run into an old friend. He shook his head and thanked me and smiled. He wasn't any more ashamed of his face than he was of the lube running pinkish with traces of blood and shit between his legs. He wasn't ashamed of the sick noises rattling around in his throat, or how ugly he looked: contorted, plastic, monstrous. What good would shame have done him? Paul had moved beyond it, toward yet another place I had never been.

Paul had come to me for *cathartic suffering.* I couldn't say if he truly reached catharsis. Maybe he emailed his next mistress down the line, still searching. But as he hung there from the cross, I saw him leave me at shame and go somewhere else, beyond it. He looked beautiful, the way ugly things can be sometimes, and I wanted so badly to go with him. But the money was still waiting for me in the pocket of his jeans. He must have forgotten; I never did. I wedged a pair of safety scissors between the plastic and his skin, freed Paul's nose, and latched the gag again, tighter than it had been before, ratcheting his jaw out of the smile.

Just a mile or so east of the dungeon, in a seminar room on campus, we talked about shame. We talked about it like it was something that happened naturally: always on accident, never on purpose. We read the late queer theorist Eve Kosofsky Sedgwick, who wrote about shame's emergence in infancy, at the stage when a baby mirrors the expression of her caregiver. That performance is a self-conscious one, a narcissistic-yet-relational one. The dark side of peekaboo. When the caregiver looks away, misses her cue, she fails the infant's need for recognition, and that perceived rejection produces the particular kind of fear the infant will later come to know as shame. All grown up, she will wave back at someone in a crowded bar or train station, someone who is waving, she is certain, at her—only to realize that he is waving at the person behind her. Her eyes will shoot down to the floor. *Fuck*, she might mutter to herself, the exhale of the word itself a relief from the feeling. If she grew up shame-prone, she might think, *Fuck, I am so stupid, nobody sees me.* If she didn't, she might think, *Fuck, that was embarrassing, I hope no one saw me.* We all hope to grow into the latter; many of us don't.

Degradation play draws upon those foundational fears. It takes what we all carry, sloshing around deep inside us, and raises the stakes. Fear of being seen. Fear of not being seen. Fear of being seen as nothing. Paul paid me for all of that, and in accepting his money, I got it for free.

The thing about sex work is that, in the eyes of the world, it becomes who you are. Once a whore, always a whore, or so the story goes. It's why everyone wants whores to stop whoring, but when they do, they can't get hired at Starbucks or 7-Eleven. Not with a record, anyway. It's why I was afraid I would be fired from my day job if anyone ever found out about my night job.

We distinguish shame from guilt because guilt attaches to what one does, whereas shame points to what one is. I didn't learn that in graduate school. I learned that in the dungeon.

I'd have liked to applaud Paul for his acceptance of himself, stripped down to his basest form. I'd have liked to applaud him for his refusal to hide. But the truth was that he called to confirm his appointment from a burner phone. He wasn't unashamed. He could just afford privacy for it. I took his money to inflict it because I couldn't otherwise afford an apartment. If the session was cathartic for him, it never could have been for me.

After two more hours of trying my best to make sure Paul's suffering brought his catharsis, after I had cut the plastic wrap from his limbs and allowed him to shower off the spit and lube, I laid him down at the foot of the bed, zipped him into a leather sleep sack, and watched an episode of *Law & Order: Special Victims Unit* on my laptop. I got up in the middle of the night to fish my $1,200 out of his pocket. He slept on the floor beneath me—quiet, immobile, content—through all the itches he couldn't scratch.

Epilogue

• •

A man takes a seat next to me at the Mandrake's long bar.
It's a low-ceilinged local haunt, frequented by artists and de-
signers leaving work at galleries along La Cienega Boulevard,
stalling their long commutes toward the gentrifying East LA
neighborhoods they call home. He asks the bartender for
a whiskey and slides an unmarked envelope toward me. It
touches the base of my sweating highball glass, condensa-
tion blooming onto the no-longer-crisp white paper. I pick
it up, make eye contact, and work my finger into the crease.
I count the cash discreetly before stuffing it into my purse.

I am pleased that he is young. Almost as young as me.
He looks older the closer you get to his face—I notice when
I lean in to thank him for the cash. He has a ruddy complexion, deep pores pooling oil, and a crooked nose with a
lavender scar across the bridge. Not a real fighter; he's too
doughy. Probably overzealous at CrossFit or Krav Maga. But
his age doesn't blow my cover. That's what's important. A
reasonable person might believe that we matched on Tinder,
that I am meeting him for a date.

The man wraps his thick fingers around his bourbon,
takes a sip before tipping the bartender and shimmying his

wallet back down into his pocket. Then he sets his eyes on me. This initiates the role-play.

He leans in toward me, takes the pose of a town gossip.

"Come here often?" he asks.

"Is that all you got?" my reply.

I stir my drink with a straw. It's sweet, gin versus lavender, with the lavender winning. I want a beer, but I don't drink beer in front of clients.

The client fumbles his words.

"Ah . . . ah."

He laughs nervously, takes a drink, taps his whiskey back on the table like we'd just done some elaborate cheers that he learned in his fraternity, drinks again. He's not adept at improv. Instead of trying a new line, he lets a moment pass and says it again.

"Come here often?"

I smile, a concession. I'm happy that the scene will be short and sweet and I won't be facing an hour with a man who can't keep up. I nod my head and bat my lashes. The batting takes effort. My lashes are heavy under synthetic fiber, paint, and glue.

"I do. I come often."

A smirk pulls at the corners of his mouth. This is the script he wanted, one we all know all too well. I judge his fantasy: *simple*. No, not simple, *basic*. My judgment boosts me up onto my high horse, a good place to be for this particular scene.

I lick my lips and get them right up close to his ear. His ear feels hotter than an ear should be.

"I come . . . often."

I lean back, shift my weight again so I'm set squarely upon my own barstool. I watch his mouth widen from smirk to smile. He's a little boy about to tell a naughty joke. He knows his mama's gonna bust his ass, but he just can't help it. He turns toward me; I toward him: a face-off. He spreads his legs and scoots himself up on his stool so that I can see his erection pushing against the zipper of his khaki chinos. He reaches his hand between his legs to adjust it, to make sure I saw, as if not seeing were a possibility. I look over my shoulder to see who's behind me, to see who else can see.

"I would love to watch you come," he says, and takes a satisfied drawl of whiskey. For a moment, he looks calm. He's read his lines; he's delivered. He knows what's next. We discussed the choreography of the scene over the phone, just two hours before we sat down. He turns back to face the bar and stares straight ahead, quivering in anticipation of the response he can see coming, a kid who's just grown tall enough to ride the biggest roller coaster in the park, grappling suddenly with the fact that he's strapped in and it's about to take off. No turning back. I'm dreading the takeoff as much as he is.

I let a moment pass.

The next part of the story happens fast.

I mimic the strange ritual I saw him practice when he took a drink of his own cocktail: swig from the glass, tap the glass on the bar, swig from the glass a second time. Maybe it's a good-luck charm, like slapping the roof of your car when you pass an oncoming vehicle burning just one headlight. I learned that from Becca. Or maybe from Katie. Or from David. Maybe Grace. Probably Sam. Or I taught it to each one of them—I can't remember.

I stand and straighten my dress. Then, I yell loud enough for the entire bar to turn, "I wouldn't have sex with you if you were the last man on earth!"

As I turn to go, my purse snags on my seat and the barstool makes this ugly scraping sound as it drags across the ground, louder than I had yelled. This is more humiliating than anything that preceded it, but I stop the stool from toppling over behind me, save the cash from hitting the vodka-soaked floorboards. I glance at the man, and his cheeks are flushed red as anything. This is the feeling for which he has paid. I got it for free.

I had planned to pour my drink on his crotch like they do in the movies, but now that I'm faced with the barback and the DJ and the girl in the nice yellow dress sitting one stool down from the man, I lose my nerve. I don't want to make a mess for the bartender, who didn't agree to participate in this humiliation scene in the first place. The yelling alone will ruin the bar for me, and it's just down the street from the dungeon. It was the place where I had my first date with Catherine, the place where I had my birthday party a few years back. But I know my own humiliation threshold well enough to know that I won't be able to step foot inside here again, not for a long time, anyway. I should have picked another spot, I scold myself, farther from home. But I didn't want to get on the freeway at rush hour.

"Wait, I'm sorry, I—" the man stutters, stands up. He stumbles, catches himself, a step behind me, in pursuit.

"No!" I shout, turning and raising my hand to his face. I shove it right at his mouth, where he's no longer smiling. I storm out of the bar and into the unseasonably warm night. The door slams behind me, and he doesn't follow. I pull the envelope from my purse and count again—three hundred dollars—on the walk to my car.

During my own commute home, I replay a conversation I had with a friend a week before, in another dim-lit cocktail bar where I could only afford to drink because I did things like I'd just done. She recounted the frustration of dating straight men from Tinder, the hours she'd spent that weekend locked in tedious conversation with an unkempt man who looked nothing like his profile photos. I asked her why she didn't just get up and leave.

"I couldn't," she said. "I was afraid."

I sit in traffic, feeling like I've gotten away with something. It's not just the money. It's that I get to say no.

The dominatrix is the id of American femininity. She says the words that we all wish we could say when we find ourselves frozen in the presence of men. *No* is principal among them.

No is a speech act, a word that does things. Like *I do*, or *I'm sorry*. I didn't learn that in the dungeon. I learned that in graduate school. It doesn't always work, though, any more than *I do* or *I'm sorry*. The ability to say no is both powerful and complicated. I didn't learn that in the dungeon. I learned that in middle school.

To use the word *no* is to disrupt femininity itself. Women are supposed to be nice, pleasing, compliant, available. *No* is the utterance that disrupts all of that. It is the failure of femininity to do as it's told.

My clients paid me for that disruption. They paid me to flip the script, to undo everything men and women were supposed to be, but only for the span of one hour, after which they would put their watches and their wedding bands back on and I would open the dungeon door just a crack and warn them that it's still bright outside, it's going to take your eyes a minute to adjust. The fact that they could do it with such ease—that they could pay me, that they could step back into the light and they could rely on their eyes to adjust—was proof that the script could never really be flipped, that nothing we had done in the dungeon disrupted the men they were and would be outside of it.

I knew that, of course. I knew that female supremacy was manufactured in the dungeon. Still, when I was in there, it did sometimes feel good to say no.

But when I stepped back outside, back into the light, back into the world of men, my eyes never quite adjusted. What I had done in there had changed me.

• •

Before I tried it myself, the only time I'd seen a sex worker in real life was when I was seventeen and my mom drove David and me to Cincinnati to see the all-female metal band Kittie. After the concert, Mom got us lost, as she always got us lost. She never consulted a map, just drove and drove until she saw signs for the interstate. She told us the signs would always come, if you were patient.

We stopped at a red light in what would have been called, in Vegas or Amsterdam, a red-light district. In Cincinnati, Ohio, street prostitution was addiction and coercion and didn't offer much in the way of tourist allure. Two women stood on the corner wearing heavy winter coats and shitty sneakers, accompanied by a man my mom was convinced was their pimp.

"Girl, you better get your education," she warned me. "If you don't, you'll end up selling your ass just like those two."

Never mind that my mother hadn't gone to college, and as far as I could tell she wasn't selling hers.

After all was said and done, I never felt like I sold my ass either, but I did feel like I'd rented it out by the hour. I can't say for sure if I would have dropped out of school, or if I would have figured out another way to stay, but either way, my mom's advice didn't account for the fact that getting an education doesn't always change matters all that much, and selling your ass isn't always all that terrible. That's also easy for me to say—I didn't have a pimp.

I had gotten my education and been teaching writing for more than a decade before a student turned in an essay about selling her own ass to stay in school. I read it and wondered if she had found out about me. I wish I could say that I told this student that she wasn't alone. But the truth is that I was still afraid of what might happen to me if I was caught corrupting innocents, was caught colluding in doorways, was caught making do. So I didn't tell her that she wasn't alone. But I hope that, somehow, she knew.

Acknowledgments

Thank you to my agent, Jade Wong-Baxter, for seeing the book that this would become, and to my editor, Carolyn Kelly, for seeing it through.

Thank you to the team at Avid Reader/Simon & Schuster who contributed to this book's making: Alison Forner, Sydney Newman, Clay Smith, Annie Craig, Rafael Taveras, Meredith Vilarello, Lauren Wein, Amy Guay, Jordan Rodman, Alex Primiani, Katherine Hernandez, Morgan Hart, Lewelin Polanco, Alicia Brancato, and Erica Ferguson.

Thank you to Leigh Stein for knowing I was writing a memoir before I knew it myself, and for shepherding me through the wilderness of book publishing.

I am grateful for the Tin House Summer Workshop, Saeed Jones, and the Saeed workshop crew, who were among my first readers. The Mendocino Coast Writers' Conference and Lisa Locascio Nighthawk, its fearless leader, who gifted me the opportunity to discuss *The Bachelor* over wine with Sharon Olds. Thank you to Jeannie Vanasco for reading my work at Mendocino and seeing something good there. Thank you to all of the writers who taught the classes and led the workshops that kept me writing through the pandemic: T Kira Madden at the Center for Fiction, Alex Marzano-Lesnevich at Catapult, Melissa Febos at Corporeal Writing, Kali Fajardo-Anstine at Tin House, and Garth Greenwell at the Shipman Agency. Thank you to the Barbara Deming Memorial Fund. The Money for Women grant gave me the literal space I needed to push through this book's most difficult chapters. Thank you to Erin Keane at *Salon*, and Stella Cabot Wilson and Allisen Lichtenstein at Catapult, who edited early work that would make its way into this book.

Thank you to those who listened and guided: Sarah Kessler, Karen Tongson, Grzegorz Stępniak, Vanessa Carlisle, Kate Litterer, Sam Cohen, Lauren Hadaway, Trish Bendix, Carmen Maria Machado, Rachel West, and the Hookers Army.

Thank you to my family, especially my mother, Regina, for your unwavering love and support, and for all of my best stories.

Thank you to my first reader, Kristen Mortensen, for teaching me to celebrate the small victories, and for holding my hand every night while I wrote this book.

To my students at USC: your bravery on the page inspires mine.

Thank you to every sex worker I have ever known, and every sex worker I will never know.

About the Author

Chris Belcher is a writer, professor, and former sex worker. She completed a PhD in English at the University of Southern California, where she is now Assistant Professor (Teaching) of Writing and Gender Studies. Under her working name, Natalie West, she edited the acclaimed anthology *We Too: Essays on Sex Work and Survival*. Born and raised in West Virginia, she now lives in Los Angeles.

Avid Reader Press, an imprint of Simon & Schuster, is built on the idea that the most rewarding publishing has three common denominators: great books, published with intense focus, in true partnership. Thank you to the Avid Reader Press colleagues who collaborated on *Pretty Baby*, as well as to the hundreds of professionals in the Simon & Schuster audio, design, ebook, finance, human resources, legal, marketing, operations, production, sales, supply chain, subsidiary rights, and warehouse departments whose invaluable support and expertise benefit every one of our titles.

Editorial
Carolyn Kelly, *Assistant Editor*

Jacket Design
Alison Forner, *Senior Art Director*
Clay Smith, *Senior Designer*
Sydney Newman, *Art Associate*

Marketing
Meredith Vilarello, *Associate Publisher*
Caroline McGregor, *Marketing Manager*

Production
Allison Green, *Managing Editor*
Morgan Hart, *Production Editor*
Alicia Brancato, *Production Manager*
Lewelin Polanco, *Interior Text Designer*
Ritika Karnik, *Desktop Compositor*
Cait Lamborne, *Ebook Developer*

Publicity
Katherine Hernández, *Publicity Assistant*

Publisher
Jofie Ferrari-Adler, *VP and Publisher*

Subsidiary Rights
Paul O'Halloran, *VP and Director of Subsidiary Rights*